The Psychology Major's Handbook

The Psychology Major's Handbook

FOURTH EDITION

Tara L. Kuther
Western Connecticut State University

Australia • Brazil • Mexico • Singapore • United Kingdom • United States

CENGAGE Learning

The Psychology Major's Handbook, Fourth Edition
Tara L. Kuther

Product Director: Jon-David Hague

Product Manager: Timothy Matray

Content Developer: Michael B. Kopf (S4Carlisle Publishing Services, Inc.)

Content Development Services Manager: Greg Albert

Product Assistant: Kimiya Hojjat

Marketing Manager: Melissa Larmon

Art and Cover Direction, Production Management, and Composition: Lumina Datamatics, Inc.

Manufacturing Planner: Karen Hunt

Cover Image: Indivision/DEX Image

WCN: 01-100-101

Library of Congress Control Number: 2015935710

ISBN: 978-1-305-11843-0

Cengage Learning
20 Channel Center Street
Boston, MA 02210
USA

Printed in the United States of America
Print Number: 01 Print Year: 2015

To FHM

—TKM

Brief Contents

Contents

Chapter 4

Study Tips: Tools for Academic Success 81

Chapter 6

Writing an Empirical Paper 143

Chapter 7

What Can I Do with a Bachelor's Degree in Psychology? 166

Chapter 8

Finding a Job with Your Bachelor's Degree 183

Chapter 9

What Can I Do with a Graduate Degree in Psychology? 207

Chapter 10

Applying to Graduate School in Psychology 223

Preface

Psychology is consistently among the most popular college majors, with over 110,000 baccalaureate degrees awarded in 2012. *The Psychology Major's Handbook* provides practical information to help students decide whether to pursue psychology as a major, including an overview of the competencies acquired by psychology majors, as well as career options at the undergraduate and graduate level. Chapters discuss how to succeed in college, develop an active learning style, hone study skills, and become more self-aware. New college students often are surprised by the autonomy required of students. Perhaps the biggest difference between high school and college is that college requires students to take an active role in their education. *The Psychology Major's Handbook* is intended to help students recognize their role in steering their own education. No book can replace the guidance of a faculty advisor, but *The Psychology Major's Handbook* is a helpful resource for students who seek general assistance as well as may serve as a springboard for student–advisor discussions.

The fourth edition of *The Psychology Major's Handbook* emphasizes active learning by including additional exercises and writing prompts to help readers consider how the material applies to them and what actions they might take to shape their own professional development. Each chapter includes at least eight opportunities for assigning student writing as in-class or take-home assignments. Exercises and writing prompts appear as stand-alone assignments throughout each chapter, accompany checklists, quizzes, and tables within each chapter, and appear at the end of each chapter.

The *Psychology Major's Handbook* has been thoroughly updated to include current, relevant information on careers available to bachelor's, master's, and doctoral degree holders in psychology. The chapters on careers in psychology have been reorganized and streamlined to emphasize the many settings in which psychology majors work and the generalizable skills relevant to each setting. Every chapter has been reviewed, updated, and, often, rewritten to highlight major concepts critical for success in college and beyond. For example, Chapter 1 now includes a brief section on becoming a psychologist and Chapter 2 information on career assessments, such as the MBTI and Strong Interest Inventory as well as Internet resources for learning about majors and careers. Chapter 3, on taking an active role in one's education, now includes a discussion of what is learned in college and the value of out-of-class experiences, such as conducting independent research and attending psychology conferences. Chapter 4, on study skills, is entirely rewritten to include the importance of attitude and mind-set as well as reflect the ways technology influences studying. The chapter on finding jobs with a psychology degree (Chapter 7) has been fully rewritten to include updated résumé samples and coverage of the impact of the Internet on job hunting (e.g., how to create a LinkedIn profile and how to prepare a text résumé that can be cut, pasted, and e-mailed). Chapter 10, on applying to graduate school, has been rewritten to include information about the revised GRE exam, using technology and the Internet in learning about and applying to programs, interviews, and more.

Since the first edition of *The Psychology Major's Handbook*, released at the turn of this century, technology has become a ubiquitous, unescapable part of life for young people. Each chapter of the fourth edition acknowledges students' everyday use of technology and provides tips and advice for applying technological and Internet tools to aid academic and professional development. Technology and Internet topics include tools for time management and organization, reference management tools, analyzing and cleaning social media profiles, job hunting, and conducting interviews over Skype.

The Psychology Major's Handbook is organized to accompany students on their journey from Introductory Psychology through the college years. Chapter 1 introduces students to the scope of psychology, including subspecialties, the wide range of places where psychologists work, and academic degrees. Chapter 2 aids students facing the challenge of choosing a college major by discussing self-assessment as a tool for learning about oneself and providing a series of exercises to help students discover their interests and abilities in order to determine whether psychology is the right choice.

Chapters 3 through 6 are intended to accompany students through the college years, serving as a resource to periodically review. Chapter 3 examines the skills that are honed in college and helps students identify and take advantage of the resources at their schools so that they can get the most from their college years. Specifically, the chapter covers how to develop relationships with faculty and how to obtain research and applied experiences. The chapter also surveys the range of presentation and publication opportunities available to undergraduates in psychology. Chapter 4 emphasizes the roles of mind-set, active learning, and study skills as keys to college success and provides detailed tips and strategies to improve time management, reading, note taking, studying, and test taking. Chapter 5 examines the psychology term paper or literature review: how to choose a topic, narrow it, locate information, understand the format of research articles, take notes, avoid plagiarism, write the first draft, and revise it. In Chapter 6, the empirical paper is demystified. Readers learn about the structure of the empirical paper, what to include in each section, and APA style; a template describing and illustrating APA style is provided at the end of the chapter.

Chapters 7 through 10 offer specific information for psychology majors and students who are considering psychology as a major. Chapter 7 examines careers for psychology majors. Readers learn about the value of a liberal arts degree, what employers look for, how to acquire useful skills, and jobs for psychology majors in business, human resources, and social service fields. Learning about jobs is one thing; getting them is another. Chapter 8 provides advice on how to obtain a job after graduation: finding positions, completing applications, résumés, cover letters, and interviews.

Chapter 9 provides information about careers that require a graduate degree, takes a close look at the master's degree with specialties in psychology and related fields, and discusses careers for master's and doctoral degree holders. The final chapter, Chapter 10, provides advice for students who are interested in attending graduate school. Readers are encouraged to examine their reasons for applying to graduate school. Specific advice is provided on gathering program information, evaluating programs, preparing for the GRE, completing admissions essays, acquiring recommendation letters, and succeeding in interviews.

It is my hope that *The Psychology Major's Handbook* will help students determine the path that is right for them and guide them on their journey. I hope to aid faculty in encouraging students to make informed decisions about their major and to help faculty support and guide students through the college years.

Acknowledgments

The Psychology Major's Handbook has benefited from the input of many. All of what appears in these pages has been inspired by interactions with my students and colleagues at Western Connecticut State University, who I thank for sharing their experiences, questions, ideas, and enthusiasm. I am appreciative of the constructive comments and helpful suggestions offered by colleagues, instructors, students, and readers over the last one and one-half decades. Thanks to Victoria Monzillo for her comments, proofreading skills, and work on the test bank. It is my pleasure to work with the folks at Cengage: Tim Matray and Nicole Sala on this fourth edition, and Jon-David Hague on the third edition. I thank Vicki Knight for her guidance on the first and second editions. My parents, Philip and Irene Kuther, have provided unwavering support and guidance. I thank my amazing husband, Fred Martell, who is exceedingly patient and supportive while I pound the keys and stare at the screen, D & D too.

Dear Student

Welcome to the world of psychology! *The Psychology Major's Handbook* is intended to accompany you on your journey through college. A comprehensive book such as this can sometimes be overwhelming, so here are some guideposts to help you find your way:

- **Are you wondering, "What's psychology?"** Check out Chapter 1, which explains the scope of psychology, including the many subspecialties, degrees, and the wide range of places where psychologists work.
- **Not sure what to major in or whether psychology is for you?** In Chapter 2, you'll learn about yourself through exercises and activities that help you to identify your skills, abilities, and interests.
- **Wonder what you can do to get the most out of college?** Feeling confused with the lack of guidance? Chapter 3 explains the hidden curriculum in college: how you can take control of your education by getting involved with faculty, research, and field experience.
- **Does it seem as if you study and study and still don't get the grades you want?** In Chapter 4 you'll learn about essential study skills, including time-management tips, suggestions on how to read more effectively, advice on note taking, study tips, and guidance for taking tests with ease.
- **Have a big paper assignment and don't know where to start?** Turn to Chapter 5 for tips on how to choose a paper topic, where to get ideas, how to find information, take notes, write the paper, and revise it.
- **Taking Experimental Psychology or a laboratory class and don't know how to write a lab report?** Chapter 6 demystifies the empirical paper or research article. You'll learn about the special structure of empirical articles, what to include in each section, and APA style. A template appears at the end to help you conquer APA style.
- **Wonder what you can do with a psychology major?** Want to major in psychology but have no clue what to do after graduation? Chapter 7 dispels the myth that psychology majors are unemployable. You'll learn about the value of a liberal arts degree, what employers look for, how to acquire useful skills, and jobs for psychology majors in business, human resources, and social service fields.
- **Getting close to graduation and starting the job hunt?** Turn to Chapter 8 and learn how to obtain a job after graduation. Everything you need to know is covered, including how to find positions, complete applications, prepare a résumé, write cover letters, and ace interviews.

- **Wondering what you can do with a graduate degree?** Think you might want to continue your education but aren't sure of your options? In Chapter 9 you'll learn about graduate degrees in psychology and the variety of careers for graduate degree-holders in psychology.
- **Ready to apply to graduate school?** So you think graduate school is for you? Chapter 10 tells you how to gather program information, evaluate programs, prepare for the GRE, complete admissions essays, acquire recommendation letters, and manage the many decisions and tasks that are entailed in applying to graduate school.

The Psychology Major's Handbook

CHAPTER

1

What Is Psychology?

Chapter Outline

Close your eyes and envision a psychologist at work. What do you see? What is he or she doing? Does your image include any of the following?

- Conducting research with monkeys
- Monitoring a magnetic resonance imaging (MRI) machine to understand what parts of the brain are active when people view pictures of various items and situations
- Creating and administering a survey on employee perceptions of their work environments
- Developing and evaluating an intervention for families with a history of domestic violence
- Helping educators learn about how the mind works and how to teach most effectively
- Counseling a client who suffers from depression
- Teaching physicians how to understand the emotions that accompany illness in order to communicate more effectively with patients
- Developing and implementing training programs for employees
- Helping police departments by providing information about criminal behavior, assisting officers in managing stress, or explaining the limitations of eyewitness testimony

If you answered yes to any of these examples, you would be right because psychologists engage in all of these activities and more. Are you surprised? Although psychologists are most often portrayed in the media as therapists in private practice settings, psychologists do much more than provide therapy. In this chapter we discuss the broad range of activities and responsibilities that fall under the umbrella of psychological science.

What Is Psychology?

Broadly speaking, psychology is defined as *the scientific study of behavior.* Behavior refers to anything an animal or a person does, feels, or thinks. Many students are surprised to learn that some psychologists work with animals. Psychologists often study animal physiology and behavior to extend what they learn to humans. As scientists, psychologists apply precise methods of observation, data collection, analysis, and interpretation to learn about what makes people and animals behave the way they do. Psychologists generate hypotheses, or educated guesses, about what might cause a particular behavior or phenomenon, and conduct careful scientific research to test those hypotheses. The field of psychology examines interactions among the brain, the environment, psychological functioning, and behavior. Topics of psychological study include social relationships, the brain and the chemicals that influence it, visual and auditory perception, human development, the causes of normative and atypical behavior, and much more. Psychologists conduct a variety of activities in many settings. Of course we cannot forget that psychologists also work directly with people, applying psychological science to help improve people's lives.

Most people are most familiar with psychologists' role as service providers, providing psychological therapy and treatment to clients. However, fewer than 40% of new psychologists work in service provider roles (Michalski, Kohout, Wicherski, & Hart, 2011). What do the rest do? Some psychologists are employed as professors at universities, community colleges, and high schools. Others work as researchers in university, hospital, corporate, and government settings. Psychologists work as administrators, managing hospitals, mental health clinics, nonprofit organizations, government agencies, businesses, schools, and other settings. Most psychologists perform more than one of these roles. For example, a psychologist who works as a college professor might also have a private practice or conduct research with a social service agency.

Psychology's Breadth

A wide range of topics fall under the umbrella of psychology and each topic is its own specialized field of study. The following sections present the most common specialties within psychology. In each of these areas, some psychologists spend most of their time conducting research to expand the knowledge base, some practice or apply research findings to help people and communities, and some do both, as scientist-practitioners. In addition, over one-third of psychologists teach and conduct research at colleges and universities.

Real Tips for Real Students

The Briefest Taste of Psychology

Many students find the Introductory or General Psychology course challenging. There's a good reason for that: Introductory Psychology presents the entire field of psychology at a whirlwind and dizzying pace. As you learn, try to remember that each chapter of the book presents an entire subfield of psychology—an area in which psychologists specialize and spend their entire lives working. If you find a particular chapter interesting, note that your college offers at least one and often more than one course in that area. If you find a chapter (and thus subfield) uninteresting, the good part about the Introductory Psychology course is that you'll move on to a different chapter and different subfield in just a week or two.

Clinical Psychology

Clinical psychologists study, diagnose, and treat persons who experience emotional, behavioral, and psychological problems or disorders. The problems may range from normative difficulties like helping someone deal with grief or a crisis to more serious and chronic disorders such as anxiety and mood disorders. They also specialize in particular populations, such as children or older adults. Others specialize in particular problems, such as depression or anxiety. Some psychologists are generalists and treat people of all ages and with all types of problems. Most people are familiar with the practitioner role of a clinical psychologist as it is commonly depicted on television, but many clinical psychologists conduct scientific research. For example, some study risk factors for mental disorders, such as the contributions that genetic and environmental factors make in developing a disorder. Others might study treatments, such as the effectiveness of a given medication, therapy, or intervention. Finally, clinical psychologists work in universities as professors and researchers.

Cognitive Psychology

Cognitive psychology is the scientific study of mind and mental processes. It examines the nature of thought, known as *cognition*, and how it works. Cognitive psychologists study how we think—specifically, how we take in information, store it, learn, and use it to make decisions. Topics of study include attention, memory, learning, and decision making. Some cognitive psychologists study these processes in animals and apply what they learn to humans. Some specialize in particular age groups, such as studying attention in infants or memory in older adults. Cognitive psychology is part of a larger interdisciplinary field of *cognitive science*, which includes findings from other research disciplines such as neuroscience, anthropology, and linguistics. Cognitive psychologists and scientists are found in academic settings as professors and researchers. They are also found in applied settings where they assist companies to apply what is known about cognition to products. For example, Internet companies that seek information about how people scan webpages or companies that develop video games might work with cognitive psychologists.

Counseling Psychology

Counseling psychologists engage in many of the same activities as clinical psychologists, but focus their activities on normative functioning, rather than psychological disorders. As researchers, counseling psychologists study how to help people manage everyday life issues, such as divorce, remarriage, career changes, and transitions to and from college. Practicing counseling psychologists help people adjust to life changes and provide vocational assessment and career guidance. Like clinical psychologists, counseling psychologists work in academic settings as professors and researchers and in community settings such as mental health clinics, halfway houses, college counseling centers, criminal justice settings, and social service agencies.

Developmental Psychology

Developmental psychologists study human development across the life span. In academic settings, developmental psychologists teach and conduct scientific research on the emotional, intellectual, and physical development of children, adolescents, and adults. Research topics include a diverse array of issues such as whether most adults experience a midlife crisis, how babies learn to crawl, or what factors influence adolescent drug use. Developmental psychologists also work as researchers, consultants, and program evaluators in applied settings, such as pediatric hospitals, geriatric centers, and nonprofit organizations. A developmental psychologist might provide advice on how to design a nursing home that meets the needs of older adults or develop and evaluate early childhood education programs. Some developmental psychologists, known as *applied developmental psychologists*, engage in practice activities, such as conducting developmental assessments of children to ensure that they are timely in meeting developmental milestones.

Educational Psychology

Educational psychologists study how people learn and apply that knowledge to educational settings. They develop methods and materials to increase the efficiency and effectiveness of educational programs and curricula designed for people of all ages. Educational psychologists work in academic settings and conduct research on learning and instruction. Some study how people learn to read, or complete math problems. Others train teachers and develop methods of instruction to enhance the educational setting.

Experimental Psychology

Experimental psychologists specialize in conducting scientific research. While all psychologists are trained in scientific research, experimental psychologists' education emphasizes methodology and statistics skills. They are experts in conducting research. Experimental psychologists usually focus their research on one topical area within psychology such as cognition, perception, human performance, or social psychology. Some experimental psychologists study animals to apply what they learn to humans, or simply because animal behavior is interesting. Most experimental psychologists are employed in academic settings, teaching and conducting research. Others work as researchers for businesses, corporations, and the government.

Forensic Psychology

Forensic psychologists study legal issues from a psychological perspective. They conduct scientific research on topics such as the reliability of eyewitness testimony, juror selection, and how to interview eyewitnesses without contaminating their testimony. Forensic psychologists apply research findings by providing expert testimony on cases in criminal, civil, and family courts. They may evaluate prisoners, assist in making parole decisions, and assess defendants to determine whether they are competent to provide testimony. Forensic psychologists work not only with lawyers and judges but also with police departments to select, train, and evaluate police officers. Forensic psychologists are found in academic settings as well as applied settings, such as law firms, government agencies, and policy settings.

Health Psychology

Health psychologists study how psychological, biological, and social factors influence health and illness. They conduct scientific research on health-related topics, such as whether relaxation techniques and social support can help people overcome illness more quickly, or how to change people's attitudes about smoking. Health psychologists design, assess, and modify programs to promote health and wellness (e.g., stress management, smoking cessation, and weight loss). They work in academic and research settings such as universities and medical schools, as well as in applied settings such as hospitals and clinics.

Human Factors Psychology

Human factors or engineering psychologists study how people interact with machines, environments, and products. They conduct research on how people understand and use machines to increase people's safety, efficiency, and productivity. Human factors psychologists might work on designing a computer monitor to prevent user fatigue and eyestrain, or they might arrange the instruments on a car's dashboard to enhance access and safety. Human factors psychologists design, evaluate, and modify military equipment, airplanes, computer terminals, and consumer products. Most human factors psychologists work in industry and government; some work in academic settings.

Industrial-Organizational Psychology

Industrial and organizational psychologists apply psychological principles and scientific research findings to the workplace. They are concerned with the relation between people and work. Industrial and organizational psychologists often work for companies, corporations, and the government, studying how to recruit, select, train, and evaluate employees. They conduct applied research on questions like what personality factors make a good employee, how to improve worker productivity, and characteristics of effective leaders.

Industrial and organizational psychologists develop programs to improve employee morale and make the workplace more efficient and pleasant. Others teach and conduct research as members of academic departments in psychology and business.

Behavioral Neuroscience

Behavioral neuroscience refers to the psychological and physiological study of brain and behavior. How do neurotransmitters influence our behavior? What part of the brain is responsible for motivation, language, or emotion? Behavioral neuroscientists conduct research to answer questions about how the brain influences our emotions and behavior. They teach and conduct scientific research in academic settings, as well as train medical doctors, clinical psychologists, and other health professionals. Some behavioral neuroscientists conduct applied work as part of a health care team assessing and treating persons with brain injuries within neurology, psychiatric, and pediatric units of hospitals, and in clinics.

Quantitative Psychology and Psychometrics

Quantitative psychologists study and develop new scientific methods and techniques for acquiring, analyzing, and applying information. Quantitative psychologists help other researchers in designing, conducting, and interpreting experiments. *Psychometricians*, a type of quantitative psychologist, specialize in testing. They create and revise psychological tests, intelligence tests, and aptitude tests. Quantitative psychologists and psychometricians work as researchers in academic, business, and government settings.

Social Psychology

Social psychologists study how people interact with each other and how they are influenced by the social environment. They conduct research on personality theories, attitude formation and change, persuasion and conformity, and how people relate to one another, including attraction, prejudice, group dynamics, teamwork, and aggression. Social psychologists work in academic settings as teachers and researchers, but they also work for corporations and advertising agencies, conducting marketing research and studying how consumers view products.

School Psychology

School psychologists work to foster the intellectual, emotional, educational, and social development of children. They apply the science of psychology to the school environment. School psychologists conduct research on educational topics such as how the classroom climate influences student learning, or how to promote appropriate behavior in the classroom. They work in schools to assess and counsel students, work with parents and teachers, and develop behavioral interventions.

As shown in Table 1.1, psychology is diverse and entails much more than conducting therapy with patients relaxing on leather sofas. Instead, the field of psychology offers a variety of careers in direct service, academics, government, and business. That is, not all psychologists conduct therapy or even study people. What all of the subfields of psychology have in common, however, is a concern with understanding the causes of behavior.

TABLE 1.1 **Subfields in Psychology**

Subfield	Emphasis
Clinical Psychology	Understanding and treating emotional, behavioral, and psychological problems or disorders
Counseling Psychology	Understanding normative functioning and promoting healthy adaptation
Developmental Psychology	Understanding and optimizing human development across the life span
Educational Psychology	Understanding how people learn and modifying educational settings accordingly
Forensic Psychology	Applying psychology to inform and study legal issues
Health Psychology	Understanding and applying psychological, biological, and social influences on health and wellness
Human Factors or Engineering Psychology	Understanding and applying information about how people interact with machines, environments, and products
Industrial and Organizational Psychology	Applying psychological principles and scientific research findings to the workplace
Quantitative Psychology	Developing and studying new scientific methods and techniques for acquiring, analyzing, and applying information
Social Psychology	Understanding how people interact with each other and how they are influenced by the social environment
School Psychology	Understanding and fostering the intellectual, emotional, educational, and social development of children in school setting

Real Tips for Real Students
Start Your Own Personal Database

One of the first things psychology students often learn is that the field is constantly evolving and changing. Create your own database of resources to help you keep up to date in an ever-changing field. How do you keep track of the field? Cultivate a list of bookmarks, subscribe to newsletters, and follow researchers, psychologists, and organizations on Twitter and/or Facebook. Organize your sources of information as well as what you learn and you'll not only expand your knowledge of psychology but you'll also gather ideas for future papers and projects. Students who keep track of interesting findings and ideas find it easier to come up with topics for class papers. When you find an article or idea worth saving, save the link or article in a folder on your computer, phone, app, or cloud service, like Evernote, Google Keep, Dropbox, or OneNote. Before long you will have cultivated a small library of sources and findings that can help you learn more about the topics that interest you and serve as resources for ideas for paper and research assignments.

EXERCISE 1.1
Subfields of Psychology

Choose three subfields of psychology. For each subfield:

1. Explain the subfield in more detail than provided here.
2. Identify at least one psychologist and discuss his or her work.
3. Describe two other topics of research conducted by psychologists in the subfield.

BECOMING A PSYCHOLOGIST

Students major in psychology because they are interested in understanding human behavior. Some students choose a psychology major believing that they can become a psychologist after earning the degree; however, this is not true. One of the most important things that psychology majors must understand is that the bachelor's degree in psychology *does not* prepare graduates to be psychologists. It typically takes another five to eight years of study after the bachelor's degree to become a psychologist. A career in each of the subfields of psychology that we have described requires a graduate degree. What is a graduate degree? Let's begin by considering the undergraduate degree, a bachelor's degree.

Bachelor's Degree in Psychology

The bachelor's degree, a bachelor's of arts (BA) or bachelor's of science (BS) degree, typically is the culmination of four years of undergraduate study. Whether a student earns a BA or BS often depends on the university they attend rather than the program's rigor. Psychology students are awarded BA degrees in some universities and BS degrees in others, yet their education is identical. Most students who earn bachelor's degrees enter the work world after graduation, working in business and human service settings (see Chapter 7 for more information about careers with a bachelor's degree). Some enter graduate school to earn a master's degree or doctorate.

Master's Degree in Psychology

The master's degree is a graduate degree that typically requires two years of study beyond the bachelor's degree. There are many different types of master's degrees, most commonly the MA (master of arts) and MS (master of science). Requirements for service-oriented fields such as clinical, counseling, and school psychology usually include practical experience in an applied setting, which may span longer than the two years of coursework.

What can you do with a master's degree? Depending on the program and curriculum, a master's degree enables graduates to: (a) teach psychology in community colleges or universities (usually part-time); (b) become more competitive for jobs in government and industry; (c) practice industrial/organizational psychology in business settings; (d) obtain certification to practice school psychology (depending on state); and (e) obtain certification as a counselor or marriage and family therapist and practice counseling. Can master's trained individuals provide effective therapy? Studies have shown that there are no convincing differences in therapeutic outcomes as a function of the practitioner's level of training (Atkins & Christensen, 2001; Seligman, 1995). A far greater number of students pursue master's degrees than doctoral degrees in psychology. Students who are interested in graduate study for the sole purpose of becoming a therapist might give a master's degree very careful consideration as it is a quicker and cheaper alternative to a doctoral degree that can fulfill certification requirements to practice as a counselor. See Chapter 9 for more information about careers with a graduate degree.

Doctoral Degree in Psychology

A doctoral degree provides a greater range of flexibility and autonomy than the master's degree, but it usually requires five to seven years of graduate work to complete (and for some individuals as many as eight or nine years).

In clinical, counseling, and school psychology, the requirement for the doctoral degree generally includes a year or more of internship or supervised experience. A doctoral degree requires a great commitment of time and money.

Why do students seek doctoral degrees? Generally students pursue doctoral degrees for any of the following reasons: (a) to teach college; (b) to conduct research in a university or private organization in industry or business; (c) to practice therapy as a psychologist; or (d) to engage in a variety of consulting roles allowing autonomy. There are two types of doctoral degrees in psychology; each provides training that prepares students for specific professional activities. The PhD refers to the doctor of philosophy. Like the master's degree, the PhD is awarded in many fields. It is a research degree that culminates in a dissertation based on original research. PhD graduates may work as researchers and as practitioners in a variety of settings. The PsyD refers to the doctor of psychology. It is offered only in clinical and counseling psychology and is considered a professional degree, much like a JD (doctor of jurisprudence, a lawyer's degree). The PsyD emphasizes practice; students become expert practitioners but do not become researchers. The doctor of education (EdD), a third doctoral option for psychology students, is not as popular as the PhD and PsyD. The EdD is offered in departments of education, rather than psychology. Typically EdD graduates work in the field of education and educational psychology as researchers, administrators, and professors.

In short, there are many levels of education in psychology and many educational paths that will prepare you to work with people. Not all psychology majors will become psychologists. In fact, the vast majority will not.

Why Major in Psychology?

If a bachelor's degree in psychology doesn't make you a psychologist, why major in psychology? As many majors explain—because it is interesting. More importantly, because you will learn how to adopt a scientific perspective and way of thinking that may influence all areas of your life. A background in psychology will change how you see your world. As you learn more about psychology you will become able to see the world through the lens of psychological science, offering a unique perspective and understanding of people. Although you will not be a psychologist with a bachelor's degree, you will learn about psychological principles you can apply in your day-to-day life. A psychological perspective can shape much of what you do. For example, the ethical guidelines that psychologists follow can inform your consideration of how the information about ethical issues and responsibilities of psychologists applies to you.

EXERCISE 1.2

Internet Scavenger Hunt

Use the Internet to answer each of the following questions about specialties in psychology. Provide the search terms used, the website, and your response.

1. In what states can psychologists prescribe medication?
2. How is forensic psychology different from psychology and the law?
3. Identify three applied psychology subfields.
4. During World War II, psychologists used their skills in new ways to help the war effort. In what ways did psychologists contribute? What field of psychology developed from these contributions?
5. What is Principle A of the American Psychological Association *Ethics Code*?
6. What subfield(s) is (are) concerned with a biopsychosocial model? What is a biopsychosocial model?
7. When was the PsyD born?
8. Discuss two subfields of experimental psychology.
9. Identify three ways in which psychologists can contribute to businesses and corporations.
10. What is *Eye on Psi Chi*? What did it replace?

ETHICS AND PSYCHOLOGY

Psychologists affect people directly and indirectly through their work as researchers, teachers, writers, and therapists. Psychologists have a responsibility to act professionally and both protect and promote the welfare of others. Therefore, psychologists' attention to ethics, or principled conduct, is paramount. The following section examines some of the ethical issues that psychologists face.

Ethical Dilemmas Experienced by Psychologists

Psychologists in all subfields confront ethical challenges each day. For example, psychologists who provide therapy must balance challenging their client to confront issues plaguing them with the need to protect the client from self-harm. Establishing professional boundaries with clients is another challenge that practicing psychologists face. For example, is it ever appropriate to hug a client?

Psychologists also encounter ethical issues that are unique to their subfield. For example, when a forensic psychologist assesses a defendant to determine his or her capacity to stand trial, who is the client? To whom is the forensic psychologist responsible—the court, the defendant, the prosecuting attorney? Consider the industrial-organizational psychologist working in a business setting who must advise employers in making decisions about whom to lay off. Should the psychologist consider the individual's performance alone or also consider his or her personal life? Should the employee's marital and family status influence the decision?

Psychologists who conduct research manage another set of ethical issues. How do psychologists balance the benefits of research against the possible harm that can occur to participants—the mental, emotional, and physical risks of research participation? One critical way in which participants' rights are protected is the federal requirement that researchers seek informed consent from participants before conducting a study. Informed consent is a participant's informed, rational, and voluntary agreement to participate. By informed, it must be made with knowledge of the risks and benefits of participation. Researchers are obligated to explain the scope of the research and whether the potential for harm exists. By rational, it must be made by a person capable of making a reasoned decision. Parents provide parental permission for their minor children to participate because we assume that minors are not able to meet the rational criteria of informed consent. Finally, consent must be voluntary, meaning that it must be made freely and without coercion.

Researchers' responsibilities continue after the research is completed. Scientists' work ultimately can impact society. In reporting results, psychologists should be mindful of the social and political implications of his or her work (Society for Research in Child Development, 2007). Researchers must consider how their findings will be portrayed in the media and must work to correct misinterpretations. Researchers must attempt to foresee the inferences that people may draw about their findings and prepare to correct misinterpretations.

Ethics and You

How do psychologists navigate the ethical issues that may arise in their work? The American Psychological Association (2010), a professional organization of psychologists, has published an *Ethics Code* that articulates psychologists' responsibilities and ethical obligations. The basis for the *Ethics Code* is the following five General Principles. Although intended for psychologists, the General Principles outline a model of behavior that is applicable to all. What are the principles and how might they apply to you?

Beneficence and Nonmaleficence Psychologists work to help others, benefit them, and not harm them. In addition, psychologists attempt to be aware of their own mental and physical health and how their health influences others. Psychology students can apply this principle to their own lives by seeking to help others—friends, family, and the community—with whom they come in contact and to do no harm. Our own functioning—physical and mental—influences our interactions with others. An awareness of this can help us to make decisions and act in ways that help and not hurt others.

Fidelity and Responsibility Psychologists are aware of their professional and scientific responsibilities to people, communities, and society at large. They uphold ethical standards, take responsibility for their actions, and are concerned about their colleagues' behavior. Applying this principle as a student entails choosing a set of ethical principles by which to live. Become aware of your responsibilities to others—family, friends, pets, and more—and work to behave in accord with your principles. Finally, be aware of others' behavior and show concern when friends, for example, show inappropriate behavior.

Integrity Psychologists are accurate and honest in their work as scientists, teachers, and practitioners. Psychologists do not lie, cheat, or steal, and they keep promises. Psychology students show integrity in much the same way as psychologists. They are honest in their work as students, but also in their everyday nonacademic life.

EXERCISE 1.3

Can You Identify Academic Dishonesty?

Circle the responses that exemplify academic dishonesty and inappropriate academic behavior.

1. Copying a sentence from an article, noting the author but not enclosing the material in quotation marks.
2. Listing facts, statistics, or other information without citing the source.
3. Reviewing another student's paper to learn about writing style and how to organize your paper on a different topic.
4. Copying a graph from an article and listing the source and page number.
5. Listing information and citing a reference that was not the source of the material
6. Citing articles and books that were not read.
7. Being unsure of the source of a particular piece of information, so listing a likely source.
8. Changing the data in your study, by mathematically doubling the number of participants, for example, to improve your research findings.
9. Copying from another student's test.

10. Reading another student's paper and rephrasing his or her responses in your own paper.
11. Writing important points on your desk to use during an exam.
12. Working with other students to complete a take-home exam despite the professor's instructions to work independently.
13. Copying a sentence from an article, enclosing the copied material in quotation marks and listing the author, year, and page number.
14. Submitting a paper that you wrote for one class as an assignment in a different class.
15. Writing a paper for someone else.
16. Writing a paper by explaining ideas found in many articles and books and citing each.
17. Explaining an idea or theory from a book in your own words, without listing the source.
18. Participating in an online class discussion as someone else.
19. Cutting and pasting information from a website into your paper or discussion post in an online class.
20. Copying your tests from a particular instructor and class to share with friends who currently are enrolled in that class.

Answer: All *but* the following items are examples of academic dishonesty: 3, 4, 13, 16

Justice Psychologists work to ensure that people they come into contact with are treated with fairness and justice, permitting them equal quality in services. Psychologists are aware of their own biases, competencies, and limitations and work to ensure that all people they come into contact with are treated fairly and equitably. Students treat others fairly. They are aware of their own perspectives and biases and how those might influence their interactions with others.

Respect for People's Rights and Dignity Psychologists recognize and respect the inherent worth of all people and their rights to privacy and self-determination. They are aware of the role of individual differences, such as culture, ethnicity, gender, age, sexual orientation, and more, and consider them in their work with individuals. Psychologists attempt to be aware of their own biases, eliminate biases in their work, and do not condone biases in the work of others. Psychology students who respect the dignity and value of others and work to eliminate biases in their thought and behavior will grow into model citizens who can positively influence others around them.

EXERCISE 1.4

Psychology in the Media

Locate a magazine article or website describing research findings having to do with psychology.

1. Provide a brief summary of the findings.
2. Explain what subfield of psychology the research represents.
3. Identify one potential ethical issue related to the research topic.
4. Reconsider the findings described in the article. What further questions do you have? What questions should be addressed next? If you were the researcher whose work was mentioned in article, what would you try to learn next?

OVERVIEW OF *THE PSYCHOLOGY MAJOR'S HANDBOOK*

Now that you have had an introduction to the field of psychology, let's talk about what you can expect from this book. Your first step in choosing a major and preparing for a career is to get to know yourself. Chapter 2 will introduce you to new ways of understanding yourself. A major theme of this book is that *you* play a major role in determining your success in college and beyond. Chapter 3 will show you how to take an active role in your education and shape your own future. Regardless of your major, you'll need to learn how to study and how to write papers. Chapters 4 through 6 will introduce you to time management and study tips as well as specific information about how to write college papers—and specifically, psychology papers.

The remaining chapters of this book encourage you to look ahead and consider your future. What can you do with a bachelor's degree in psychology, and how do you look for a job after graduation? Chapters 7 and 8 address these questions. In Chapter 9 you'll learn what careers are available with a graduate degree in psychology and Chapter 10 provides an overview of how to apply to graduate school. The college years offer opportunities and challenges. The *Psychology Major's Handbook* will help you navigate these years and keep the big picture—your future—in mind.

SUGGESTED READINGS

Gernsbacher, M. A., Pew, R. W., Hough, L. M., & Pomerantz, J. R. (2009). *Psychology and the real world*. New York: Worth.

Hock, R. R. (2012). *Forty studies that changed psychology*. New York: Pearson.

Ruscio, J. (2005). *Clear thinking with psychology: Separating sense from nonsense*. Belmont, CA: Cengage.

Smith, R. A. (2002). *Challenging your preconceptions: Thinking critically about psychology*. Belmont, CA: Cengage.

Stanovich, K. E. (2012). *How to think straight about psychology*. New York: Pearson.

INTERNET RESOURCES (Available at http://www.tarakuther.com)

Classics in the History of Psychology

http://psychclassics.yorku.ca/

On this website you'll find the full text of classic books in psychology, from Sigmund Freud to B. F. Skinner and more.

Psi Chi: The National Honor Society in Psychology

http://www.psichi.org

The Psi Chi website offers a variety of resources for psychology students, including full-text access to all of the articles published in *Eye on Psi Chi*, the organization's quarterly newsletter. Articles cover areas in psychology, career preparation, personal growth, and more.

APA Monitor

http://apa.org/monitor/index.aspx

The American Psychological Association's monthly magazine includes articles on the latest research findings, psychology's influence on the government, practice-related findings, and resources for students.

APS Observer

http://www.psychologicalscience.org/index.php/publications/observer

The monthly magazine published by the Association for Psychological Science digests the latest research into interesting articles accessible to the lay public. It includes monthly columns for students.

About Psychology

http://psychology.about.com

Posts articles about all areas of psychology and the most up-to-date psychology links on the Net.

APA: Careers in Psychology

http://www.apa.org/careers/resources/guides/careers.aspx

This brochure, from the American Psychological Association, provides an excellent overview of the diverse fields within psychology, complete with salary data and interviews from established professionals in each field.

Psychology Today

http://www.psychologytoday.com/

Psychology Today is a magazine available in print and online. While it is not a scientific journal, it digests research findings for a lay audience and may be a source of interesting ideas to pursue.

CHAPTER 2

Choosing a Major: Is Psychology for You?

Chapter Outline

"What's your major?" As a new college student, this is likely one of the most common questions you'll encounter from your friends and relatives. If you haven't yet chosen a major, this may also be a particularly frustrating question. Don't fret. You're not alone in your frustration. Choosing a major is one of the most difficult decisions you'll face in college. After all, how do you decide what to do with your life? Fortunately you don't need to have your life plan laid out in order to choose a college major that fits you. A common misconception about college is that one's choice of major determines one's career. It's no wonder that students who buy into this myth find selecting a major daunting. Luckily, this common belief is not true.

Choosing a major is not the same as choosing a lifelong career, yet this myth persists. For example, many people assume that students who major in humanities, sciences, and social science fields, including English, history, biology, sociology, and psychology are either not qualified for any jobs or qualified only for careers in those specific areas. This isn't true. A history major does not have to become a historian, a biology major does not have to become a biologist, and a psychology major does not have to become a psychologist in order to be gainfully employed. This is especially fortuitous as each of these careers require years of graduate study beyond the baccalaureate degree. Students who earn undergraduate degrees in these fields find jobs in business, research, human resources, teaching, the military, and a variety of other occupations (see Chapter 7 for more information about careers with a bachelor's degree in psychology). Your major will not limit you to only one career choice and graduate study is not a prerequisite to find a career you love.

Although the question of what major to pursue may feel pressing, realize that your choice of majors does not limit your opportunities. Within ten years after graduation, most people work in careers that are not directly connected to their undergraduate majors. In addition, new types of jobs are emerging each year, and most of us have no way of knowing what those jobs will be or what type of education will be needed in order to qualify for them. For example, fifteen years ago, most people had never heard of a patient advocate or a web developer—and social media managers and app developers didn't exist! It's likely that other careers will evolve over the coming years. Consequently, career counselors recommend that college students focus on developing general transferable skills that employers want and that graduates will need in order to adjust to a rapidly changing world, such as writing, speaking, computer, problem solving, and team building. Choose a major that reflects *your* interests and abilities, and provides you with opportunities to develop and hone skills that are useful for a variety of careers. The exercises in this chapter will help you to learn more about yourself; assess your interests, skills, and abilities; and determine which major is right for you.

CHOOSING A MAJOR

As you begin the process of selecting a major, remember that there is no bad choice. Every college major offers training in communication, information management, and critical thinking skills as well as opportunities to develop a unique blend of skills and competencies. However, majors differ in the specific set of competencies emphasized. For example, the emphasis on scientific reasoning and problem solving, coupled with a focus on understanding how people think and behave, is what makes psychology unique among majors. Carefully consider your options, your skill set, and your interests to select a college major. At the end of this process you may find that psychology is the major for you—or you may make another choice. Listen to yourself and make the decision that is right for you, but also recognize that many students change their major sometime during their college years. It is not set in stone. Follow these steps to ensure that you're true to yourself in choosing the college major that is right for you and one that you'll stick with throughout your college years.

Become Informed of Your Options

The first step in making any decision is to become informed of your options. What majors does your college offer? Some majors, such as psychology, English, and economics, are available at all colleges and universities. Other majors, such as engineering, can be found only at some institutions. What options does your college offer? Flip through your college handbook and look at each department and each major. Take a moment to review each program, even if you think it isn't interesting or right for you. Sometimes we have preconceived biases and incorrect information about a discipline or major. For each major, ask yourself the questions in Table 2.1 and note your responses in writing so that you can easily revisit your work and compare majors later.

TABLE 2.1 LEARNING ABOUT MAJORS: QUESTIONS TO CONSIDER

- ❑ What is this field? What does it study?
- ❑ Do I have any experience in this area?
- ❑ Have I taken a class in this subject? If so, what did it cover? What was the class like?
- ❑ What classes can I expect to take as a major?
- ❑ What other experiences do majors typically obtain, for example, internships and/or research experiences?
- ❑ What jobs have recent graduates obtained?

Real Tips for Real Students

Don't Let Profs (Negatively) Color Your Perspective

As you go about the process of considering majors and your experiences in various fields, remember that sometimes a professor can color your view of a discipline. For example, a professor who you find unappealing may make a subject that you'd otherwise find interesting seem boring. When you evaluate a field negatively, take a moment to consider what experiences have led to this evaluation. If it's the result of a single classroom experience, consider giving the discipline another shot before you rule it out.

It is likely that you will not find answers to all of these questions in your college handbook. Examine the department website to find information about the program, faculty (including their research interests and involvement with students), and opportunities for graduates. Most department webpages will provide answers for many of these questions. After completing this task, list all of the majors that sound interesting to you, without making judgments. Then, for each major, gather information from a variety of sources, such as the following.

Seek Information from Others

Internet research can get you only so far. In order to learn about majors and career options it's essential to gather information from knowledgeable people. Students, graduates, career counselors, and professors can offer invaluable information and perspectives.

Speak with Current Students Ask other students how they chose their major and why they think it's a good choice. What do they think about their courses, the topic, professors, and opportunities after graduation? What are the required courses like? Every major has its most challenging set of courses: What are those courses? Why are they considered challenging? What about the professors? Do students have out-of-class interactions with faculty? What kind? What out-of-class experiences are available? Is there a student club?

Speak with Recent Graduates Ask recent graduates about their experiences in college and afterward. Ask them some or all of the questions you asked current students. Also ask about their experiences after graduating. Consider the questions in Table 2.2.

If you don't know any recent graduates, visit the department and/or your college's career center. Most college career centers maintain records of recent graduates and can put you in contact with a few graduates to help you learn more about their work and career experiences.

TABLE 2.2 LEARNING ABOUT MAJORS: WHAT TO ASK RECENT GRADUATES

- ❑ What was the job search like?
- ❑ What kinds of jobs did they seek?
- ❑ How were they received by potential employers?
- ❑ Where were they hired?
- ❑ How well does their job match their expectations?
- ❑ What are the positive and negative features of their work?
- ❑ What role, if any, did their major play in their job search and career?
- ❑ Do they feel that their major prepared them for their jobs?
- ❑ If they could do it again, what major would they choose? Why?

Speak with a Career Professional Visit your college's career center to seek advice. Tell the career counselor about what you've learned about yourself in completing the exercises in this chapter (consider bringing your responses and writing). Your college's career counseling professionals can help you narrow your choice of majors and provide additional opportunities to learn about yourself by completing additional personality and interest assessments. Take advantage of this important (and free!) resource.

Speak with Professors Don't forget to talk with professors to learn more about majors. Visit the office hours of a professor in whose class you are enrolled, who seems approachable, or who works in a field of interest to you. Talk with him or her. Ask questions about the undergraduate major and what kinds of jobs recent graduates have obtained. Do some homework beforehand to ensure that your questions are informed. For example, read the department website to learn a little bit about the major, basic course requirements, and, if possible, what courses the professor teaches. Visit the professor's website to learn about his or her courses and research. It will be easier to know what to ask if you know a little bit about the program and the professor. You might begin by explaining that you're thinking about majoring in his or her discipline and would like to know more about the field. Use the question in Table 2.3 as a starting point, but tailor them to your own needs.

As you can see, there are multiple sources of information about any given major. Approach the task as if you were solving a puzzle. Each person and source provides a unique bit of information and perspective. Sources may disagree about particular qualities or characteristics of a major. Compile all of the information and weigh it based on the person's perspective (e.g., as student, graduate or faculty), perceived accuracy (Does the information seem accurate? What is the source's perspective?), and perceived similarity

TABLE 2.3

LEARNING ABOUT MAJORS: WHAT TO ASK PROFESSORS

- ❑ What do graduates do?
- ❑ Are there formal opportunities to work closely with faculty, such as research courses with small enrollments or independent study courses?
- ❑ Do many students interact with faculty outside of the classroom, for example, assisting with research?
- ❑ Do students tend to participate in clubs and outside activities, such as group trips to conferences?
- ❑ Are there opportunities to participate in off-campus applied activities, such as internships?
- ❑ How did the professor choose his or her major?
- ❑ What are important attributes for a successful student?
- ❑ Any advice on choosing a major?
- ❑ What advice would the professor give for a new student in the major?

(How similar are your and the source's views?). Once you have gathered information and decided on several majors that may be a good fit for you, it's time to shift your attention inward and learn about yourself.

EXERCISE 2.1

Learning about Majors: Summing It Up

After evaluating one or more majors and speaking with degree-seekers, degree-holders, and professionals, what have you learned?

1. What majors did you evaluate?
2. What are some of the opportunities for students and graduates in this major, according to students?
3. What are some of the opportunities for students and graduates in this major, according to professors and other professionals?
4. Do students and professors share the same views on the challenges of this major? If not, where do they diverge? Why do you think they disagree?
5. What was the single most commonly mentioned positive aspect of this major?
6. From your perspective what are the most important positive and negative features of this major?
7. How well do you think you could overcome the negative features?

How to Learn about Yourself

An essential part of choosing a major that will provide the preparation that you desire is knowing your own interests and aspirations. Specifying them, however, is challenging. How do you know what you want? How can you anticipate your interests over the next few years? How do you tackle such an amorphous topic as choosing an area of study? I won't lie: Learning about yourself and uncovering your interests and aspirations isn't easy and can even feel uncomfortable. This is especially true if you view it as one burning task that has a strict deadline. Don't force it. You have time to explore and find what's right for you.

Learn about Yourself through Reflective Writing

After completing the exercises earlier in this chapter and book you may have noticed that writing is a useful way of organizing your ideas and recording what you learn about various majors. Writing is also useful for learning and organizing what you know about yourself. Always good advice, understanding yourself is critical to choosing a major that will satisfy your intellectual curiosity and fulfill your career goals. Consider keeping a log of your thoughts and experiences. Some might call this record a log, journal, or diary. Whatever you call it, reflective writing—capturing your thoughts and perspective in writing—can help you learn about yourself. Your log is a collection of your creative activity and can be saved in a simple notebook, computer file, or even in your phone. Your log is a private learning space where you can reflect upon yourself, your experiences, goals, dreams, and anxieties—learn more about who you are. Recording your thoughts can serve many purposes and aid you throughout college and your career. As you proceed in college you may find it useful to use your log to record ideas for papers and, if your program requires it, thesis topics. There is a benefit to being mindful and your log can help you. If you are still wondering what writing—maintaining a log of your thoughts can do—let's consider some of the benefits of writing for reflection.

Uses of Reflective Writing Writing is a way to explore your thoughts about yourself and the world around you. Sometimes we're not aware of our thoughts and feelings until we capture them with the written word. Expressing your ideas and feelings in words forces you to focus your thoughts, identify your opinions and values, and clarify your sense of identity. Here are three ways that you can use regular self-reflective writing.

Record your experiences, reduce stress, and gain insight into yourself. A reflective log provides a record of your life and your thoughts. Days, weeks, and months pass all too quickly. Memory is fallible. Return to your writing to help you to remember events, experiences, feelings, and intentions. Your log is a place to record accomplishments, hopes, and dreams as well as to retain details that you would probably otherwise forget. After a long day or a difficult experience reflective writing can give you a private opportunity to consider your feelings and release stress. From a therapeutic perspective, looking back over your writing permits the opportunity to reflect on patterns of experience, interaction, and emotion, providing insight into yourself and your perspective on life. How have you changed and grown? You can gain insight about yourself by reviewing your writing.

Reflective writing as an organizational tool. Your writing does not have to be particularly deep. Some people use their reflection logs for creating lists and plans. Perhaps the easiest way to begin keeping a log is to use it as a place to record lists of immediate tasks to be accomplished. With regular use, writing becomes a habit and can grow beyond making lists to include reflection, planning, and goal setting. You can write about your goals and document the steps needed to achieve them, as well as your progress. In this way, your log can help to organize your daily life.

Reflective writing as a problem-solving tool. Writing is an effective tool for problem solving because writing is thinking. The next time you find yourself confronted with a problem or a big decision, try writing about it. Explain the problem in words: What do you know about it? Discuss your feelings about the problem and analyze it. Writing may lead you to brainstorm potential solutions. Then your writing might shift toward analyzing each solution. Expressing ideas in written form requires a different thought process than simply pondering an issue. We think in new ways when we write. This allows us to conceptualize problems differently and come to solutions more quickly.

Tips for Beginning a Reflection Log If you find the benefits of reflective writing enticing, try it yourself. Your log can take many forms. It might be a plain notebook, a file on your computer, a file synced to a cloud service, or an app in your phone. The form your log takes doesn't matter—what matters is that it's readily accessible and easy for you to use. The cardinal rule of reflective writing is to remember that your log is for your eyes only. Don't let spelling, handwriting, and grammar be major concerns. Get your feelings and experiences down in writing, any way that you can. No one else will review or grade it. To get started, consider the following:

Don't over think it: Just write. There are no rules. You can write about anything that comes to mind, like ideas for papers and projects, everyday items such as lists of accomplishments and tasks to be completed, and even creative writing ideas such as story or poetry ideas, if that's your thing. Write about your problems or everyday frustrations. Observe your life. If you're having difficulty you might even write about the trouble that you're experiencing. You can write your thoughts as they come, even if you're writing that you don't know what to write.

Try a third-person perspective. If you are having trouble getting started, try writing about events that are happening to you or around you, from a third-person perspective, using pronouns such as he and she, as if you are observing someone else. For example, begin writing with the phrase, "It was a time when . . . ," and then describe the situation in detail, using as many of your senses as possible. What are the sounds, smells, sights, and feelings present? This exercise can help you to put things into perspective; it is especially effective when writing about life changes (like the transition to college), relationships (like that argument with your boyfriend or girlfriend), and events that you found upsetting (like finding out that you didn't do so well on that test). Throughout this book, you'll find plenty of topics and ideas to write about in your log, which will help you learn more about yourself and make plans for your future.

Write for brief periods, often. The goal of keeping a reflective log is to capture your thoughts. The more often you write, the more you'll learn about yourself. Keep your log close at hand. If you have fifteen minutes between classes, write. You might write about what you've learned in your prior class and how it relates to your experience, which will make it more likely that you learn and retain the material. Or simply about what you're thinking or feeling, whether you're hungry, tired, or antsy. Try to get into the habit of writing each day, even for just a few minutes. Try writing at bedtime or right after waking up. It doesn't take much time. You'll be surprised at how much you can capture in just a few minutes if you don't censor yourself. Also try to write some longer entries, because they will give you the opportunity to flesh out your thoughts and make insights about yourself.

Avoid expectations. Your log is whatever you choose to create. It does not have to be filled with descriptions of monumental experiences. Entries don't have to be well written or scholarly. Don't let these myths rob you of the chance to benefit from reflective writing. Also note that reading is not required. Some people reread their logs as chronicles of their lives. Others rarely read their logs but instead use writing to process their thoughts. Remember that the information is always there should you choose to read it, but you don't have to read it.

Try reflective writing. It can help you explore who you are and discover who you hope to become. Through writing and reflecting, the mundane can become profound. Take a chance and explore yourself through writing.

Learn about Yourself through Assessment

By now you likely realize that understanding yourself is critical to choosing a major that keeps your interest over the college years. Reflective writing is an important tool, but choosing a major requires a thorough self-assessment. It sounds technical, but *self-assessment* is simply the process by which you examine your skills, abilities, motivations, interests, values, experience, and accomplishments. In other words, it's how you learn about yourself, which will help you make decisions about your major. The following exercises will help you to better understand yourself, but remember that a useful self-assessment is not generated instantaneously. It takes time, hard work, and honesty.

Assess Your Interests and Traits Who are you? What characteristics best describe you? Understanding your unique personality traits will help you to choose a major that is right for you and, later, a job that complements your characteristics and is rewarding. Exercise 2.2 will help you to get a better understanding of your personality, which is essential to choosing a major that you'll be happy with. The reflection prompts can help you process what you have learned.

EXERCISE 2.2

Assess Your Personal Traits

Check off those traits that describe you. Include additional traits if needed. Take your time to think about each one, and be honest with yourself. Then complete the questions that follow.

- ❑ Academic
- ❑ Active
- ❑ Accurate
- ❑ Adaptable
- ❑ Adept
- ❑ Adventurous
- ❑ Affectionate
- ❑ Aggressive
- ❑ Alert
- ❑ Ambitious
- ❑ Analytical
- ❑ Appreciative
- ❑ Articulate
- ❑ Artistic
- ❑ Assertive
- ❑ Astute
- ❑ Athletic
- ❑ Attentive
- ❑ Balanced
- ❑ Brave
- ❑ Broad-minded
- ❑ Businesslike
- ❑ Calm
- ❑ Candid
- ❑ Capable
- ❑ Caring
- ❑ Cautious
- ❑ Charitable
- ❑ Cheerful
- ❑ Clean
- ❑ Clear
- ❑ Competent
- ❑ Competitive
- ❑ Congenial
- ❑ Conscientious
- ❑ Conservative
- ❑ Considerate
- ❑ Consistent
- ❑ Conventional
- ❑ Cooperative
- ❑ Courageous
- ❑ Creative
- ❑ Critical
- ❑ Curious
- ❑ Daring
- ❑ Decisive
- ❑ Deliberate
- ❑ Delicate
- ❑ Democratic
- ❑ Dependable
- ❑ Detail-oriented
- ❑ Diligent
- ❑ Discreet
- ❑ Distinctive
- ❑ Dominant
- ❑ Dynamic
- ❑ Eager
- ❑ Easygoing
- ❑ Effective
- ❑ Efficient
- ❑ Eloquent
- ❑ Emotional
- ❑ Empathetic
- ❑ Extroverted
- ❑ Fair-minded
- ❑ Farsighted
- ❑ Feeling
- ❑ Firm
- ❑ Flexible
- ❑ Forceful
- ❑ Formal
- ❑ Frank

❑ Frugal
❑ Future-oriented
❑ Generous
❑ Gentle
❑ Good natured
❑ Gregarious
❑ Hardy
❑ Helpful
❑ Honest
❑ Hopeful
❑ Humorous
❑ Idealistic
❑ Imaginative
❑ Impersonal
❑ Independent
❑ Individualistic
❑ Industrious
❑ Informal
❑ Initiator
❑ Innovative
❑ Intellectual
❑ Intelligent
❑ Introverted
❑ Intuitive
❑ Inventive
❑ Jovial
❑ Judicious
❑ Just
❑ Kind
❑ Liberal
❑ Likable
❑ Literary
❑ Logical
❑ Loyal
❑ Mature
❑ Methodical
❑ Meticulous
❑ Mistrustful
❑ Modest
❑ Motivated
❑ Nurturing
❑ Objective
❑ Observant
❑ Open-minded
❑ Opportunistic
❑ Optimistic
❑ Orderly
❑ Organized
❑ Original
❑ Outgoing
❑ Patient
❑ Peaceable
❑ Perceptive
❑ Persistent
❑ Practical
❑ Private
❑ Productive
❑ Progressive
❑ Protective
❑ Prudent
❑ Punctual
❑ Quick
❑ Quiet
❑ Rational
❑ Realistic
❑ Receptive
❑ Reflective
❑ Relaxed
❑ Reliable
❑ Reserved
❑ Resourceful
❑ Responsible
❑ Reverent
❑ Risk-taker
❑ Sedentary
❑ Self-confident
❑ Self-controlled
❑ Self-disciplined
❑ Self-starter
❑ Sensible
❑ Sensitive
❑ Serious
❑ Sincere
❑ Sociable
❑ Sophisticated
❑ Stable
❑ Strong
❑ Strong-minded
❑ Structured
❑ Subjective
❑ Successful
❑ Tactful
❑ Talented
❑ Tenacious
❑ Thorough
❑ Thoughtful
❑ Tolerant
❑ Trusting
❑ Trustworthy
❑ Truthful
❑ Understanding
❑ Unexcitable
❑ Uninhibited
❑ Verbal
❑ Versatile
❑ Vigorous
❑ Warm
❑ Wholesome
❑ Wise

Prompt

Examine the list of personality descriptors that you have checked off. Carefully consider each. How well does each adjective describe you? Choose three to five adjectives that you find most important.

1. Why did you choose the descriptors? Provide examples from your experience that illustrate how each word describes you.
2. Think back to your childhood dreams. Do you remember being asked by friends and family, "What do you want to be when you grow up?" How did you typically respond? What careers did you select as a child? Why?
3. Do you still have the same career-related dreams? How have your interests changed?
4. Consider your characteristics listed in question 1. How do these traits compare with those needed for the career of your childhood dreams? How do they fit with your revised-adult view?

Identify your interests though self-assessment. Another way to use what you know about yourself to choose a major is to identify your occupational interests. Pay attention to your interests to determine the work environment that you'll find most appealing. Holland (1959) proposed that people's interests and the matching work environments can be loosely categorized into six themes or codes: Realistic, investigative, artistic, social, enterprising, and conventional. Although created half a century ago, the Holland Occupational Codes remain the most commonly used assessment of career interests (Ruff, Reardon, & Bertoch, 2007). For a brief insight into your career interests and their match with each Holland Code complete Exercise 2.3. The career development center at your college can help you determine and interpret your Holland Code. Holland Codes are the basis for the O*NET Interest Profiler, a self-assessment inventory that aids individuals in identifying their work-related interests. The O*NET Interest Profiler is a free downloadable computer program sponsored by the U.S. Department of Labor/Employment and Training Administration and the American Job Center Network (Lewis & Rivkin, 1999) and available at http://www.onetcenter.org/CIP.html. A short version of the O*NET Interest Profiler can be taken online for free at http://www.onetcenter.org/IPSF.html; http://www.mynextmove.org/explore/ip.

EXERCISE 2.3

Identify Your Holland Personality Type

Realistic

- ❑ I am mechanically inclined
- ❑ I am athletically inclined
- ❑ I like working outside with tools, plants, or animals
- ❑ I like creating things with my hands
- ❑ I am practical
- ❑ I like to see direct results of my work
- ❑ I am a nature lover
- ❑ I am systematic
- ❑ I am persistent
- ❑ I am calm and reserved

Investigative

- ❑ I like learning, observing, problem solving, and working with information
- ❑ I like solving abstract, vague problems
- ❑ I am curious
- ❑ I am logical
- ❑ I am reserved
- ❑ I am introspective
- ❑ I am independent
- ❑ I am observant
- ❑ I am interested in understanding the physical world
- ❑ I like working alone or in small groups

Realistic

- [x] I am independent
- [x] I dislike vagueness and ambiguity

Investigative

- [ ] I like to be original and creative in solving problems
- [x] I enjoy intellectual challenges

Artistic

- [x] I am imaginative and creative
- [ ] I like to express myself by designing and producing
- [ ] I prefer unstructured activities
- [ ] I am spontaneous
- [ ] I am idealistic
- [ ] I am unique
- [x] I am independent
- [ ] I am expressive
- [ ] I am unconventional
- [x] I am compassionate
- [ ] I am bold
- [x] I prefer to work alone

Social

- [x] I am compassionate
- [x] I like helping and training others
- [x] I am patient
- [x] I am dependable
- [x] I am supportive
- [x] I am understanding
- [x] I am perceptive
- [x] I am generous
- [ ] I am idealistic
- [ ] I am cheerful, well liked
- [ ] I am people-oriented and friendly
- [x] I am concerned with the welfare of others
- [x] I am good at expressing myself and getting along well with others

Enterprising

- [ ] I like to work with people
- [ ] I like persuading people
- [ ] I like managing situations
- [ ] I like achieving organizational or economic goals
- [ ] I am a leader
- [ ] I am talkative
- [x] I am extroverted
- [x] I am optimistic
- [ ] I am spontaneous and daring
- [ ] I am assertive
- [ ] I am energetic

Conventional

- [x] I am good with numbers
- [ ] I like to work with data and carry out tasks in detail
- [ ] I am persistent
- [x] I am practical
- [ ] I am conforming
- [x] I am precise
- [x] I am conscientious
- [x] I am meticulous
- [x] I am adept
- [x] I am practical
- [ ] I am frugal

(Continued)

EXERCISE 2.3 (Continued)

Enterprising	Conventional
❑ I am good at communicating	❑ I am stable and dependable
❑ I am good at selling and persuading	❑ I am well controlled
❑ I prefer tasks that require quick action	❑ I prefer task that are structured
	❑ I prefer to know what's expected
	❑ I prefer a well-defined chain of command

Prompt
Count your checkmarks to determine which sets of descriptors best match your characteristics. Most students find that two or more sets of qualities fit them. Which set(s) of descriptors best describe you?

Understanding your career interests may make it easier to choose a major because some majors are better suited to particular constellations of interests than are others. Table 2.4 lists college majors, organized by Holland Code. Remember that this simply is a guide to careers. Not all possible careers are listed, and the categories are much more fluid than they appear.

Notice that many college majors fit more than one Holland Code. College majors tap multiple interests and abilities—and foster similar skills in students, such as critical thinking and communication skills. Use this exercise as a general guide but recognize that the characteristics for success in various college majors often overlap to some degree.

Identify your interests though career assessment. While you can learn a lot about yourself through reflection and surveying your own interests, a visit to the career center at your college can provide you with an objective and detailed profile of your interests. A career counselor can administer several inventories to help determine what career path is right for you. The two most commonly administered inventories are the Strong Interest Inventory (Strong, Donnay, Morris, Schaubhut, & Thompson, 2004) and the Myers-Briggs Type Indicator (Myers, McCaulley, Quenk, & Hammer, 1998).

Administered at your college's career center, the *Strong Interest Inventory* contains 291 items that survey your occupational interests and values. It takes about forty minutes to complete and yields a detailed report that includes your Holland Code, a list of your top interests and what you find most motivating and rewarding, and comparisons of your interests with those of people working in 122 occupations. The Strong Interest Inventory also lists occupations in which people whose interests most closely match yours work. Finally your values, that is, preferences regarding work style, learning

TABLE 2.4 **CAREERS BY HOLLAND PERSONALITY TYPE**

Realistic	Investigative	Artistic
Agriculture/Forestry	Animal Science	Advertising
Criminal Justice	Anthropology	Art History
Engineering	Astronomy	Art Education
Health and Physical Education	Biochemistry	Architecture
Plant and Soil Sciences	Biological Sciences	Communications
Architecture	Chemistry	English
Recreation and Tourism Management	Computer Science	Foreign Language
Environmental Studies	Engineering	Graphic Design
Geology	Geography	History
Medical Technology	Geology	Interior Design
Exercise Science	Mathematics	Journalism
Sport Management	Medical Technology	Music
Engineering	Medicine	Music Education
	Nursing	Speech/Drama
	Nutrition	
	Pharmacy	
	Philosophy	
	Physical Therapy	
	Physics	
	Psychology	
	Sociology	
	Statistics	
Social	**Enterprising**	**Conventional**
Audiology	Advertising	Accounting
Counseling	Broadcasting	Business
Criminal Justice	Communications	Computer Science
Elementary Education	Economics	Economics
History	Finance	Finance
Human Development	Industrial Relations	Mathematics
Library Sciences	Journalism	Statistics
Occupational Therapy	Law	
Nursing	Management	
Nutrition	Marketing	
Philosophy	Political Science	
Political Science	Public Administration	
Physical Education	Speech	
Psychology		
Religious Studies		
Sociology		
Social Work		
Special Education		
Urban Planning		

environment, leadership style, risk taking and team orientation, are listed. A summary provides a graphic representation of your results. The career counselor will discuss your results with you. Remember that although a number of compatible careers are listed, you are free to pursue whatever career appeals to you. The Strong Interest Inventory simply provides a more detailed look at the aspects of career assessment that we have discussed in this chapter. It's especially useful if you have tried the activities in this book and still find yourself puzzled with regard to what really interests you.

Another assessment option available in your college's career center is the *Myers-Briggs Type Indicator* (MBTI). With over 100 items, the MBTI assesses individuals' perceptions, preferences, and judgments in interacting with the world. Created by mother and daughter, Katharine Cook Briggs and Isabel Briggs Myers, the MTBI is based on Carl Jung's theory that there are sixteen personality types in which people may be categorized based on their preferences along four dimensions or subscales. The MBTI contains several subscales. The extraversion/introversion subscale refers to the degree to which you turn outward or inward, that is, the degree to which you are oriented toward people and actions or the internal world of thoughts and ideas. The sensation/intuition subscale examines how you prefer to understand information: Do you focus on the facts or do you prefer to interpret and add meaning? Do you focus on logic and reasoning when making decisions or do you first look at circumstances and people (thinking/feeling)? Your preferences for structure is assessed by the judging/perceiving scale that examines whether you prefer to make decisions or remain open to new ideas and options. Finally the measure categorizes test takers into a "personality type" suggesting their own set of preferences. If you choose to take the MBTI remember that it is simply a tool to help you learn about yourself. It is up to you to determine whether the results make sense to you. Finally note that although useful for self-exploration, some psychologists have argued that there is insufficient research to conclude that the MBTI is effective (Pittenger, 2005).

The question that you must answer is: What interests you? The happiest and most successful students choose majors that they find engaging. Many students decide on a major before considering their interests and values. They take courses for a semester or two and then realize that they've chosen a major in which they have minimal interest. Identifying your interests early in your college career can save you from changing majors and wasting time. What appeals to you? An effective way of assessing your interests is to write about your personal history. Consider Exercise 2.4.

Exercise 2.4

Review Your Personal History

1. List and write about all of the times that you can think of when you have encountered a problem (regardless of its size) and have taken action to solve that problem. In other words, write about all of your accomplishments.

2. List as many as you can. Don't stop when it becomes difficult, but probe further. If you're stumped, try free writing about your achievements. Free writing entails writing whatever comes to mind, without censoring or editing it. Keep the ideas flowing, or even write about the difficulty you're experiencing in coming up with ideas. Looking over the exercises in this chapter can help. Eventually you'll produce a number of interesting items to reflect on.
3. The accomplishments that you list need not be monumental. Accomplishments can be small, and they don't have to be recognized by other people. Write about the achievements that are personally relevant to you and of which you are most proud.
4. Next examine your accomplishments carefully. Which have brought you the most satisfaction? Which do you value most highly? Why?

This exercise helps you to identify your strengths and is a fantastic self-esteem builder because it illustrates your accomplishments—the things that make you special. By understanding which achievements you cherish, you'll have a better idea of your interests and values, which is essential to choosing a major or career that's right for you.

Assess Your Skills In addition to understanding your interests, your choice of major should reflect your skills and abilities. What are your skills? What activities do you do best? If you're unsure, try writing an experiential diary to get a better grip on your skills. An experiential diary lists all the jobs, leadership positions, and extracurricular activities that you've engaged in, and then lists all the tasks comprising each of these activities and jobs. Once you've created a master list, write down all of the skills required to perform the tasks on your list. For example, if the task was answering the phone, it probably entailed the following skills: communication skills (the effective use of language), problem solving, and the ability to direct inquiries. Also identify specific skills that you've learned, like the ability to use computer programming languages or speak a foreign language. Even with an experiential diary, it is sometimes difficult to list and remember all of your skills and abilities. Exercise 2.5 will help you to better understand your skills.

EXERCISE 2.5

Assess Your Skills

Check off all of the skills that apply to you, then complete the activity below.

❑ Acting or performing
❑ Administering
❑ Advising
❑ Analyzing data
❑ Applying
❑ Arranging social functions
❑ Budgeting
❑ Calculating
❑ Checking for accuracy
❑ Coaching
❑ Collecting money

(Continued)

EXERCISE 2.5 (Continued)

- ❑ Communicating
- ❑ Compiling statistics
- ❑ Conceptualizing
- ❑ Controlling
- ❑ Coordinating events
- ❑ Counseling
- ❑ Creating new ideas
- ❑ Decision making
- ❑ Designing
- ❑ Dispensing information
- ❑ Dramatizing ideas or problems
- ❑ Editing
- ❑ Entertaining people
- ❑ Evaluating
- ❑ Expressing feelings
- ❑ Finding information
- ❑ Fund raising
- ❑ Generalizing
- ❑ Goal setting
- ❑ Handling complaints
- ❑ Identifying problems
- ❑ Illustrating
- ❑ Implementing
- ❑ Improving
- ❑ Initiating with strangers
- ❑ Innovating
- ❑ Interpreting
- ❑ Interviewing
- ❑ Investigating problems
- ❑ Judging
- ❑ Leading
- ❑ Listening to others
- ❑ Managing
- ❑ Measuring
- ❑ Mediating
- ❑ Motivating
- ❑ Navigating
- ❑ Negotiating
- ❑ Observing
- ❑ Organizing
- ❑ Painting
- ❑ Persuading
- ❑ Photographing
- ❑ Planning
- ❑ Problem-solving
- ❑ Programming
- ❑ Promoting
- ❑ Proofreading
- ❑ Questioning
- ❑ Reading
- ❑ Reasoning
- ❑ Recording
- ❑ Record keeping
- ❑ Recruiting
- ❑ Researching
- ❑ Scheduling
- ❑ Selling
- ❑ Singing
- ❑ Sketching
- ❑ Speaking
- ❑ Supervising
- ❑ Synthesizing information
- ❑ Teaching or training
- ❑ Team building
- ❑ Thinking logically
- ❑ Tolerating ambiguity
- ❑ Translating
- ❑ Troubleshooting
- ❑ Visualizing
- ❑ Writing

Prompt

1. What skills did you check?
2. Can you think of examples of how each skill has developed or how you've used it to achieve a goal?
3. Based on your consideration, choose the top three to five skills and explain your choices. These skills are your strengths.
4. Now look at all of the skills that you checked, including those for which you found it difficult to think of supporting examples.
   a. Do any of these skills need further development?
   b. Which of these skills do you prefer using? Why?
   c. Which are you interested in using in the future? Why?
   d. Which skills do you dislike? Why?
5. Are there any skills that you don't currently have, but would like to develop? Explain.

By now it should be apparent that you already have an array of skills. Are you interested in using and pursuing those skills? We tend to like and be interested in things that we are good at. Is that true for you? You may not be skilled in a particular area, but if you find it interesting, you can seek the education and training to become skilled. Don't let your current competence levels dictate your choices. If you are willing to work, you can make great strides and learn many skills that can help you meet your career goals.

Assess Your Values While choosing a major does not tie you to a particular career, it is useful to consider your career aspirations and life goals in order to seek the educational experiences that will prepare you for them. What do you want out of life? How do you define success? Would you rather live in a city or in a rural area? Is personal time and flexibility important to you? Would you like a family (and if so, large or small)? Is financial success important? Values are the things that are important to you, that you see as desirable in life. Spend time thinking through your priorities. Reflective writing can help you to understand and clarify your values. Consider the following collection of values, categorized by theme. Check off the ones that appeal to you.

EXERCISE 2.6
Identify Your Values

Service	Adventure	Leadership
❑ Active in community	❑ Excitement	❑ Influence people and opinions
❑ Help others	❑ Risk taking	❑ Supervise others
❑ Help society and the world	❑ Travel	❑ Power authority and control
❑ Work with and help people in meaningful way	❑ Drama	❑ Make decisions
	❑ Exciting tasks	❑ Direct work of others
	❑ Good health	❑ Leadership
	❑ Travel	❑ Coordinate people data and stuff
		❑ Hiring and firing responsibility

(Continued)

EXERCISE 2.6 (Continued)

Creativity	Relationships	Financial Reward
❑ Aesthetic appreciation ❑ Artistic creativity ❑ Creative expression ❑ Develop and express new ideas ❑ No set routine ❑ Work on own or as creative team ❑ Flexible working conditions	❑ Organization affiliation ❑ Work friendships ❑ Family ❑ Work with others—teamwork ❑ Public contract ❑ Friendly work atmosphere ❑ Work with people you like	❑ High earnings ❑ Commission-based work ❑ Material possessions ❑ Very high salary ❑ Extra pay for extra work ❑ Long hours
Prestige	**Meaning and Purpose**	**Variety**
❑ Recognition ❑ Status ❑ Respect ❑ Professional position ❑ Responsibility ❑ Income	❑ Spirituality ❑ Personal fulfillment ❑ Work related to ideals ❑ Make a difference ❑ Express inner self in work ❑ Integrate belief system into work	❑ Changing work responsibilities ❑ Diversity of tasks ❑ New projects ❑ Varied tasks ❑ Meet new people ❑ Range of settings and situations
Security	**Independence**	**Physical Activity**
❑ Stability ❑ Predictability ❑ Low pressure ❑ Job assurance ❑ Guaranteed annual salary ❑ Retirement benefits ❑ Live in familiar location	❑ Freedom ❑ Autonomy ❑ Work alone ❑ Set own pace and working conditions ❑ Flexible hours ❑ Choose team or work alone	❑ Outdoor work ❑ Physical challenge ❑ Physical fitness ❑ Desk job

Intellectual Challenge	Productivity	Advancement
❑ Address challenging problems ❑ Pursue/obtain knowledge ❑ Constant updating of information/ working with new ideas ❑ Work with creative and intellectually stimulating people ❑ Acknowledged expert ❑ Research and development	❑ Competence and proficiency ❑ Fast-paced work ❑ Efficient work habits ❑ Hard work is rewarded ❑ Quality and productivity is rewarded by rapid advancement	❑ Promotions ❑ Work under pressure ❑ Competition ❑ Limited only by energy and initiative

Prompt

1. What values did you check? Do your selected values cluster into a few areas?
2. How have these values influenced your choices and behaviors? Consider your extracurricular activities and interests.
3. How might these values inform your career choices?

Draw Conclusions

Now that you're aware of your traits, interests, skills, and values, compile this information to get a comprehensive view of yourself. Review the lists and descriptions of majors in your college handbook. Do any seem to fit your set of traits, skills, and interests? Some majors and careers will match many of the personal traits and skills that you possess, and others will not match your self-description. Review what you have learned about various majors and about yourself. If you are still puzzling over what major to choose, list the two or three forerunners. Use the college handbook and department websites to find additional information. Once you have narrowed down your choice of majors consider the pros and cons of each major. Table 2.5 summarizes the process of choosing a major.

TABLE 2.5

Steps to Choosing a Major

- ❑ Assess your personality and attitudinal traits
- ❑ Assess your skills and abilities
- ❑ Assess your values and life goals
- ❑ Research majors
- ❑ Explore courses
- ❑ Talk with other students and recent graduates
- ❑ Visit the career center
- ❑ Talk with professors
- ❑ Compare alternatives
- ❑ Reflect on your choice
- ❑ Remember that your major is not your career

EXERCISE 2.7

Comparing Majors

Choose a potential major (or two or three, if you're still searching) and determine the following:

1. How interested am I in this topic? Is it a new interest or a long-standing one? Do I enjoy the subject?
2. What is the curriculum for this major? What kinds of classes do I have to take?
3. How well does the major match my skills and abilities? Can I perform well in this subject? Is it too easy or too challenging?
4. Which professors teach this subject? Do I know any? Have I taken courses with any?
5. How motivated am I to study this subject? Is it inherently interesting or fun? Do I dread classes or homework in this area?
6. Do I tend to seek out other students and faculty in this department for discussions and other informal interactions?
7. What kinds of jobs do graduates hold? Will the major prepare me for the kind of career I desire?

Choosing Psychology

After completing the exercises in this chapter, speaking with others, seeking outside information, and doing some careful thinking, you may have narrowed down your choices of majors. If that's true for you, fantastic! If not, keep working and thinking; you will find what is right for you. Remember that your major choice isn't set in stone. You can change your mind. All majors offer important educational opportunities. In that sense, you can't choose a "wrong" major. That said, there are some majors that will better fit your interests and aspirations than others. Let's take a closer look at psychology: What skills and knowledge are acquired with the psychology major?

Skills Acquired with a Psychology Major

The psychology major prepares graduates for "lifelong learning, thinking, and action" (McGovern, Furumoto, Halpern, Kimble, & McKeachie, 1991, p. 600). Like other liberal arts majors, psychology students gain knowledge and skills that generalize to the world outside the classroom. The emphasis on learning and applying principles of psychology to understand human behavior makes the degree unique (American Psychological Association, 2013). As a psychology major you will have the opportunity to develop the following.

Knowledge of Human Behavior Undergraduate education in psychology is intended to expose students to the major facts, theories, and issues in the discipline. Understanding human behavior entails learning about physiology, perception, cognition, emotion, development, and more. Consequently, psychology majors construct a broad knowledge base that serves as the conceptual framework for lifelong learning about human behavior as well as the capacity to apply their understanding in everyday situations.

Information Acquisition and Synthesis Skills The knowledge base of psychology is constantly expanding. Successful psychology students learn how to gather and synthesize information. Psychology students learn how to use a range of sources including the library, computerized databases, and the Internet to gather information about an area of interest. More important, psychology students learn how to weigh and integrate information into a coherent and persuasive argument. In addition, successful psychology students apply their advanced understanding of cognition and memory to enhance their own processing and recall of information.

Research Methods and Statistical Skills Psychology students learn how to apply the scientific method to address questions about human behavior. They learn how to identify a problem, devise a hypothesis, choose and carry out scientific methods to gather information about the problem, conduct statistical analyses to evaluate a hypothesis, and interpret data summaries to devise a conclusion. In other words, psychology students become able to pose and answer questions about human behavior and experience.

Critical Thinking and Problem-Solving Skills Exposure to the diverse perspectives within psychology trains students to think flexibly and to accept some ambiguity. Introductory psychology students often ask for the "right" answer; they soon learn that answers often aren't black or white, but many shades of gray. Psychology students acquire skills in thinking critically about complex problems. They learn to weigh multiple sources of information, determine the degree of support for each position, and make a reasoned decision about which position has more merit and how a problem is best solved.

Reading, Writing, and Speaking Skills Psychology students develop reading, writing, and presentation skills for effective oral and written communication. They learn how to think critically about what they read, as well as comprehend and present arguments from a psychological standpoint. Moreover, their understanding of human behavior aids students in constructing arguments that are easily comprehended by others. Information derived from psychology regarding cognition, memory, listening, persuasion, and communication enhances psychology majors' ability to communicate orally and in writing.

Interpersonal and Intrapersonal Skills Psychology students develop the ability to communicate their ideas and use their knowledge of human behavior to devise persuasive arguments. Successful students are able to lead, collaborate with others, and work effectively in groups. Psychology students are primed to be effective communicators because they are trained to be sensitive to issues of culture, race, class, and ethnicity. Students of psychology also develop intrapersonal awareness, or self-knowledge. They are able to monitor and manage their own behavior, which is critical in succeeding in academic and interpersonal tasks.

Adaptability Psychology students quickly learn that the perfect experiment is an unattainable goal toward which all researchers strive. Students learn how to design the best research studies possible, given limited resources. The capacity to evaluate and adapt to changing circumstances is highly valued in today's volatile economy and workplace.

An undergraduate education in psychology will provide you with the opportunity to develop these skills, which, incidentally, is not an exhaustive list. The combination of liberal education and training psychological science is what makes the psychology major very special. The psychology major satisfies the objectives of a liberal arts education, which include critical and analytical thinking, independent thinking, leadership skills, communication skills, understanding how to learn, being able to see all sides of an issue, and understanding human diversity (Roche, 2010). Training in research design and statistical analysis, as well as human behavior, is what makes the psychology major unique among liberal arts degrees.

If you choose to major in psychology, you will develop and expand your knowledge of human behavior. You'll become increasingly able to discriminate relevant from trivial information. You'll learn how to find and pull together, what professors often refer to as *synthesize*, information from a variety of sources. You'll learn about psychological theories, concepts, and terms that will help you to understand and influence the world around you. If you study and take college seriously, you'll develop advanced critical thinking, communication, and interpersonal skills, which are valuable to all careers, regardless of whether they are directly related to psychology.

What to Expect as Psychology Major

What, specifically, can you expect as a psychology major? Like all college students, you can expect to complete a range of courses required by the university, often referred to as General Education requirements because they're intended to provide you with a broad education covering many subjects that are essential to a well-rounded and capable thinker. Whereas the General Education curriculum provides breadth of knowledge, your major is intended to provide depth of knowledge in a specific area. As a psychology major you can expect to learn about human behavior and the methods that psychologists use to study human behavior. Specific requirements may vary by university; however you can expect to complete the following:

Introductory Psychology/General Psychology. Your first course in psychology will provide a whirlwind tour of the field and its dizzying array of subfields. Some students find Introductory Psychology challenging, overwhelming, or even boring because it is often a fast-paced experience intended to provide an overview of the entire field—all of the subdisciplines mentioned in Chapter 1—within a single semester. Every chapter in the textbook and every week in the course introduces a new subfield—and it is likely that the Psychology Department at your college offers at least one course in each of those fields. Some students are put off by the fast pace—once they become interested in a topic it's time to move on to the next chapter and the next subfield. Perhaps the most helpful way to consider the Introductory Psychology class is as a primer to the field and a way to learn more about what areas you may want to learn more about in the future.

Methodology and Statistics. It is the methodology courses that will teach you how psychologists learn about human behavior—the methods we use to make discoveries. Students learn the research methods that psychologists use to ask and answer questions about human behavior. They also learn statistics and the methods psychologists use to compile and draw conclusions from the information that they collect. Finally students gain experience in designing and carrying out research studies that give them practice in asking and answering questions about human behavior.

Breadth Courses. Just as the college General Education curriculum is designed to provide students with a broad knowledge base for a well-rounded education, the Psychology breadth requirement imparts psychology majors with a well-rounded education in human behavior. The particular sets of courses vary across psychology departments, but all will require you to enroll in courses in the Developmental, Cognitive, Biological, and Social/Personality subfields. Others may include required courses in Clinical or Applied areas. Common courses offered by Psychology departments are listed in Table 2.6. The below courses may be grouped in several ways, depending on department. Some psychology courses are required for majors at nearly all schools, while others are electives found at a handful of schools.

TABLE 2.6 COMMON PSYCHOLOGY COURSES

Applied
Family Psychology
Health Psychology
Industrial Psychology
Organizational Psychology
Psychology and Law
Sport Psychology
Consumer Psychology

Biological and Neuropsychology
Physiological Psychology
Sensation and Perception
Psychopharmacology

Clinical
Clinical Psychology
Abnormal Psychology
School Psychology

Developmental
Adolescent Psychology
Adulthood and Aging
Life-Span Development
Developmental Psychopathology
Child Psychology

History, Methods, and Statistics
Research Methods
Experimental Psychology
Psychological Statistics
History of Psychology

Learning and Cognitive
Psychology of Learning
Psychology of Creativity
Educational Psychology
Behavior Modification
Cognitive Psychology
Cognitive Neuroscience

Personality, Social Processes, and Measurement
Group Dynamics
Social Psychology
Psychology of Motivation
Psychology of Personality
Psychological and Educational Testing
Psychology of Adjustment
Psychology of Gender
Psychology of Women
Cross-Cultural Psychology

Elective Courses. You can expect to take several elective courses in your major—courses that are not required, but are your choice. These courses are opportunities to explore your interests or gain knowledge and skills that you think will be helpful in the future.

Capstone Course. The capstone course is intended as the crowning achievement for majors, a course that requires them to synthesize all that they have learned to demonstrate that they have mastered the material. It is an advanced course that is intended to require you to bring together your knowledge about how to study psychological phenomena: how to ask research questions, devise methods of addressing questions, and draw conclusions. You might conduct an independent research study or write a lengthy review paper or senior thesis. Ask your professors to learn more about the capstone requirement and get advice so that you can plan ahead and take the courses that you believe will best prepare you for this experience.

Real Tips for Real Students

Plan Ahead for Your Capstone Course

Most departments offer a handful of capstone courses in different subfields of psychology. For example, one department may offer capstone seminars in developmental psychology, cognitive psychology, social psychology, and experimental psychology. Usually these capstones have different prerequisites. For example, the developmental psychology capstone may require students to have completed specific courses in developmental psychology and likewise for the other capstone courses. Be aware of this early to ensure that you have the time and opportunity to take the prerequisite courses to gain admittance into the capstone course you desire.

Is psychology right for you? Only you can answer that question. Psychology offers many opportunities, but other majors offer different sets of opportunities. You are the only expert in choosing your major. No one else can do it for you, and no test provides all of the answers. While parents, friends, professors, and counselors might offer assistance and advice, ultimately this is your decision. Your major will not lock you into one career path—there are many roads and a psychology major can be the first step toward a variety of careers.

Suggested Readings

Bolles, R. N. (2014). *What color is your parachute? 2015: A practical manual for job-hunters and career-changers*. Berkeley, CA: Ten Speed Press.

Johnston, S. M. (2013). *The career adventure: Your guide to personal assessment, career exploration, and decision making.* Upper Saddle River, NJ: Prentice Hall.

Kuther, T. L., & Morgan, R. D. (2010). *Careers in psychology: Opportunities in a changing world.* Belmont, CA: Wadsworth.

Lore, N. (2008). *Now what? The young person's guide to choosing the perfect career.* New York: Fireside.

Shatkin, L. (2011). *Panicked student's guide to choosing a college major: How to confidently pick your ideal path.* Indianapolis, IN: Jist Works.

INTERNET RESOURCES (Available at http://www.tarakuther.com)

An Online Resource to Enable Undergraduate Psychology Majors to Identify and Investigate 172 Psychology and Psychology Related Careers

http://teachpsych.org/Resources/Documents/otrp/resources/appleby14.pdf

Maintained by Dr. Drew Appleby, this list of careers includes links to O*NET information and more.

*O*NET Interest Profiler*

http://www.mynextmove.org/explore/ip

Online Holland Code assessment.

Career Assessment

http://www.quintcareers.com/career_assessment.html

This is an excellent and comprehensive site with articles, tools, and other resources for assessing your career interests.

Self-Directed Search

http://www.self-directed-search.com

Available for a fee, this self-report questionnaire assesses your personality type, according to Holland's theory.

College Board's Big Future: What Are You Into?

https://bigfuture.collegeboard.org/explore-careers

Contains information about a wide range of majors and careers as well as how to tell what majors fit with your interests.

Career Key

http://www.careerkey.org/english/

The Career Key is a free website with assessments to help you with career choices, career changes, and career planning, job search, and choosing a college major or training program.

Reflection Prompts

My Questions

This exercise helps you to identify unanswered questions and gives you prompts for future reflection entries. Use your writing to formulate and record questions that you wonder about. What questions do you have about your schoolwork, personal life, values, or current events and items that you've read about in newspapers, magazines, or books? As a college student, what do you need to know? Identify three to five questions that you believe address essential information. How will you search for the answers? Brainstorm three sources of information.

Self-Review

Once you've amassed several weeks or months' worth of entries, you might use your log to reflect on how you're changing. Read over earlier log entries. How have you changed? Do you have different ideas about the entry? Do you have new interpretations of events? Do you disagree with an earlier entry? Try to track how you think, and how your thinking is changing. Can you draw conclusions about yourself from what you've written?

Why College?

Why did you decide to attend college? What did you hope to gain? What have you learned since beginning college? Do you still have the same reasons for attending?

CHAPTER

3

Take an Active Role in Your Education

Chapter Outline

Get Involved in the Discipline

Attend Psychology Conferences

Disseminate Research

Participate in Professional Organizations

Exercise 3.6 Academic and Professional Organizations

Suggested Readings

Internet Resources

Reflection Prompts

One of the biggest differences between high school and college is that college requires you to take an active role in your education. Whether you take anything of substance away from your college years, whether you learn anything, is up to you. Your own interest, motivation, and hard work will make or break your college years. Students often are surprised by this new level of autonomy, and they often are unsure of how to take control of their education. This chapter will help you to take advantage of the resources in your department, college, and field so that you can get the most from your college years.

What Do You Learn in College?

The first step in taking an active role, steering your own education, is to be aware of the range of competencies that a college degree imparts. Students of all majors have the opportunity to develop these skills as they are what encompass a well-rounded education and what are expected of knowledgeable individuals. The liberal arts constitute a range of subjects including the humanities (such as history, literature, and philosophy), social sciences (such as psychology and sociology), and natural sciences (such as biology and physics). Most colleges require students to complete a variety of courses in the liberal arts that are often referred to as General Education courses and intended to impart broad general knowledge and intellectual skills and expose students to a world of ideas, people, cultures, and history. Students of all majors learn how to consider multiple perspectives and examine ideas, explore their possibilities and challenge their assumptions.

No matter your major, you will learn from two sets of curricula during your college years. You will learn the specific content of your major, the material that's printed in the course catalog, including specific facts, concepts, and theories that college courses are designed to impart. However, you will learn much more than the specific information, or content, of your courses. College also entails a covert curriculum, a subtle set of skills, of which students are often unaware, such as how to acquire information, think, and learn—skills that are more important than any set of facts you might learn (Appleby, 2001). College students have the opportunity to develop the following competencies that will prepare them for their careers after graduation.

Communication Skills

The ability to communicate in a clear, organized, and persuasive way is a skill that is useful to all careers and can be applied throughout life. All of your college courses provide opportunities to develop and strengthen your oral and written communication skills but some courses, such as in English composition, public speaking, and writing, offer specialized practice. Many students approach writing and communications courses as simply requirements to complete. Instead, these courses are an important foundation for communication skills—the capacity to get a message out to the world and be heard. Savvy students take additional courses in writing or public speaking, because no matter the career, the ability to be understood in a clear and persuasive way is invaluable. Remember that each course you take contributes something unique to your education. No course is a "joke" or simply something to endure.

Reading Skills

The ability to read complex material quickly, understand it, extract the relevant material, and use the information to solve problems are skills that students hone in college and will use in their careers (Appleby, 2001). For example, employees in business, management, and advertising must keep abreast of the literature in their field by reading books, magazines, and trade publications to help them to perform their jobs more efficiently. Savvy students quickly recognize that they must adapt their reading to the content at hand and take a different approach when reading scientific articles as compared with reading fiction. Students who recognize the covert curriculum, the lifelong skills that they will develop in college, approach assignments as opportunities to learn and sharpen their reading comprehension skills, as well as adapt their reading styles to the material to be read.

Listening and Note-Taking Skills

The ability to take accurate notes and identify the arguments and important points that emerge from discussion are just as important to success after graduation as they are in college. Successful employees and graduate students have the ability to listen carefully and attentively and to understand and follow instructions. Lectures and class discussions offer valuable opportunities to develop active listening and note-taking skills that stretch beyond the content of the course.

Computer Literacy

We interact with technology every day and it is an inevitable part of the workplace. Today's college students are often referred to as *digital natives* because they have grown up immersed in a world of technology. Unlike prior generations, young people today developed basic technology skills such as typing, texting, and web searching at an early age. Although many college students were introduced to word processing, spreadsheet, and presentation software in high school, these skills are honed in college when students learn to use them to complete advanced projects. All students will encounter new programs to learn, including course management software such as Blackboard, and new Internet and database searching skills. College students become more proficient at adapting to new technology and learning new skills.

Critical Thinking and Problem-Solving Skills

The most important skill that a college education imparts is the ability to think. Certainly, you're able to think well before you enter college, but the quality of thinking improves radically over the college years with practice analyzing complex problems, thinking critically, and constructing arguments that are supported by evidence. Critical thinking refers to the ability to gather, comprehend, analyze, evaluate, and apply information to solve problems. These thinking skills are essential to making wise decisions throughout life.

Self-Management Skills

College is often the first time that students are independent and responsible for their own behavior. At first it is very difficult. Students may be late for class, forget about assignments, or neglect to do their laundry. It is often mistakes that encourage learning. Successful students don't dwell on mistakes: They learn from them. With time, students become more independent, responsible for their actions and well-being, and more organized—all skills that prepare them for today's demanding work environments. College students face new pressures and multiple demands: classes, projects, outside activities, meetings with professors, athletic practice and games, socializing with friends, part-time work, and volunteer work, for example. Part of the unwritten curriculum of college is developing the ability to regulate or control one's emotions and behaviors in order to manage the multiple conflicting demands of life (Appleby, 2001). Students learn to become more punctual, reliable, mature, and respectful—skills critical to a happy, healthy, and productive adulthood.

College is not simply about learning the content of your major. The covert curriculum is perhaps even more important. A college education provides the tools for students to learn how to think independently and critically, develop mature and reasoned decision making, solve complex problems, effectively communicate their ideas with others, and exercise self-control (Bare, 1988). Become engaged with your education and you'll develop thinking, analysis, and self-management abilities that last a lifetime. This is true no matter your major. If you put in the time and hard work, you will receive a broad and fulfilling education. One example of how students can play a role in their own education is to make the effort to get to know their professors.

Get to Know Faculty: Professors, Advisors, and Mentors

Many students don't take advantage of their school's most valuable resource: the faculty. Sure, they attend class, take notes, and learn the content of their discipline, but learning occurs in many places outside of the classroom. When students take an active role in their education, they soon realize that there is much to learn from professors, learning that can extend beyond mere content knowledge. Perhaps one of the most important pieces of advice in this book is to get to know your professors. Establish relationships with faculty.

Professors help your professional development in more ways than lecturing, overseeing class discussions, and bestowing grades. Professors also can help you to enrich your college years through a variety of learning experiences outside the classroom. For example, professors can involve students in their research, providing opportunities to assist them in making new discoveries and generating new knowledge. Faculty aid students' professional development in other ways too, such as by introducing students to others who can help them to meet their goals (e.g., a professor in a graduate department to which you might apply). Professors also can help their students obtain special opportunities such as internships, summer positions, and teaching assistantships. Finally, job and graduate applications often require several letters of recommendation from faculty. Recommendation letters discuss more than just grades; they discuss students' abilities and aptitudes from academic, motivational, and personal perspectives. Of course, persuasive recommendation letters should not be your only reason for developing relationships with faculty members, but helpful letters are an important motivator and reward.

Interact with Professors

If you would like to develop out-of-classroom professional relationships with faculty, note that professors want to engage with students who are bright, motivated, committed, and enthusiastic. The first step in getting to know professors is making yourself someone that your professors want to know better. All relationships are two-way streets and relationships with faculty are no different. Who do you like to interact with? What characteristics do they show? Most people prefer to interact with others who are respectful, attentive, kind, inquisitive, and genuine. These characteristics also attract faculty.

Your behavior both in and out of class can attract or deter a professor from developing a professional relationship with you. Do you display behaviors that faculty appreciate? Take the quiz in Exercise 3.1 to assess your knowledge about appropriate in-class and out-of-class behavior. Exercise 3.2 presents some of the top behaviors that professors clearly *do not* want to see in class. Some of the items may appear humorous, but (believe it or not) they are regularly seen in class.

EXERCISE 3.1

Do You Display Appropriate In- and Out-of-Class Behavior?

Circle Yes or No to the following items. Be honest!

1.	Yes	No	I attend presentations and programs sponsored by the department.
2.	Yes	No	During class, I often send e-mail or text.
3.	Yes	No	I smile and say hello when I see professors.
4.	Yes	No	I take more than one makeup exam.
5.	Yes	No	I stop by during professors' office hours to discuss something from class that sparked an interest or seek assistance with class material.
6.	Yes	No	I let my phone ring during class.
7.	Yes	No	I help other students by sharing lecture notes and forming study groups.
8.	Yes	No	After missing class or arriving late, I often ask my professor to e-mail his or her notes and a complete explanation of what I missed.
9.	Yes	No	I sit toward the front of class.
10.	Yes	No	I often hand in assignments late.
11.	Yes	No	I rarely miss class.
12.	Yes	No	When the professor asks, "Are there any questions?" I often ask "Is this going to be on the test?"
13.	Yes	No	When my professor gives a particularly interesting lecture, I often offer a compliment and ask additional questions afterward.

(Continued)

EXERCISE 3.1 (Continued)

14.	Yes	No	After each exam I often nitpick over test questions, trying to get additional points.
15.	Yes	No	I participate in departmental events, clubs or activities, such as Psi Chi or the psychology club.
16.	Yes	No	I often read other books or newspapers in class.
17.	Yes	No	I prepare before class.
18.	Yes	No	I often leave class at break.
19.	Yes	No	I try to offer good answers to the professor's questions during class discussions.
20.	Yes	No	I use group time in class to catch up with my friends.
21.	Yes	No	I participate in class, but try not to dominate class discussions (i.e., I let others speak too).
22.	Yes	No	I often interrupt my professor's lecture with, "But you said..."
23.	Yes	No	I try to show interest in the course and remain attentive during class.
24.	Yes	No	I often arrive late to class.
25.	Yes	No	I try to ask well-reasoned and well-formulated questions during class.

Scoring:

Add up the number of times your "yes" responses to odd items and "no" responses to even items. The higher your score, the greater number of appropriate behaviors you display and the more likely that professors view you favorably.

Prompt

1. Given your score, how favorably do you think are professors likely to view you? Why?
2. How might your in- and out-of-class behavior influence your ability to develop professional relationships with faculty?
3. How can you improve your in- and out-of-class behavior? Discuss at least three ways in which you can improve your behavior.

EXERCISE 3.2

What Not to Do: Fifteen More Behaviors That Turn Off Faculty

1. Socialize in class, such as pass notes or chat.
2. Near the end of class, close your books firmly and jingle your car keys to help remind your professor that time is just about up.
3. Attempt to make term papers look longer by adding blank pages after the front and back pages, using large font, and huge margins.
4. Be rude to classmates.
5. Roll your eyes.
6. Engage in non-class behaviors, such as reading a book, playing with a phone, checking out Facebook, or sleeping.
7. Ask: "Is this going to be on the test?"
8. Let your phone ring, chirp, or beep during class.
9. Use technology inappropriately (that is, for non-class activities such as viewing videos or social networking).
10. Speak without being called on and/or interrupt your professor.
11. Repeatedly miss classes, arrive late, or leave early.
12. After missing class or arriving late, ask the professor to go over what you missed or ask, "Did I miss anything important?"
13. Visit a professor's office for the first time at the end of the semester, after receiving a poor mark, to ask for extra credit.
14. Expect differential treatment, for example, that rules about late assignments don't apply to you.
15. Nitpick over test questions after each exam, being more interested in getting points than learning.

Prompt:

1. Have you noticed any of these behaviors in class? What message do you think they convey?
2. Imagine that you are giving a presentation to the class and your peers are attending to their phones as they listen. How might you feel?
3. How might poor classroom behavior interfere with your professional development in and out of the classroom?

Effective Use of E-mail to Contact Professors

One of the most common ways that students interact with professors outside of class is through e-mail. Most professors use e-mail to schedule meetings with students, answer brief questions about content, and address questions specific to the student, such as about late assignments, grades, or makeup work. The content of your e-mail message sends a message to faculty about your maturity and professionalism. The e-mails you send to faculty should look very different than the casual messages you may send to family and friends. Addressing the professor appropriately, using proper grammar, and avoiding slang and accusatory language is important to having your message be interpreted as you'd like for you to be taken seriously. Always reread your message before sending it. Succinct messages like, "Why did you give me a C for that assignment?" can be interpreted as accusatory rather than a genuine question. Err in providing more explanation than less. Better yet, consider the advice in Real Tips for Real Students.

Real Tips for Real Students
E-mailing Professors about Grades

Should you e-mail your professor to ask questions about your grades? Even professors who rely on e-mail heavily often have different policies for discussing grades. Check the course syllabus for information about a professor's e-mail policies but recognize that sensitive topics such as grades are often best discussed in person. For example, a professor is best able to answer your question about a paper grade by referring directly to the paper. Questions about grades often become learning opportunities—and that requires face-to-face contact. Likewise, questions about grades often are interpreted differently when vocalized in person as compared with read in an e-mail. Asking in person requires more time and effort on your part and sends the message that you are serious about learning. Also, a verbal explanation to a student with a paper in hand often takes less of a professor's time than an e-mail, especially when writing the e-mail requires that professor to look up the student's grade and work, consider it, then reply. Bottom line: E-mail professors to set appointments to discuss grades, but consider discussing grades themselves in person.

Pay attention to your professor's policy about e-mail. Some professors prefer that students e-mail before calling or visiting office hours. Others use e-mail only to make appointments. Some don't use e-mail at all. The course syllabus usually lists the professor's preferences with regard to e-mail—when to do so, how to do so, and so on. Learn about these preferences early so that you know how to contact your professor should you need to.

Perhaps the most important thing to remember is that e-mail to faculty is a formal communication. Keep this in mind and the following tips are easy to anticipate.

1. **Use your institutional e-mail address.** Most institutions list it as the official method of contact. Frequently e-mails from other senders might get caught in spam filters. Also, a silly e-mail address, like butterflygrrrl@email.com is unprofessional and sends the wrong message.
2. **Use the subject line.** The subject line is used to identify the purpose and summarize what's in the e-mail. For example, "PSY100 Assignment Question."

3. **Be formal.** Address your professor as Professor Smith, Dr. Smith, and so on. Many professors include information on the class syllabus about how they wish to be addressed. Use it. If you are unsure whether your professor holds a doctorate and can be called Dr., err on the side of caution and refer to him or her as Professor. Moreover, note that most female faculty do not wish to be called Mrs. and often feel that it is inappropriate.
4. **Identify yourself and your course.** Remember that your professor teaches multiple courses, so stating, "This is John Smith from your psychology course," is not as helpful as, "This is John Smith from your Research Methods course." Professors often teach more than one section of a course, so it's helpful to also include the course number and section, such as, "I'm John Smith from your PSY201-01 Research Methods course," or "your Monday 10:00 A.M. Research Methods course."
5. **Keep your message short.** Instructors can receive dozens of e-mails each day. Make it easy for them to grasp your question and they can respond.
6. **Proofread.** Check spelling and grammar. Errors can be interpreted as a sign of carelessness. Do not write in all capital letters; in e-mail, it is interpreted as shouting.
7. **Do not use slang, emoticons, or abbreviations.** What is acceptable in texts and instant message communications is not appropriate for communicating with your instructor.
8. **Don't expect an immediate response.** Do not expect your instructor to reply during evenings or over weekends. Wait 24 to 48 hours for a response. Frequently professors include information on their syllabus about how long students can expect to wait for a response.
9. **Resend, if needed.** If you must resend the message, forward the original message with a quick note indicating that you're following up on your message in case it was missed.
10. **Follow up.** A simple "thank you" in response to a reply is usually appreciated.

EXERCISE 3.3

E-mailing Professors

Consider the following e-mail from a student to his or her instructor:

> I was wondering was there anything else I can do to get a C in the course!!!!! im workin on playin on da team for the school next term!!!!???? I got sick real bad there notting!!!!!!!!!!!!!!!!!! i had got sick real bad and i have a letter for u if u like!!!! i spent 6 hours at health center and my fever was real high so they would let me go and it was hard to get up and do anything if ukno what i mean!!!! ????????????????? Im just missing a few point to earn a C- 2 point it is!!! that better then a D+

(Continued)

EXERCISE 3.3 (Continued)

1. What is the student attempting to communicate? Where did he or she go wrong?
2. Imagine that you are a professor reading this message from a student. What is your likely response?
3. Rewrite this e-mail message to best convey the student's concerns and get a helpful response from the faculty member.

We use technology to communicate with our friends and families each day. The informal nature of instant messages and texts helps us communicate more quickly and can convey warmth and humor in our interactions with others. However, it is critical to remember that business communication is formal—and e-mails to faculty should be formal to be taken seriously. Everyday communications with your professors will influence their opinions of you, which can influence the range of opportunities that come your way.

Your Academic Advisor

When students select a major, they are assigned an academic advisor. An academic advisor is a faculty member whose role is to help students select courses and other learning opportunities to provide them with a well-rounded education and preparation for their chosen career. Your advisor may assist you with academic advising, which focuses on issues such as course scheduling and availability, meeting prerequisites, fostering academic success, and graduation requirements. He or she may also assist you with career advising, which emphasizes your short- and long-term career goals and will occur during multiple discussions over your years in college. The advisor–student relationship is a two-way street; you should come prepared to discuss your interests, needs, and goals. Your advisor may have dozens of other students to advise, so use your scheduled time with him or her wisely. Help your advisor to help you by following the tips in Table 3.1.

Your academic advisor likely is quite busy, but advisors make time for their students. Specifically, your advisor's posted office hours are explicitly for your use. Your advisor might ask you to reserve time beforehand or simply stop by. Ask for his or her preference. Consult with your advisor when you are having academic difficulties, or considering adding or dropping a course, changing your major, withdrawing from school, or transferring to another college. Stop by during office hours to ask a quick question, but if your questions are of a serious nature, such as whether to change your major, schedule an appointment so that you have the time to openly discuss your concerns. Your advisor has your best interests in mind and will provide you with the advice that you need to make sound decisions. When making big decisions such as whether to change your major, drop out of school, or go to graduate school, your advisor may suggest that you seek additional input and feedback from other sources such as other

TABLE 3.1 **ADVISING CHECKLIST**

- ❑ Know who your advisor is
  - Advisor name: ______________________________
  - Location: ______________________________
  - Phone number: ______________________________
  - E-mail: ______________________________
  - Office hours: ______________________________
- ❑ Schedule an appointment at least one week prior to your registration date.
- ❑ Study the university handbook to determine what courses are required of your major.
- ❑ Write down questions as they arise.
- ❑ List the courses that you have taken. Most departments have a worksheet for majors to complete that lists all general education and major requirements. Complete this sheet and keep an up-to-date copy filed away some place safe.
- ❑ Examine the registration website or booklet to choose potential courses.
- ❑ Prepare a tentative schedule with several course alternatives.
- ❑ Be prepared to explain how the courses you have selected fulfill the curricular requirements of your major.
- ❑ Consider your ultimate career goals and write down any questions that you have about your plans for after graduation.
- ❑ Actively discuss your career goals with your advisor and seek advice as to how to plan to meet them.

faculty, family, friends, and the counseling center. Your academic advisor is a source of feedback and advice; take advantage of this important resource. But always remember that your academic and career decisions are your own. Seek advice and assistance in order to make informed decisions, but the ultimate responsibility for the decisions that you make is your own. While an academic advisor is assigned to you, a mentoring relationship develops more organically.

Seek a Mentor

Seek to develop a special relationship with a faculty mentor. A mentor is a person with expertise who takes a special interest in you; he or she may be a college professor, advisor, or job, research, or practicum supervisor. Mentors provide their protégés with opportunities to learn, be advised, and obtain moral support (Keith-Spiegel & Wiederman, 2000). Seek a faculty mentor and you'll have opportunities for intellectual engagement that will enhance your college career. Note that mentors are more than academic advisors; your academic advisor may or may not also become your mentor. A mentor facilitates your undergraduate accomplishments, provides intellectual and emotional support, and helps you on the path toward your career.

How Do You Find a Mentor? An important way to seek a mentor is by seeking opportunities to get involved in research. Students who are motivated and visible in their departments and who seek to get involved in faculty research will usually find it easier to meet professors who are interested in developing professional working relationships. Seek opportunities and approach professors. It may seem scary and require initiative, but the rewards are great. Tell professors that you're looking to become involved in research. Explain that you hope to work closely with someone on their research and ask questions about their work. Demonstrate honest intellectual curiosity and motivation. If you are perceived well, word will get around that you're an excellent student looking for research experience. Remember that classroom behavior is an important indicator of maturity and motivation that influences professors' views of students.

If you do well in your courses and present yourself as competent, motivated, wanting to get involved, and committed, you may even be approached by a faculty member who wants to mentor you. Students with excellent literature searching, critical analysis, and writing abilities are helpful assistants. Students with expertise and interest in research and statistical analyses are often especially appealing to faculty because they require less instruction—and therefore can become deeply immersed in research at a faster pace.

As you look for a mentor, remember that the most popular professors may have more students coming to them than they can mentor. Working closely with a student in a mentoring relationship entails a great deal of time, attention, and intellectual focus; faculty can only mentor so many students at once. Some faculty may not be able to take on additional students. Remember that popularity, whether a particular professor is liked by the majority of students, should not be your main criterion for selecting a mentor. Look to faculty who are actively involved in research and whose interests parallel yours as closely as possible. Visit during office hours to ask a question or two about graduate school or your career interests; get a feel for the professor's approachability. If he or she seems interested in discussing these questions, express your desire to gain some experience in research. In the vast majority of cases, there is no pay involved for assisting professors with their research. Instead, you'll get a free learning experience that will improve your skills and abilities as well as make you more appealing to graduate schools and employers. Sometimes you may earn course credit for your work. Finally, volunteer to work closely with a professor only if you have the time to commit. Remember that falling behind or dropping out will reflect negatively on you—much more so than if you hadn't become involved at all.

What to Look for in a Mentor The role of a mentor is to provide guidance so that students are aware of resources and opportunities and understand their options. Successful mentoring relationships are not an accident. Mentoring relationships are most successful when students make careful and conscientious efforts to find mentors who possess certain characteristics and who complement their needs. A successful mentoring relationship requires chemistry, the ability to work together.

In order to find a helpful mentor, be aware of your needs and career goals. Where are you now, in terms of skills? Who do you want to become? How must you grow and what skills and experiences must you obtain to do so? A well-chosen mentor can help you to find the answers to those questions, while a poorly chosen mentor might leave you hanging, frustrating you with more questions than answers. Effective mentors are professionally skilled but also have positive attributes and are skilled interpersonally (Appleby, 1999). Some desirable characteristics to look for in mentors are listed in Exercise 3.4. No one person will have all of these characteristics; you must decide which are most important to you and find someone who approximates them.

EXERCISE 3.4

Choosing an Effective Mentor

Check off the characteristics that match the attributes of a faculty member from whom you are considering seeking mentorship.

Effective mentors are interpersonally skilled. They:

- ❑ Are responsive, warm, and encouraging
- ❑ Are nonjudgmental
- ❑ Help students develop positive self-concepts
- ❑ Help to open doors to career and graduate school opportunities by telling others of the positive aspects of protégées
- ❑ Provide emotional support
- ❑ Challenge and motivate students to attempt new tasks that stretch their abilities.

Effective mentors have positive personal attributes. They are:

- ❑ Mature and wise
- ❑ Providers of accurate and useful advice—and enjoy providing advice
- ❑ Friendly, optimistic, and positive in their life outlook
- ❑ Admired and respected by students and peers
- ❑ Trustworthy and dependable
- ❑ Ethical and have high moral standards

(Continued)

EXERCISE 3.4 (Continued)

Effective mentors have attained professional competency. They are:

- ❑ Qualified, competent, and experienced
- ❑ Knowledgeable with up-to-date information
- ❑ Able to communicate well
- ❑ Actively involved in professional or academic organizations
- ❑ Involved in research
- ❑ Interested in lifelong learning

Prompt

Learn about the faculty in your department. Visit the Psychology Department website and review faculty biographies. Visit their websites. Review their lists of publications.

1. Choose two or three faculty to study in more depth. Who are they and why did you choose them?
2. Look up the abstracts of articles that sound interesting. Review their research. What type of work do they do? Write a two-sentence summary of his or her area of expertise and research. Do you find it interesting? Why or why not?
3. If you're interested in their work, read more and devise three questions to ask about their work. List them.
4. Visit the professor's office hours to speak with the professor about his or her research. What did you learn?
5. Consider your overall impressions: How comfortable do you feel speaking with this faculty member? If you're uncomfortable, try to identify why.
6. Complete this process for each faculty member, and you'll begin to get ideas about which faculty you're more inclined to work with. Discuss the results of this exploration.

As you consider potential mentors, ask yourself the following questions:

1. Is the professor in a position to share his or her time and advice?
2. Does he or she have a reputation for producing high-quality and timely research?
3. Is the professor interested in mentoring you?
4. Are you comfortable with the professor's demeanor and personality? Does it fit your academic style and needs?
5. From your perspective, does the professor exhibit the ability to communicate openly and clearly?

Chose a mentor who you admire and with whom you can communicate and whose interpersonal skills and interactional patterns work well with your own.

Get Research Experience: Be a Research Assistant

While you can gain research experience by volunteering to help your mentor, a research assistantship is a more formal research opportunity. A research assistantship is an opportunity for undergraduate students to assist a faculty member in his or her program of research. Assisting a faculty member in research is an exciting opportunity to do the research rather than just read about it.

Why Become a Research Assistant?

Research generates new knowledge. When we engage in research, we make new discoveries and learn new things. Sure you read about psychology research, but carrying it out is an altogether different animal that will help you learn more than you have in any class. It's an opportunity to be on the cutting edge of psychology. Aside from the thrill of generating new knowledge, assisting a professor with research provides many other valuable opportunities, such as (Grover, 2006; Landrum & Nelson, 2002)

- Gaining specialized skills and knowledge by working one-on-one with a faculty member
- Exposure to methodological techniques that will be helpful in completing your senior thesis or, perhaps, graduate work
- Practicing written and oral communication skills by learning how to express research findings and preparing papers for submission to, and presenting at, professional conferences and journals
- Developing a mentoring relationship with a faculty member
- Obtaining experiences that will enhance your applications to employers and graduate programs
- Acquiring outstanding letters of recommendation as faculty who work closely with you can write more detailed letters that fully demonstrate your capacities and strengths.

Engaging in research is a worthwhile experience for all students because it provides opportunities to learn how to think, organize information, and solve problems, as well as demonstrate commitment to a project—all skills coveted by employers and graduate admissions committees (Sleigh & Ritzer, 2007). In fact, graduate school admissions committees rate research experience as a "very important" factor in the admissions process and more important than GPA (Keith-Spiegel & Wiederman, 2000; Mayne Norcross, & Sayette, 1994; Walfish & Turner, 2006).

What Does a Research Assistant Do?

What will be expected of you as a research assistant? We cannot predict the specific tasks that you will be assigned, as a research assistant's tasks will vary by faculty member, project, and area of psychology. Some might be involved in data collection by administering surveys, or maintaining and operating lab equipment. Others might code and enter data, make photocopies, or write literature reviews. Here are some general tasks that research assistants perform (Landrum & Davis, 2010).

- Collect data by administering surveys, interviews, or running research protocols.
- Score, code, and enter data into a spreadsheet or statistical analysis program.
- Conduct library research including literature searches using databases (e.g., PsychInfo, Social Sciences Citation Index, PsychArticles), making copies of articles, and ordering unavailable articles and books through interlibrary loan.
- Assist the faculty member to develop new research ideas.
- Use computer skills such as word processing, spreadsheet, scheduling, and statistical analysis programs.
- Assist in preparing submissions for local or regional conferences and, if accepted, work on poster or oral presentations for professional conferences.
- Assist faculty in preparing a manuscript to submit the results of collaborative research to a scientific journal.

Frequently students who work with faculty members as research assistants develop their own ideas for research projects that stem from the faculty's work. For example, one of my students worked with me on several related projects and developed her own hypothesis to extend my work by adding additional variables. She carried out her project under my supervision as her senior thesis, presented it at a regional psychology conference, and together, we published it in a scholarly journal. Research assistantships provide substantial educational and professional development opportunities.

How Do You Become a Research Assistant?

First and foremost, you should perform well in class, and be motivated and visible in your department. Let faculty know that you're interested in getting involved in research, but do not send out a mass e-mail or a form e-mail notifying them of your availability. Instead, approach professors during their office hours and ask for leads on who might be looking for research assistants. Before you approach a professor you would like to work with, learn about his or her work. Read some of the professor's articles, especially the most recent ones. When you find a professor who is looking for an assistant, carefully and honestly describe what you can offer (computer skills, Internet skills, statistical skills, and the number of hours per week you're available). Let the faculty member know that you're willing to work hard (be honest). Ask thoughtful questions, such as those in Table 3.2. Ask questions about the professor's expectations and how you will be evaluated. Professors are often unintentionally vague in describing their expectations for students during the research assistantship as well as for the products of the collaboration such as a paper

(Landrum, 2008). The specific expectations will likely vary from project to project and from student to student, but a student might expect to be evaluated on at least some of the following abilities listed in Table 3.3.

TABLE 3.2 Questions to Ask about a Research Assistantship

- ❑ Are the work hours set or is there some flexibility? Might I expect to sometimes work overtime and other times finish early?
- ❑ What will I do? What are specific kinds of examples?
- ❑ Will I be evaluated? How?
- ❑ Will I be asked to submit a paper or other project at the end of this experience?
- ❑ How long will the project last?
- ❑ How long is the commitment (full semester, part semester)?

TABLE 3.3 Sample Faculty Expectations for Research Assistants

Research Methods and Data Analysis

- ❑ Generate research questions
- ❑ Determine ways to measure phenomena
- ❑ Create surveys
- ❑ Collect data
- ❑ Enter data into statistical software
- ❑ Use statistical software to analyze data

Communication Skills

- ❑ Conduct literature searches
- ❑ Manuscript preparation
- ❑ Prepare submission to conferences
- ❑ Present at conferences
- ❑ Preparation of tables, graphs

Interpersonal Skills

- ❑ Leadership
- ❑ Teamwork
- ❑ Communication skills
- ❑ Listening skills
- ❑ Relationship with faculty member

Self-Management

- ❑ Time management
- ❑ Organization
- ❑ Ethical behavior

It may be tempting to consider turning the professor down because the hours don't fit your schedule or the research isn't interesting enough, but the opportunity to work as a research assistant is a coveted prize that will enhance your academic and professional development in many ways. Don't be hasty in turning down such an important opportunity. You may not work on a project that you find endlessly stimulating, but you will obtain excellent experience. Also, research projects often become more interesting once you're immersed in them. Your academic interests most likely will change as you gain more experience and education.

Why Do Professors Seek Student Research Assistants?

You're now aware that there are many benefits of getting involved in research. Did you know that there are benefits for faculty too? They get a hardworking student to do some labor-intensive parts of research. Faculty, especially those at undergraduate institutions without graduate programs, often depend on undergraduates to further their research programs (Cooley, Garcia, & Hughes, 2008). Many faculty members have ideas for studies that they don't have time to conduct. Motivated students can help them to carry out these studies. If you develop a relationship with a faculty member, you might be able to help him or her conduct a project that may otherwise remain shelved for lack of time.

Involving undergraduates in research also offers the opportunity for faculty to develop a relationship with a student and witness his or her professional growth, which most professors find quite rewarding. There are other benefits for faculty who involve undergraduates in their research (Davis, 1995). They:

- remain current by conducting reviews of the current literature in a particular research area,
- keep analytic skills active through the design and completion of research,
- maintain and expand professional networks through attending conventions to present research completed with students, and
- bring research into the classroom and enhance teaching effectiveness through active involvement in research.

Student–professor research relationships offer benefits to all involved; however, the commitment to become a research assistant is a big one. You will be given responsibility to ensure that aspects of the project get done. The faculty member will count on you to be responsible and complete your assignments correctly. This includes asking questions and seeking assistance if you don't understand the task. Your performance as a research assistant can give a professor lots of good things to write in a letter of recommendation, including specific examples of your skills, competencies, and personal characteristics. If you complete tasks competently, you might be asked to take on more responsibility, and you will learn more as well as earn a reputation as an excellent student and potential future colleague (and thereby earn excellent letters of recommendation). However, there is a positive payoff from conducting research with faculty only if you consistently perform competent work. If you don't take the commitment seriously, are unreliable, or make repeated mistakes, your relationship with the professor will suffer (as will your standing in the eyes of other faculty because professors often share information about their experiences with students). If you decide to work with a faculty member on his or her research, treat it as a primary responsibility.

Get Research Experience: Conduct a Research Study

Taking an active role in your education entails looking for opportunities to learn and develop useful skills. We have seen that engaging in faculty research promotes a host of abilities and skills that employers and graduate programs seek. Another way to obtain research experience is to carve out your own opportunity by conducting an independent study. As you're aware, research generates new knowledge. When we engage in research, we make new discoveries and learn new things. Sure you read about psychology research and may have assisted faculty with their research, but carrying out your own study to examine your own hypothesis is an altogether different animal that will help you learn more than you have in any class.

Although student-developed studies are often referred to as *independent studies*, they are far from the isolated experiences that the name conveys. All are closely supervised by faculty. Some psychology departments require students to carry out their own research projects in order to demonstrate their competence; these studies often take place in capstone courses.

If you are interested in developing and conducting your own study, take the steps we have described to find a faculty member whose interests match yours and who is willing to oversee your study. Together you will determine your research question and how to address it. Frequently students' ideas for independent studies come from their work on faculty projects. It is often said that research generates more questions than answers. These are often the best studies to conduct as they already have a faculty member's attention and interest. However, you may also consider approaching a professor with whom you have not conducted research. The specific steps entailed in designing and conducting your research study will be determined by the topic and by your interactions with your faculty supervisor. Choose a professor with interests similar to yours and with whom you have had positive contact in the past. Pay attention to the advice in this chapter about how to choose and make contact with faculty.

EXERCISE 3.5

Seek Out-of-Class Opportunities

Many students want to get involved in research and other psychology-related extracurricular activities. Some opportunities are highly visible, such as participating in the Psychology Club. Others are much more subtle. Scout out the opportunities available to you in the Psychology Department.

1. Is there a psychology-related student club?
2. Is there a Psi Chi chapter? What are the requirements to join?
3. How many faculty members are in the department? What are their specialties (such as developmental, cognitive, clinical, etc.)?
4. Does the department schedule outside and in-house speakers regularly? Are any scheduled for this semester?
5. Are there any department activities scheduled for this semester?
6. Locate the department webpage. What information is provided about course scheduling? Research opportunities? Grad school prep? Internship and practica opportunities? Tutoring?
7. Do any professors have webpages? Visit each webpage. Does the professor explain his or her research? Are publications listed? Write a two-sentence summary of his or her area of expertise and research. In what ways is it interesting? Is there anything unappealing? Why?
8. Are there formal classes designed to provide one-on-one interaction with a professor? For example, a guided readings course in which a student and professor jointly choose a collection of readings about a topic or an independent research study in which a student completes a project under the guidance of a faculty member. If so, what are the prerequisites and requirements to enroll? Do all faculty participate? If not, identify faculty who supervise students in one-on-one coursework.

GET TEACHING EXPERIENCE

Taking an active role in your education entails seeking opportunities for personal and professional development. As you consider your own academic and professional development, attempt to gain experiences that will round out your competencies. Research experience is an important contribution to your academic development, but applied experiences, such as working as a teaching assistant or completing field experiences such as internships or practica, also build important competencies.

Although less common than research assistants, teaching assistants have opportunities to learn a variety of skills. Many professors, myself included, observe that teaching a topic helps them to develop a new, more complex, understanding of that topic. Explaining material to another person helps you identify gaps in your own knowledge—and prompts learning.

What do undergraduate teaching assistants do? They work with a faculty for at least one semester, offering assistance with a specific course. They may help an instructor plan discussion questions or in-class group assignments, run discussion or laboratory sessions, and serve as class assistants. More specifically, a teaching assistant might do any of the following, depending on the instructor and institution:

- Attend lectures
- Conduct review sessions for exams
- Facilitate discussions
- Prepare lectures as needed
- Request or acquire necessary equipment
- Hold regular office hours
- Tutor students
- Manage and respond to course-related e-mail
- Update course webpages
- Participate in online discussions
- Organize assignments
- Proctor exams
- Maintain course attendance records
- Attend instructor/TA meetings
- Act as liaison/mediator between student and professor

Not every department and college offers teaching assistantships. Some departments have formal programs with application procedures that entail completing forms, submitting a statement of intent, and soliciting recommendation letters. Others have no formal program, but students informally assist faculty as volunteers. Still others offer teaching assistant opportunities as an independent study course in which a student earns course credit for working as a teaching assistant and completing an academic project, such as a paper examining his or her experiences. Ask your professors if teaching assistant opportunities exist. Ask even if no one you know has worked as a teaching assistant. Sometimes opportunities exist, but they are largely unadvertised. Ask and you may be pleasantly surprised. At any rate, asking never hurts and will only make you appear motivated and eager to learn and gain experience.

Real Tips for Real Students
Consider Tutoring

If your department does not offer teaching assistantships consider getting some teaching experience by tutoring other students. Check whether your department has tutoring facilities or a program. If not, check with the study skills center and student services center to locate your university's tutoring program. Tutoring is an opportunity to learn, to help others, and to determine if further study in psychology is for you. Couple tutoring with research and applied opportunities to round out your experience.

GET FIELD EXPERIENCE

Field experiences in the form of internships or practica involve students in relevant academic experiences and provide a useful service to agencies and communities (Jessen, 1988). Examples of field placements include being an intern at a social service agency (where you might observe or assist in intake of clients, psychological testing, report writing, and behavior modification) and working in a human services department of a company or business (where you might observe and learn to administer structured interviews, write performance appraisals, and coordinate special projects or programs). As an intern, you have a chance to get an idea of what it is like to work in a particular setting. For example, you might sit in on a group therapy or parent training session or help personnel plan sessions and analyze the outcomes of sessions. You may learn new skills and hone others—and come to recognize that you have skills to contribute to practical settings.

Why Seek Field Experience?

There are many benefits to participating in field experience. If you hope to become a mental health professional and provide services to others, it is important to seek practice opportunities as an undergraduate in order to clarify your interests (Walter, 2007). It is not uncommon for a student to believe that clinical or counseling psychology is for them until they gain some experience and realize that they don't like working with people. Therefore, one of the most important reasons for seeking field experience is to become more certain of your career choice. Working in the field helps you to identify not only what work-related outcomes you value (e.g., pay, autonomy, responsibility) but also what interests and abilities you need to be satisfied in that work (Taylor, 1988; LoCicero & Hancock, 2000). It is a job tryout. You'll learn about a particular job environment, duties, and support. You'll learn about typical clientele you might work with and what you can expect in terms of resources. If you choose to apply to graduate school, field experiences will suit you well. Admissions committees and directors of applied subfields of psychology, such as clinical, counseling, or school psychology, look favorably on field experience because it is a good indicator of a student's interest, motivation, and competence in applied settings.

Other benefits of field experience include the opportunity to apply what is learned in class in a real-world setting, acquire knowledge and new skills, and learn about the practice of psychology (Jessen, 1988; LoCicero & Hancock, 2000). Depending on the placement, you may learn more about psychological problems, ways of helping, agency functioning, professional relationships, interviewing techniques, psychological testing, report writing, consultation, behavior modification, and group therapy. Field experience gives you a chance to develop useful skills that may be hard to practice and develop in class, and it helps you to integrate what you've learned. Personal benefits include developing responsibility, maturity, and confidence (LoCicero & Hancock, 2000).

Aside from educational and personal benefits, field experience offers professional benefits. These include gaining a realistic understanding of work environments, developing professional contacts, and enhancing your résumé (Landrum et al., 2000; Jessen, 1988). Interns get formal and informal job sources and contacts, are evaluated positively by recruiters, earn higher salaries in the workplace, and report greater satisfaction in jobs (Taylor, 1988). Students who work as interns are more likely to be satisfied with their jobs after graduation—and may even have a job lined up before graduating (National Association of Colleges and Employers, 2014a). They also remain in their jobs longer than the students who do not obtain field experience. Students who obtain field experience are able to consider the match between their academic preparation and work requirements while they are in school. Some recent graduates feel poorly equipped for the stresses of work, including politics, difficult clients, and the conflict between theory and application. Field experience, however, gives students time to learn more and to resolve the conflicts early. Therefore it may not be surprising that after graduation, students who obtain field experience often have a smoother, easier transition to work, without the "reality shock" that other graduates often experience (Taylor, 1988).

How Do You Get Field Experience?

The organization of field experiences varies by institution and department. Many departments have a faculty member who serves as a campus coordinator for field experience and internship programs. He or she makes sure that internship sites are appropriate, develops working relationship with them, and evaluates student performance. Other departments may not have one coordinator; in some cases different faculty are responsible for each internship site, depending on their relationship with the site. Some colleges have an office that specializes in placing students in internships. Sometimes these offices and opportunities are referred to as cooperative education.

Your department may require that you obtain an internship through the cooperative education office. Sometimes a department may require a student to find his or her own practicum site. If you are in this position, begin at least two to three months early as locating a site, making contact and meeting with the director, obtaining a faculty supervisor and getting permission to proceed requires time. Look up the social service agencies in your area, such as women's centers, shelters, and not-for-profit agencies that help individuals and families. E-mail the director and explain that you are a student and looking to volunteer and perhaps get course credit for your work. Attach a résumé. Alternatively you might call and ask if they'd like more information. Anticipate meeting and interviewing with the agency staff. Be prepared to have a faculty speak with the agency, vouching for you and taking responsibility of providing academic supervision. Field experience is a challenging experience that will test your knowledge and will help you learn much about yourself.

GET INVOLVED IN THE DISCIPLINE

Research, teaching, and field work offer important educational opportunities, but there are many other ways to learn and advance your competencies. Show your interest in psychology and open up new avenues of learning by seeking opportunities to get involved in the field as a whole. Disseminating the results of research—formally telling others about what you have found—requires another set of competencies and offers many benefits. Another way of becoming active in the field is to become active in a local or national psychology organization, as described in the following sections.

Attend Psychology Conferences

Conferences are good places to see what psychology research is all about. Professional organizations such as the American Psychological Association and Association for Psychological Science hold annual meetings in various cities around the United States. Psychologists from all types of settings attend to share and learn about the latest research—as well as socialize. National conferences attract thousands of people. National conferences usually take place at hotels in cities near airports so that attendees can easily arrive and leave, as well as have a place to stay as most conferences last several days. Regional psychology associations also hold annual conferences, some of which might be within driving distance. These conferences are smaller, with a few hundred people depending on the conference. A list of regional psychology associations is in Table 3.4.

TABLE 3.4 REGIONAL PSYCHOLOGICAL ASSOCIATIONS

Eastern Psychological Association (EPA): http://www.easternpsychological.org

Southeastern Psychological Association (SEPA): http://www.sepaonline.com

Southwestern Psychological Association (SWPA): http://www.swpsych.org

Rocky Mountain Psychological Association (RMPA): http://www.rockymountainpsych.org/

Western Psychological Association (WPA): http://westernpsych.org/

Midwestern Psychological Association (MPA): http://www.midwesternpsych.org/

New England Psychological Association (NEPA): http://www.nepsychological.org/

Prompt:
Visit the webpage of the psychological association that represents your area of the country. What kinds of resources are offered? When is the annual conference? Where?

What can you expect to do at a conference? You'll listen to presentations by researchers who will discuss their latest work, usually work that is not yet published. You'll also view poster sessions. Posters are another format for presenting research in which the study's purpose, methods, results, and discussion are presented on posterboard. The author of the study stands by to answer questions and to talk informally about the work. Poster presentations are a great opportunity to make contacts with students and faculty who share your interests. Most conferences also have practical presentations on topics such as getting into graduate school, publishing, and teaching. Other reasons to attend conferences are to peruse and purchase the latest books in the field and to social network. You'll have opportunities to meet student researchers, possible advisors, and possible employers. If you are interested in graduate school you may have opportunities to talk to current students in programs you're considering and possibly meet faculty with whom you'd like to work. Many students find attending their first conference an eye-opening experience because it's a glimpse into the world of research psychology and academia. Distinguished researchers you've studied become real people, lecturing about their latest work, right in front of you.

If you are interested in attending a conference speak with students and faculty involved in the department club or Psi Chi. Many departments organize informal trips to conferences. If your department is not sponsoring an informal trip, seek another interested student or two and consider attending together.

Disseminate Research

If you conduct research with a faculty member and the results of the research project turn out favorably, the next step in the project is to disseminate the results and tell the scholarly community about your findings. Most commonly, research results are disseminated through presentations at professional conferences or articles in scholarly journals. Most students obtain their first experiences with research dissemination through presentations at local or regional professional conferences. Presenting research results at a conference is a wonderful learning opportunity that is an impressive addition to a résumé or graduate school application.

Typically, conference presentations take two forms—papers and posters. A paper is a twelve- to fifteen-minute presentation made to an audience in which you describe your research concisely, with the aid of handouts, overheads, or slides. Table 3.5 offers suggestions for paper presentations. Posters are more common formats for student presentations. A poster presents your research concisely on a 3-by-5- or 4-by-6-foot

TABLE 3.5

Checklist for Preparing Effective Paper Presentations

Preparation: Before Your Talk

- ❑ Carefully plan your talk. Recognize that you can make a limited number of points in your ten- to twelve-minute time frame.
- ❑ Be aware of your audience's attention and comprehension limits; don't overwhelm them.
- ❑ Consider the "big picture." What are the main ideas and findings of your project?
- ❑ Minimize the extraneous details.
- ❑ Create a detailed outline to guide your talk.
- ❑ Remember that your goal is to tell a coherent story about your data. State the point of your research, what you found, and why it matters.
- ❑ Record your practice sessions and analyze your presentation.
- ❑ Practice giving your talk to an audience, and accept their constructive feedback.
- ❑ If you are using presentation software such as PowerPoint, check the order of slides, transitions, and be sure that you know how to work your laptop.
- ❑ If you prepare handouts, include your name and how to cite the material.
- ❑ Try to visit the room that you will be speaking in beforehand to familiarize yourself with its layout.
- ❑ Place a copy of your handouts on a cloud service such as Dropbox so that you can share the link rather than print out or e-mail copies.

During Your Talk

- ❑ Do not read your talk; use your outline as a guide.
- ❑ Speak loudly and clearly.
- ❑ Look out at the audience.
- ❑ Understand that there will be distractions, such as people getting up and leaving or reading—don't take it personally.
- ❑ Try to be enthusiastic and focused; look away from distracting stimuli.
- ❑ End on time, and be prepared for questions if time permits.
- ❑ Bring copies of your paper and the link where audience members can download the paper on their own

Adapted from Karlin (2000); Mathie (2006); Adler (2010).

freestanding bulletin board. All posters are displayed in a large room for a period of time (usually one and a half to two hours), and the audience wanders through, browsing posters of interest. A poster presentation offers opportunities for lots of one-on-one interaction, as audience members stop at posters of interest to them, and ask questions about the project. Designing an effective poster isn't easy; Table 3.6 offers some advice on how to create an informative poster.

If the research that you are conducting with a faculty member turns out especially favorably, you might prepare the results for submission to a scholarly journal. While professional journals in psychology abound, there are a handful of journals that specialize in publishing the work of undergraduates.

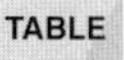

TABLE 3.6 Tips for Preparing Effective Poster Presentations

- ❑ Remember that your goal is to tell a coherent story about your data in very limited space.
- ❑ Your poster should reveal the point of your research, what you found, and why it matters.
- ❑ Present only what is necessary to tell your story—only essential details.
- ❑ Remember that you are there to answer readers' questions. Your goal is to engage the reader and have a conversation about the study.
- ❑ The components of your poster should be clearly visible from three feet away.
- ❑ Include the title, authors, affiliation, and an abstract of the research.
- ❑ Use a large font (at least 18 point and preferably 24 point).
- ❑ Pictures, tables, and figures are helpful.
- ❑ If possible, use color in your figures and pictures.
- ❑ Bring thumbtacks and tape.
- ❑ Place a copy of your handouts on a cloud service such as Dropbox so that you can share the link rather than print out or mail copies.
- ❑ Bring several dozen copies of a handout to provide additional information about the study and contact information.
- ❑ Be sure to include identification information on your handouts: your name and how to cite the material.
- ❑ Be on time. Often poster sessions are scheduled back to back, so it is important that you end on time and take your poster down because someone else will be waiting.
- ❑ Never take your poster down early.
- ❑ Have your name badge prominently displayed, and be ready to answer questions.

Adapted from Karlin (2000); Mathie (2006); Adler (2010).

The most prestigious of the undergraduate journals is the *Psi Chi Journal of Undergraduate Research*, which is sponsored by Psi Chi and published quarterly. Submissions to the *Psi Chi Journal of Undergraduate Research* are reviewed by three psychology professors. Other undergraduate journals and criteria appear in Table 3.7.

If you decide to submit to a journal, recognize that it will take a great deal of time and effort. The time it takes to prepare a paper for submission is always longer than anticipated. Once the paper is submitted, there will be a long wait (typically several months) to hear from the publisher. Even if a paper is accepted, it is usually under the condition that further revisions be made. It is important to understand that not every paper submitted to a journal is published. The standards for publication are much higher than those for getting an "A" in a course. Journal editors expect articles to make a contribution to the literature, and "nonsignificant results are typically not a big contribution in their eyes" (Powell, 2000, p. 28). Despite these cautions, the rewards of publishing are great. Publishing in a scholarly journal is a major achievement that employers and graduate schools look upon favorably.

TABLE 3.7 UNDERGRADUATE PSYCHOLOGY JOURNALS

Journal Title	Publication Schedule	Requirements	Contact Info
Journal of Psychology and Behavioral Sciences	Annual print journal	Authors must be undergraduate or graduate students. Publishes empirical and theoretical papers.	http://view2.fdu.edu/academics/becton-college/psychology-and-counseling/jpbs/
Journal of Young Investigators	Monthly online journal	Publishes original scientific research and literature review articles in the sciences and social sciences.	http://www.jyi.org
Modern Psychological Studies	Two print issues a year, in fall and spring	Primary author must be an undergraduate student. Publishes empirical papers only.	http://www.utc.edu/psychology/mps/ http://modernpsychologicalstudies.weebly.com/
Psi Chi Journal of Undergraduate Research	Quarterly print journal	Print journal. Authors must include a Psi Chi student. Submissions accepted on an ongoing basis. Publishes only empirical research.	http://www.psichi.org/?page=journal_main
Undergraduate Research Journal for the Human Sciences	Annual online journal	The primary author of a submitted paper must be an undergraduate student. Experiments, surveys, case studies, and documentary research are permitted.	http://www.kon.org/CFP/cfp_urjhs.html
University of California Los Angeles Undergraduate Psychology Journal	Annual online journal	Accepts empirical and review papers.	http://www.studentgroups.ucla.edu/psychjournal/
Yale Review of Undergraduate Research in Psychology	Annual online journal	Publishes empirical and review articles.	http://www.yale.edu/yrurp/

However, not every student has research experiences that lend themselves to submitting to scholarly journals. Fortunately there are respectable nonrefereed outlets for students to demonstrate initiative and writing skills. Newsletters published by psychology departments, student organizations, and other groups on campus offer opportunities to write about topics related to psychology. Professional organizations such as APA, APS, and regional psychological associations (such as EPA, NEPA, WPA) have student publications or member publications that are open to student writers. Finally, Psi Chi and Psi Beta offer opportunities for students to contribute to their newsletter magazines. Although these publications are not peer reviewed, and the articles are not empirical, they demonstrate initiative, writing ability, and interest in psychology—all valued by employers and graduate admissions committees.

Participate in Professional Organizations

One of the simplest, most effective, yet underappreciated ways of forming an identity as a lifelong student of psychology is to get involved in professional organizations, on and off-campus. Likely the most visible resource for psychology students on your campus is Psi Chi, the National Honor Society in Psychology, a psychology organization designed for students. Founded in 1929, its purpose is to encourage, stimulate, and maintain excellence in scholarship and to advance psychology as a science. Students enrolled at institutions that have a chapter must meet minimum qualifications and apply for membership to Psi Chi. Students at community colleges are eligible to apply to Psi Beta, the sister organization of Psi Chi.

Get involved in your institution's chapter of Psi Chi and you'll have the opportunity to get to know other psychology students, develop leadership skills, and get involved in departmental activities. It also offers opportunities for students at the regional and national levels. Psi Chi sponsors sessions at most regional and national conferences that promote the research and scholarly achievements of undergraduate psychology students. In other words, Psi Chi sponsors opportunities for students to present their research. Psi Chi offers programming relevant to psychology students at these conferences, such as presentations on careers in psychology and how to apply to graduate school. Another important benefit of membership in Psi Chi is the quarterly magazine, *Eye on Psi Chi*. Each issue includes articles on psychology as well as practical advice on how to pursue a career in psychology. The *Psi Chi Journal of Undergraduate Research* is also published by Psi Chi; it's a national peer-reviewed scholarly journal that is dedicated to research conducted by undergraduate students. Because there are so many benefits to becoming a member of Psi Chi, if your institution does not have a chapter, discuss with a faculty member the possibility of starting a chapter.

Another opportunity to get involved in psychology and promote a campus culture oriented toward psychology is to get involved with (or start) a psychology club. Most psychology clubs are open to anyone with an interest in psychology, regardless of major. Many students who do not meet the academic criteria to join Psi Chi get involved in a school's psychology club. Frequently the psychology club and Psi Chi work together to organize psychology-related activities for students.

When considering ways of getting involved in psychology-related activities, don't forget to pay attention to what's happening in your department. Departments often invite guest speakers to campus or faculty members give presentations on their research interests. Attend these activities to support the department's efforts and to demonstrate your interest and commitment to learning more about psychology.

Finally, the American Psychological Association and the Association for Psychological Science offer resources that are helpful to students. Both offer advice on entering the field of psychology and student affiliate memberships that permits you to join at a reduced fee and obtain discounts on psychology journals and books. As discussed earlier, APA and APS sponsor annual conferences in which thousands of psychologist researchers and practitioners gather to learn about the latest research, attend workshops, and network. Attend either of these conferences, or any of the conferences sponsored by regional psychological associations, for an amazing learning opportunity.

There are a variety of ways to take an active role in your education, but all involve stepping back and recognizing the covert, unstated, college curriculum (Appleby, 2001); you can learn much more in college than just theories and facts. Taking an active role in your education means that you must seek out opportunities to learn and enhance your skills. It means that you must develop relationships with faculty and do more than just attend class. Though taking an active role in your education takes effort—it's much easier to sit back and just attend class—the benefits are immense.

EXERCISE 3.6
Academic and Professional Organizations

Several professional organizations offer opportunities for students to learn about the field of psychology and make contacts with other students and professionals.

1. Visit the Psi Chi website (http://psichi.org). What is the purpose of the organization? Under the publications link, what is *Eye on Psi Chi*? Browse the collection of articles organized by category. Read three articles from three different categories (such as career preparation, fields of psychology, or promotion of research). Write a one- to two-sentence summary of each article.

EXERCISE 3.6

2. Visit the American Psychological Association website (http://apa.org). Locate the Students page. Identify two helpful resources. What are they? How are they helpful? Can students join APA? What are the benefits? How much does it cost?
3. Visit the Association for Psychological Science website (http://psychologicalscience.org). Locate the Students page. Can students join APS? What are the benefits? How much does it cost? Identify two ways of getting involved in APS.

SUGGESTED READINGS

Beins, B., & Beins, A. (2008). *Effective writing in psychology: Papers, posters, and presentations.* Hoboken, NJ: Wiley.

Halonen, J. S., & Santrock, J. W. (2013). *Your guide to college success: Strategies for achieving your goals.* Belmont, CA: Wadsworth.

Landrum, R. E., & Davis S. F. (2013). *The psychology major: Career options and strategies for success*. Upper Saddle River, NJ: Prentice Hall.

Nist-Olejnik, S. & Holschuh, J. P. (2007). *College rules! How to study, survive, and succeed in college*. Berkeley, CA: Ten Speed Press.

Silvia, P. J., Delaney, P. F., & Marcovitch, S. (2009). *What psychology majors could (and should) be doing: An informal guide to research experience and professional skills.* Washington, DC: APA.

Wegenek, A. R., & Buskist, W. (2012). *The insider's guide to the psychology major: Everything you need to know about the degree and profession*. Washington, DC: APA Press.

INTERNET RESOURCES (Available at http://www.tarakuther.com)

Psychology Student Network

http://www.apa.org/ed/precollege/psn

Published by the APA Education Directorate, this newsletter is published twice a year, in spring and fall as well as archived on this page. It is designed for precollege and undergraduate psychology students and features articles about careers and interesting topics in psychology, with a focus on opportunities for students.

APS Observer Student Notebook

http://www.psychologicalscience.org/apssc/news.cfm

Monthly column written for graduate students in psychology, but valuable to undergraduate students as well.

Psi Chi

http://www.psichi.org

National Honor Society in Psychology webpage. Review the *Eye on Psi Chi* articles for help with all aspects of student development (research, field experiences, graduate school, and more).

GradPsych

http://www.apa.org/gradpsych

Quarterly magazine for undergraduate and graduate students in psychology, published by APA.

Reflection Prompts

My Advisor

Who is your advisor? Write down the contact information for your advisor. Now reflect on your meetings with him or her. Did you set up an appointment or just visit during office hours? What kind of advice has he or she given you? Do you feel comfortable interacting with your advisor? Identify questions to ask during your next meeting.

Relationships with Faculty

Explore your feelings about interacting with faculty. How often do you interact with professors? List the professors you interact with. Explore the context of your discussions. For example, is it after class or in the professor's office? Are your discussions focused on the course material or do you talk about other things, like life and career goals? What, if anything, is holding you back from interacting with professors? Explore your feelings. How can you overcome these obstacles?

My College Career

An important part of taking an active role in your education is planning your course work. Look through your college handbook, and write down the requirements for your major. What courses are required? Are any other experiences required? Now list all the courses that you have taken. Make a list of all the courses that you need to take. In what ways have you been active in shaping your education to match your goals? What steps can you take to be more active?

CHAPTER

4

Study Tips: Tools for Academic Success

Chapter Outline

Have you ever spent hours studying for a test, only to get a mediocre grade? Meanwhile, your friend says he only studied for an hour and got an A. What's the deal? Consider this scenario:

> Tom gets home from his part-time job and fixes himself a snack. It's almost 6 P.M., and he knows that he has to start studying for tomorrow's test. It's been a rough semester and he's gone to all of his classes, but doesn't have a lot written in his notebooks. Tom finds that his mind wanders in class and it's difficult to understand the point of the professor's lectures. He usually doesn't read before each class because it's hard to keep up with five classes while working over 20 hours a week. Tom decides to complete the reading tonight, hoping that he'll remember some of it for tomorrow's test. He brings his snack to the kitchen and clears a space among the breakfast dishes piled on the table. He tries to read while eating his snack. He begins reading but finds it difficult to concentrate. "Those dishes!" Tom exclaims, "That's why I can't focus." He takes a break to wash them. Twenty minutes later, after washing the dishes and clearing off the counters and stove, Tom sits down to read. Thirty minutes into his reading, his roommate comes home and begins a long story about his horrendous day. Nearly an hour later, Tom realizes that his studying isn't working, but he's hungry, so he and his roommate order a pizza. He vows to study after dinner. "This will be an all-nighter," he thinks to himself.

Sound familiar? Tom has good intentions and is motivated to study, but he's developed poor study habits, such as cramming. He's having trouble keeping up with his classes and is simply studying in the wrong place at the wrong time. Tom's predicament is common, but don't fall prey to this damaging cycle.

An important theme of this chapter is somewhat counterintuitive: Spending lots of time studying will not guarantee you good grades. Instead, it's the *quality* of your studying that counts. It doesn't do you much good to spend countless hours poring over your books if you don't retain anything. Work hard, but also work smart. This chapter describes techniques to help you manage your time, get organized, and improve your study habits so that you don't find yourself in Tom's shoes. Improving your study habits will take time and effort but the work that you put in now will pay off. Learn to make the most constructive use of your time, and you will accomplish more in less time. With effort and consistent practice, you'll find that you can study more efficiently and be more productive.

Are You Prepared to Succeed?

Before you can improve your study skills you must take a hard look at yourself. Knowing yourself—your habits, skills, preferences, and needs—is critical to devising study strategies that work for you. In this chapter we discuss general strategies but you will need to tailor these ideas to fit your own needs and capacities. There is no one right way to study. However, the most successful students are self-aware. They monitor their learning to figure out what works for them.

How do your study skills rate? If you're like most students, they can use improvement. Complete the study skills assessment in Exercise 4.1 to learn more about your study needs.

Exercise 4.1
Study Skills Assessment

Use the following scale to respond to the study skills assessment below. Be honest!

1 = none of the time
2 = some of the time
3 = most of the time
4 = all of the time

Do you:

________ 1. Manage your time to meet school and job responsibilities, as well as relax

________ 2. Set and monitor academic and personal goals

(Continued)

EXERCISE 4.1 (Continued)

__________ 3. Read your textbooks before class
__________ 4. Pause to think about how well you understand something
__________ 5. Maintain attention during classes
__________ 6. Use active listening in class
__________ 7. Take notes that are useful for later studying
__________ 8. Study well ahead of exams
__________ 9. Use a variety of strategies for recalling information
__________ 10. Test yourself to determine whether you understand the material
__________ 11. Have a well-defined study space
__________ 12. Distinguish essential and nonessential information in lectures
__________ 13. Identify the main points in your reading.
__________ 14. Take notes on readings
__________ 15. Vary your learning and study strategies according to the material at hand.

Scoring:
Add the points for each item. Higher scores indicate more effective use of study skills.

Prompt:

1. Consider your score. How well do you think it reflects your skills?
2. Choose three items/activities that you use most often. Provide an example of each. How have these skills benefited you?
3. Choose three items that you use least often. How might employing these skills improve your academic achievement?
4. After reading this chapter, identify opportunities to use the activities noted in item 3. Discuss specific strategies to employ.

Carefully consider your answers to Exercise 4.2 and you may glean clues about where to focus your efforts to improve your studying. No one can do this part for you. You'll need to develop your own formula for academic success, based on your understanding of yourself. Once you learn what works for you, you'll increase your academic efficiency and get more work done in less time.

Do You Have Helpful Attitudes and Beliefs?

How well you do in college is not just a matter of your ability—your beliefs, attitudes, and motivation also matter. What motivates you?

Motivation and Persistence

Is your academic behavior motivated by intrinsic or extrinsic goals? Is your primary reason for reading to get good grades on quizzes? Do you stick it out to complete difficult math problems because you like the challenge? The source of your motivation influences your success. Students who are intrinsically motivated focus on the internal rewards of completing tasks, such as mastering the material and increasing knowledge. Other students focus on the outside rewards that come with success, such as earning good grades, rewards, and positive attention (Ryan & Deci, 2000). People tend to be more highly motivated and persist longer when they find a task personally interesting or gratifying, when they are intrinsically motivated to succeed. The rewards that fuel extrinsic motivation often aren't enough to sustain activity in the face of overwhelming challenges. The best students study not just to earn good grades but because they want to master the material. Generally speaking, students who are intrinsically motivated tend to perform better in college than those who are extrinsically motivated.

A second factor associated with success in college and life is one's beliefs about the causes of success and failure. How people attribute their successes, failures, and circumstances of their lives is influenced by a belief pattern known as locus of control. Locus of control refers to whether a person believes internal or external forces control circumstances in his or her life (Rotter, 1990). People who adopt an internal locus of control believe that they have the power to control most aspects of their lives whereas those with an external locus of control tend to believe that outside forces are more important contributors to their circumstances. When people with an internal locus of control earn a poor grade or do not perform as well as they would like, they look within and tend to attribute it to poor effort. They take responsibility and tend to use problem-solving techniques to devise plans to improve. People with an external locus of control, on the other hand, feel that they are powerless and have no control over their performance. Outside factors such as a poor instructor, hard test, or luck are viewed as to blame and students with an external locus of control may lose their motivation to improve as they view their success or failure as out of their control.

It not simply your view of the degree of control you have that matters in determining success. Your views of your own abilities are powerful influences on your behavior. Self-efficacy refers to your belief in your ability to successfully complete a task. Is your performance under your own control? Can you improve your own abilities or are they set in stone? Students who believe that they are competent and that they are able to learn and succeed tend to persist longer in challenging tasks and ultimately earn high grades than other students (Richardson, Abraham, & Bond, 2012). Students with a high sense of self-efficacy are more motivated to complete tasks and are more likely to be successful—and, naturally, success improves students' sense of self-efficacy.

What does all of this mean? These qualities contribute to students' academic tenacity, the tendency to persist—to work hard and to work smart—to achieve goals (Dweck, Walton, & Cohen, 2011). Successful students tend to be intrinsically motivated. They are motivated to master the material and learn more rather than to simply earn a grade. They believe that they control their own success, their effort makes a difference in their performance, and that they have the ability to succeed.

Self-Talk and Motivation

Beliefs about yourself and your abilities matter in determining your success. Change the way you view your capacities and the tasks you face and you will be more likely to meet success. It requires patience, but you can train yourself to think in ways that empower you. Pay attention to how you talk to yourself. We all engage in self-talk and have an inner critic, a voice that monitors and comments on all that we do. Self-talk influences your self-esteem, confidence, motivation, and success.

Positive self-talk contains words of encouragement and support. Positive self-talk is the voice inside you telling you that you can do it. It helps you to persevere, boosts self-esteem, and is motivating. Negative self-talk, on the other hand, is deflating. It is discouraging, belittling, and negative. It pulls you down, creating and sustaining self-doubt. Negative self-talk is the nagging voice telling you that you don't have the ability or that you aren't smart enough, that you will not succeed. Negative self-talk makes us more likely to quit.

Try to pay attention to your inner voice, your self-talk. As you work on challenging math problems or read a lengthy passage, what does your inner voice say? Train yourself to recognize when you're using negative self-talk, then turn it around into positive self-talk. When you find yourself saying, "I'm just not good at this. There's no point trying," reframe your negative self-talk into motivating positive self-talk. Instead tell yourself, "I can do this. I've done so in the past and I've learned from my mistakes. I'm willing to work hard." The self-talk you use doesn't need to be sophisticated. A simple, "I can do this," is motivating. Becoming aware of and changing self-talk is challenging but is well worth it because self-talk not just indicates our motivation and sense of control and efficacy, but it can influence it. See Table 4.1 for tips to increase your motivation.

FIVE TIPS TO INCREATE YOUR MOTIVATION

1. Set learning goals. Decide what facts, concepts, or ideas you want to learn before beginning to work on a task. Setting learning goals can motivate you to put more effort into a task.
2. See the value in the task. Understanding why you are doing the task—seeing the importance of the task—can motivate you to complete it. You may also find that you have a personal interest or find enjoyment in completing the task.
3. Have a positive attitude. As you begin a task, think about similar tasks that you completed in the past. Knowing that you've done the task before can increase your self-efficacy and lead to greater motivation.
4. Use positive self-talk. When working on a long or difficult task, you may find that telling yourself that you can do it, why it's important, or that you are almost done can keep you going. Reminding yourself that you are good at math, for example, can help motivate you to study for your upcoming math exam.
5. Create interest in the task. You can also increase your motivation by making the task more interesting. If you're not interested in the material you're reading, you can create interest in the task by taking notes or generating self-test questions in the margin to make the task more interesting.
6. Learn from your mistakes. Learning why you were unable to successfully complete a particular task or achieve a specific goal can also increase your motivation. Knowing what you need to do differently can help you be more motivated to work hard after failure.

Source: Adapted from Van Blerkom (2012) *College Study Skills: Becoming a Strategic Learner* – 7th ed, Wadsworth / Cengage p. 11.

EXERCISE 4.2

Reviewing Your Positive and Negative Self-Talk

1. Identify examples of negative self-talk that you have used. In what situations did they occur?
2. How might you reframe it into positive self-talk?
3. Identify specific positive self-talk phrases that you will use during your next challenging situation.
4. Choose three tips in Table 4.1. Identify specific ways in which you can apply them.

TIME MANAGEMENT AND ORGANIZATIONAL SKILLS

At one time or another, most of us complain about feeling overwhelmed—like there is not enough time in the day to get it all done. Although we can't add more hours to the day, you often have more free time than you realize. How do you find those free hours and allocate them as you choose? Use time management strategies to regulate your use of time. Become more efficient at using your time and you'll get more done and make time for friends, family, and—most importantly—yourself.

How Do You Use Your Time?

Before you can begin studying, you must gain control over your time, as its master and not as its slave. Most students could use some help in managing their time. The first step toward gaining control over time is to understand how you use it. Take the time management quiz in Exercise 4.3 and see how you rate.

EXERCISE 4.3

How Organized Are You?

Indicate your response, True or False, to each item below.

1. ______ I do a lot of my work at the last minute.
2. ______ I use a calendar to keep track of my work and activities.
3. ______ I struggle to begin unpleasant tasks.
4. ______ At this very moment, I can identify three things that I have planned to do today.
5. ______ I often find myself daydreaming when I should be working.
6. ______ I have a work space that I can go to that requires minimal planning or set up.
7. ______ I feel like my friends are much more organized than me.
8. ______ I have a to-do list for this week.
9. ______ I check e-mails and texts as I hear the notification.
10. ______ I know what time of day I work best.
11. ______ I often feel overwhelmed with work.
12. ______ My calendar lists all of the important deadlines that I face this semester and year.
13. ______ I often attend class unprepared and wish I had done more reading.
14. ______ I prioritize my work and activities.
15. ______ I often find myself on Facebook, Instagram, or online when I should be working.
16. ______ I have time set aside to relax and have fun with my friends.
17. ______ I often forget to complete assignments.
18. ______ I write down what I need to do.
19. ______ I often lose important papers or articles.
20. ______ I rarely hand work in late.

Scoring: Give yourself 1 point for each even item marked True and 1 point for each odd item marked False. Sum your points for a total score that reflects your use of helpful time management strategies.

Prompt:

1. Is your score as high as you'd like? Look over your answers. What aspects of time management seem most challenging for you?
2. Choose three items in which you'd like to improve. Explain your choices.
3. After reviewing this chapter, discuss specific ways of improving the items you identified.

Many students and professors are poor judges of their time use. One of the most accurate ways to learn about how you spend time is to keep a time log. If you're like most people you will find the results of Exercise 4.4 surprising. That ten-minute coffee break might really be closer to forty minutes! We may not like to admit the amount of time that we spend on Facebook or playing video games, but it is important to construct an accurate picture of your time use so that you can identify areas to change (and those to keep).

EXERCISE 4.4

Keep a Time Log

For several days or a week, record how you spend each hour of the day. Specifically, do so as your day progresses to record what you're doing as you're doing it. There are many apps that can help you log your time. Run a search for time tracking or time logging app for some options. Or you might simply set an alarm to ring every thirty minutes and record what you're doing. You may find it difficult to remember to record your activity but do the best that you can. After a few days or a week, analyze your patterns of time use.

1. What do you spend the most waking time on?
2. What do you spend the least?
3. Does your time use reflect your priorities? Is there an area where you'd prefer to spend more time? Less? Explain.
4. Are you using your time most efficiently? What can you change?

Time Management Really Means Managing Your To-Do List

Some students and faculty balk at the term time management, instead preferring to keep their schedules open and allow for spontaneity. The philosophy behind time management is that by controlling or planning part of your time you are able to be more flexible with the rest of your time. However, it's not just time that we're wrangling when we engage in time management techniques: It's really our to-do lists that are managed. Time itself is not the problem. Instead it's getting everything we need to get done, actually done.

The first, most important step in getting a handle on your time is determining what has to be done. Create a to-do list. To-do lists can be created from the perspective on the day, week, month, semester, year, or even a five-year plan. Start at the semester level. Look over all of your course syllabi. Record assignments, exams, and any due dates. Add other tasks and dates to remember for work, outside activities, and your personal life. This is your master to-do list. Most of the tasks on this list, however, are likely huge and cannot be completed in one sitting. For example, that term paper due on the last day of class that requires more than one work session the night before.

Create a plan for each large task, such as paper assignments. List the actions that are required to complete the assignment. In the case of a paper it might include brainstorming topics, reading to choose a topic, selecting a topic, gathering sources, reading and taking notes, preparing an outline, writing a draft, and so on (see Chapter 5 for more on writing papers). Think about how much time you need for each task and work backward from the due date. For example, if the paper is due December 15, complete your first full draft of the paper by the November 30th write your outline by November 15th finish reading and note-taking by the 1st, and so on. Create multiple informal personal due dates for each part of each project. This sounds like a lot of work—and it is—but this planning will make your semester run much more smoothly because you will know what you need to do for each assignment and when you will do it. Table 4.2 lists some of the many benefits of developing good time management skills.

TABLE 4.2 **BENEFITS OF TIME MANAGEMENT AND TO-DO LISTS**

Know where to begin.	One of the primary benefits of creating a schedule is that you won't waste time deciding what to do. Removing the thought and planning can free your energy to actually complete what's on your list and spend your time productively.
Less likely to avoid distasteful tasks.	It's human nature: we spend time on activities that we like and that we are good at. Many students put other tasks first and find that they've run out of time to study subjects that they dislike. A schedule prevents this type of forgetfulness.
Free your mind	Recording your to-dos—tasks that you need to complete—relieves them from your mind. Once you've written an item down, there's no need to worry about forgetting it, so you're free to focus on other things.
Prioritize	What is important to you? How important is each of the classes that you are taking to your academic standing and future plans? How many assignments does each of your courses entail? What is the relative weight or value of each assignment? It's easy to spend lots of time doing busy work that is not worth much of your final grade while not allocating enough time to study for a test or prepare a major paper.
Make time for fun	Good time management skills permit you to make time for friends and enjoy leisure without feeling guilty that you're not studying. If you schedule time to do your work, you know that it will get done. Then you can enjoy "play time" without worrying or thinking about studying.

Take this same approach each week. Determine what tasks you'll complete to make progress on your major assignments, and record specific assignments and tasks for the upcoming week. What reading is due when? Homework assignments? Anything to prepare for group assignments? Then determine which of these tasks needs to be completed on each day. This is where the time management part comes in. Create a schedule and determine when you're in class, working, or engaging in other activities, and schedule specific times for completing your tasks.

Real Tips for Real Students

To-Do List Managers

If you're looking to go the digital route for maintaining your to-do list, you're not limited to the standard app that comes with your phone. There are hundreds of to-do list apps to help you organize and manage your time. Some of the most popular apps include:

Remember the Milk: http://rememberthemilk.com

Todoist: https://todoist.com

Wunderlist: https://wunderlist.com/

Any.do: http://any.do/

Toodledo: http://toodledo.com/

There is a dizzying array of ways to organize and keep up with your to-do list. However, one warning: It's easy to let searching, trying, and playing with new to-do list apps become a form of procrastination. Don't let yourself fall into the trap of spending more time searching for a way to organize your list than actually acting on the list.

Make Choices about How to Spend Your Time

Ensuring that your semester-long to-do list gets done—and that you keep on top of the rest of your life and enjoy it—takes some planning. This is where the scheduling part of time management comes in. Many of us let too much time slip through our fingers because we aren't taught how to manage it. Juggling school, a job, extracurricular activities, and a social life is difficult and nearly impossible to manage successfully without a plan. I often hear students say that if they just tried harder they'd be able to do it all. They resign themselves to all-nighters and walk around campus like zombies. This approach, trying to do everything without acquiring the skills to manage your time, will lead to burnout. Life may seem busy now, but it doesn't suddenly get easier after graduation. In fact, demands on time often increase with career and family responsibilities.

Planning your time isn't just about squeezing more activities into your schedule, it's about taking a serious look at your commitments and priorities.

Take a moment and analyze the demands on your time. Now that you've listed all of your activities, you might realize that you are quite busy—and perhaps overextended. Are you committing yourself to too many activities? Are you trying to do too much? You might love music, but can you juggle a campus jazz band, a guitar trio, and an off-campus rock band? Can you write for the school paper and maintain several blogs at once? Recognize that sometimes you can't do it all. Decide what is important and what isn't. Difficult as it might be, you must remove activities that aren't meaningful to you in order to devote time to those that are. Don't eliminate all *fun* activities—but prioritize them and make choices about what's important to you and what will help you meet your goals. Make conscious choices of how to spend your time so that you have more control over your days and your life, rather than running late on everything and constantly feeling harried and behind.

Create Your Schedule

We can all benefit from keeping a schedule and working on time management. However, the form that the time management system takes varies for all of us. Look over the possibilities and decide what works for you. Is it

- An old-fashioned analog paper set of daily, weekly, and monthly calendars?
- A plan notebook that you fashion into a personal calendar?
- Simple text file that you sync among your devices?
- Your phone's basic calendar and to-do list app?
- An online app that can sync with your phone, desktop, and tablet computers?

Whatever format you choose, make sure that it works for you, is easy to use, and always present so that you will be motivated to use it. You may find that it takes time to figure out what works—and you may try more than one system. Once you settle on a system, use it consistently. Create a plan or a schedule for each day. That is, choose what tasks to accomplish and when to accomplish them.

- Schedule time for your reading and class assignments.
- Think ahead and schedule time to work on major projects early in the semester. As we discussed, work back from the due date and create mini deadlines. Work on these each week.
- Plan short blocks of time, preferably half-hour or, at most, hour-long blocks. Give yourself breaks.
- Schedule the most difficult tasks during daylight hours, when people tend to be most alert and awake.
- Don't schedule every moment. Allow for some flexibility, last-minute changes, and play.

- Allow time for sleep. You need at least eight hours of sleep each night (this is supported by psychological research). Without sleep you are less likely to remember material, which means that you're less likely to learn.
- Know your sleep pattern and work with it. We all have a natural rhythm of times in which we are alert and awake and times in which we are less alert. Arrange your study times around your natural rhythm. Study when you're alert and sleep when you're sleepy.
- Schedule down time, exercise time, and social time. The only way to ensure that all of your needs are met consistently is to plan ahead. Care for yourself by setting aside time just for you.

By scheduling regular periods to work, you will have regular periods to think about what you are learning rather than just simply prepare for looming deadlines. Without the pressure of cramming for an exam, you have time to think about what you're studying. When you have the chance to think about a subject and how it fits with your experience and perspective, learning can become more interesting and enjoyable—and you retain it.

The cardinal rule of time management is that you must write everything down—all of your plans. Keep a record of all your assignments and obligations in one place, including class times, study times, project due dates, assignments, appointments, and social events. Consistently write everything down so that you don't forget anything—and more importantly, so that you're free to think without worrying that you've forgotten something. Always carry your schedule and to-do list, so that you can bring order to your life and have peace of mind. Make no mistake about it, this will take some time and practice; but creating a schedule produces important returns. You'll feel like you have extra time. You'll feel more in control.

Real Tips for Real Students
Capture Lost Time

Each day we lose time as we go about the tasks of our day, such as walking from one place to another, waiting in line, and traveling. This time isn't really lost. We can use it, if we choose. For example, while walking from class try to think of the main points of the lecture and how they apply to what you know. While exercising on the elliptical machine, brainstorm topics or titles for papers or think about how to organize papers. Another way to use in-between time is to carry pocket work (reading, an article, flash cards) that you can do while waiting in lines, at the bus stop, sitting, and so on. Cell phones make it easy to always have a task at hand. Ten minutes here, fifteen there, it all adds up. In addition, cognitive psychology and memory research has shown that we can recall more information if we study in short periods rather than long ones, so you just might learn more. However, also remember that you don't need to be productive all the time. Sometimes staring into space while you wait in line is a good thing.

Create a Study Environment

Improving your skills in time management means that you will set aside consistent periods for reading, writing, and studying. Setting aside time is the first step to ensuring that you keep up with your studies. Another part, however, is creating a place conducive to your work. It is one thing to set aside time, but you need to ensure that you will be productive during that time. As a psychology student you will learn about how our environment influences us. Take advantage of that knowledge and create a study environment that will support and encourage your work. Where do you work? Is it conducive to learning?

Create a place just for study. Why? We're conditioned by our environment to behave in certain ways. The more we behave a certain way in a given environment, the stronger the habit gets. This is a powerful principle of psychology that you can use to your advantage. Create a habit for yourself. Designate an area just for studying. Choose a quiet place with adequate light. Make your study area pleasant and motivating. Avoid distractions; don't set up a study area in a high-traffic place (like the kitchen). If you are prone to distraction and procrastination, be sure to set up your study area away from the television or anything else that might distract you (e.g., a big window). Create a barrier between you and the world. If possible, shut the door or at least create an invisible barrier by facing the wall. Your study area should be convenient—a place that's easy to use, so you'll use it often. Some students need light background noise to study—though be careful that it's not distracting. Before you decide that you "need" background noise like the television or radio, try spending some time without any noise to see how it feels. Many people find white noise helpful because it's simple background noise without content—subtle hissing like the motor of a fan, or static. There are a number of websites, apps, and downloads that offer free access to white noise (try Simply Noise: http://simplynoise.com).

Many students don't have an ideal work space, a place that is just for studying. What then? Create consistent circumstances that prepare you to work. Seek a barrier, whether physical or mental. Turn yourself away from others so that their activity won't disturb you. Play white noise through your earbuds. Find a handful of places where you can distance yourself and work. Don't rely on only studying in your dorm in case your roommate has friends over. Find a place in the library, but also a quiet student lounge so that you have options. Wherever you go, however, enact the same ritual to prepare to work: Lay your stuff your stuff out, find your barrier, use your earbuds, and focus. Is your study space conducive to learning? Exercise 4.5 will help you to evaluate your study area and determine if it is conducive to work.

EXERCISE 4.5

Study Environment Quiz

Check off items that you find are true for your study environment.

❑ Clutter-free table or desk with space to spread out books and papers.
❑ Good lighting.
❑ No television, music, or other loud distractions nearby.
❑ Sturdy and comfortable chair.
❑ Comfortable temperature.
❑ Calendar, schedule, and to-do lists are handy.
❑ Laptop, tablet, and phone notifications are turned off.
❑ Books and supplies are handy.
❑ Phone is silenced.
❑ People rarely interrupt me here.
❑ There are few things in my field of vision that have nothing to do with school work.
❑ I work well and feel that my studying is effective here.

Scoring:

Count your check marks. The higher your score is to 12, the better your study environment.

Reflection:

1. How does your study space rate? Reflect on your score.
2. In what ways might the quality of your work space influence your learning and academic achievement?
3. In what ways can you improve your study space to make it a place more conducive for working? Identify three strategies for improving your work space.

Remember that your work space is not just physical. Your laptop or tablet must also be prepped for work. Close out windows that are not integral to your work. Silence notifications. Sign out of Skype. If you find it hard to avoid online distractions there are a number of websites that can make your browser or specific pages unavailable for a time period you specify. Google "block distracting websites" and you'll find a range of options for different operating systems.

We've discussed the importance of creating a habit of studying by monitoring the study place and atmosphere, but you should also pay attention to the time of day. Determine your best study time—when you're more ready to work, awake and alert. Try to study at the same time each day. When you set a discrete period of time aside for studying each day, your mind gets used to the pattern. It becomes easier to work during that time. If you stick to a routine study time and place, psychological research suggests that you'll spend less time warming up and more time studying effectively.

Be Organized

Studying is easier if you're organized. Have you ever sat down to study only to realize that you needed materials from another room? Or on your tablet rather than your laptop? Not having your materials together is a time trap, because you'll need to spend extra time gathering them and risk getting sidetracked and wasting time. Save time by keeping all your study materials in one place.

Do you know where you put last week's notes? The handout from class? Do you know where to look to find your work? There are various ways of keeping your class material organized. If you prefer to use paper, follow this simple binder method. Use a three-ring binder for your schoolwork. Keep lecture notes and handouts from each class together, marked by a tab. Use one large binder for all of your classes, separating each class with tabbed dividers. You can also add a section for other necessities such as calendars, weekly schedules, lists, and phone numbers. All that you have to carry around is a single binder—not five notebooks, folders, and many scraps of paper. You're also less prone to lose handouts if they're in your binder. If your binder is full or gets too bulky, empty the contents into file folders marked for each class. At the end of the semester you'll have at least one file folder for each class.

Today there are many digital options that provide more flexibility and are more durable than the binder-paper approach. Data management websites and apps like Evernote, OneNote, or Google Keep allow you to create notes, scan handouts, and save photos of whiteboards and other presentations. Some students take handwritten notes in class and scan them into their desired app. Some apps can convert handwriting to searchable text. Notes can be tagged for easy searching. Each of these apps is available online, as desktop programs, and as phone apps syncing across all of your devices.

READING: TIPS FOR IMPROVING COMPREHENSION AND EFFICIENCY

Have you ever read a chapter, yet were unable to remember much about it? Many students have difficulty retaining what they read. We discussed how our beliefs, attributions, and attitudes influence our academic achievement. They also influence how we approach tasks such as reading. As you sit down with a textbook in front of you, stop and think about how you feel. Are you dreading the task? Are you multitasking? Sometimes students say that they hate reading, but I don't believe it's true. We read almost all day almost every day: text messages, Facebook posts, tweets, webpages. Gathering virtually any information online comes from reading. Given how most of us are glued to our smartphones, it's a safe bet to say that most people do not hate reading. Instead it is the context that sometimes turns us off to reading. Sometimes students dislike reading textbooks. While reading a textbook will never come as easily as reading an exciting fiction book or posts about your favorite musician, reading a textbook can become more enjoyable and, more importantly, you can become more efficient so that it takes less time. As you begin to read take note of your attitudes. Are you engaging in self-defeating negative self-talk? Use positive self-talk to empower you as you are accomplishing challenging tasks. Reading a textbook is very different from reading novels or magazines for pleasure, yet students often attempt to read textbooks and other scholarly books as if they were novels. Textbooks require a different set of strategies.

Reading Textbooks with the SQ3R Method

Particularly suited to reading dense college textbooks, the SQ3R method (Robinson, 1970) is designed to help students read faster and retain more. The name stands for the steps in reading: survey, question, read, recite, review. Let's examine each step of this technique.

Survey Before reading a book chapter, quickly survey it to get an initial impression of its contents. Glance through the topic headings to get an overview of the chapter. Skim the sections, and read the summary paragraphs to get an idea of where the chapter is going. Your survey should take only a few minutes, but it will highlight the main ideas of the chapter and provide an initial orientation that will help you to organize the material as you read it. Surveying a chapter gives you background knowledge to link with other material that you are learning and what you already know and have an idea of what is to come.

Whether or not you decide to employ the SQ3R method, you should always survey the material to be read. Skim the table of contents, preface, headings, and conclusions. In addition to previewing the text, stop and think about the instructor's purpose in making the assignment. What does your professor want you to get out of this reading? How does this assignment contribute to the course content? Identify your purpose for reading: What can you gain from this reading assignment? The most obvious response might be, "an understanding of the course material," but other responses might include, "consider a possible topic for my paper," or simply, "learn something new and interesting."

Question Look at the first heading in the chapter. Turn it into a question. Your task in reading the following section is to gather information and answer that question. Posing questions will help you remember information that you already know and arouse curiosity about the reading assignment, which will increase your comprehension. This step requires conscious effort, but is worth it because active reading is the best way to retain written material. For example, if the heading is "Prevalence of Substance Use and Abuse in Adolescence," you might ask, "How many adolescents use illegal drugs?" If the heading is "Multiple Personality Disorder," you might ask, "What are the characteristics of multiple personality disorder?" Asking questions focuses your concentration. Take an active role in your reading. Don't read passively: Interrogate the author.

Read Read to answer the questions you pose. Actively search for answers. If you finish the section and haven't answered the question, reread it. Read reflectively. Consider what the author is trying to say, and think about how you can use that information.

Recite (and/or Record) Now that you've read enough to answer your question, look away and try to recite the answer to your question. Use your own words and examples. If you can do this, it means that you understand the material. If you can't, glance over the section again. Record the answer in your notes. Once you've said each answer, record it. You might also reconsider your initial question, fine-tune it, write it in the margin of the text, and underline the key words that provide an answer.

Review Once you have read the entire chapter, test your memory by asking yourself the questions that you've identified. Review your notes and get a bird's-eye view of the chapter. Consider how it fits with what you know from the course, experience, and other classes. What is the significance of the material? What are the implications or applications of this material? What questions are you left with?

Some students find that the SQ3R method is too detailed for some of their reading. A shorter reading method, known as P2R (Wong, 2015) is useful for material that you don't need to cover comprehensively. There are three steps. First, preview the entire chapter. Next, read actively. Finally, review the material. The key to making P2R work lies in using an active strategy to read, such as by reciting the important points, taking notes, answering chapter review questions, or writing in the margins. Doing something active while you read ensures that you are thinking about the material and are much more likely to retain it. Reviewing the material helps to reinforce the information.

Exercise 4.6
SQ3R Practice

Practice SQ3R on your next reading assignment.

1. What activities did you perform to do each step?
2. Review the resulting list of questions and corresponding notes.
3. How well do they capture the main points of the reading?
4. How does this technique compare with your usual strategies?
5. What are the pros and cons to the SQ3R method?

More Tips on Reading

By now you understand that reading for comprehension often requires more than one pass. It usually takes two, three, or even more readings to grasp difficult concepts. Rereading takes time and may seem inefficient; however, thoroughly understanding what you have read and integrating it with your existing knowledge will save you time in the long run, when it is time to study for a test. It is easy to remember material that you understand, so you will spend less time studying.

Here are some additional pointers:

- Use a dictionary to look up unfamiliar words. If your cell phone is nearby there's no excuse for not looking up a word. After looking up an unknown word, consider its meaning in the sentence.
- Pace yourself. Note that difficult readings will require more than one pass. Permit yourself the time to read such assignments over more than one session.
- Read the chapter before attending the lecture so that you're familiar with the material beforehand. Note unanswered questions or particularly difficult material, and seek answers during the lecture.
- If you underline text, do so minimally and stay focused on the important details. Avoid the temptation to highlight every line. Heavy highlighting can be a procrastination technique because you're often marking what you should learn instead of focusing on learning it.
- Instead of underlining or highlighting, take the briefest of notes while reading by adding brackets in margins or underlining minimally. Note pages where you might want to take formal notes. After reading, take more extensive notes. Write the main points, in your own words.

As you finish each section, or even each paragraph when reading dense material, take a moment to write down what you've learned. Be sure to use your own words and not those of the author (to lift the author's words is plagiarism, as we will see in Chapter 5). Your notes will be a valuable resource when it comes time to study. However, don't write down concepts that you don't understand. Reread the section until you understand the concept, or explain as much of it as you can and indicate your questions so that you can ask your instructor for assistance. When reading and note-taking are complete, reread all of your notes, think about what you've read, and add more notes based on your reflections (Kahn, 1992).

Getting the Most Out of Lectures: Note-Taking Tips

Class is not the time to sit back and relax. If you expect to learn and retain information from lectures, you can't simply listen, you must actively do something with the material. You must take notes. Without notes, even professors find it difficult to stick to the main points they'd like to make. Your class notes are an important study resource, a sort of privately constructed textbook that may contain information that is not available anywhere else. When you take notes, you listen more actively and are more involved in the subject, promoting learning, memory, and reducing boredom. Note-taking is a lifelong skill. Most careers require at least some note-taking (e.g., how else can you remember what happened in that staff meeting). How can you improve your note-taking skills?

Come Prepared

Listening to a lecture, participating in class, and learning is easier if you are prepared. Professors assign reading prior to class to ensure that students have the background knowledge needed to help them understand the day's lecture. Read before class so that the lecture material isn't completely new. Another reason for reading beforehand is to determine how closely the instructor follows the textbook. You might take notes differently in a class where the professor follows the textbook organization as compared to one in which the professor lectures on different topics entirely. The familiarity that comes with reading before class also means that you'll be able to recognize and organize the main ideas and terms more easily (Kahn, 1992).

Be Selective

Don't write everything the instructor says. Beginning note-takers often make the mistake of trying to write every word and become frustrated when they find that it's impossible. Try to determine the main points and take notes in your own words. Identifying the main points requires active listening. Listen actively, that is, think about what you are hearing, evaluate it, determine your understanding, and make connections with what you already know.

The instructor usually provides clues to what is important. One clue is repetition: Instructors repeat important points. Repeated use of examples indicates important points. Notes written on the board or presented in PowerPoint slides offer other clues. Remember that when you copy notes from the board or follow along with the PowerPoint slides, you will need to write more than the phrase or words indicated. Also write an explanation. The instructor's tone of voice might signify important information. Pay attention to pauses that offer time for students to take notes. Finally, instructors often highlight essential information by using specific phrases. Table 4.3 lists signal phrases that instructors might use to draw attention to critical information.

SIGNAL WORDS AND PHRASES

Listen For	Type of Phrase
To illustrate, for example, for instance	Examples to make a point more clear
Before, after, formerly, subsequently, prior, meanwhile, first, second, last	Time words to note the time relationships among ideas or enumerate them
Furthermore, in addition, moreover, also	Additional information to add to a list
Therefore, as a result, if ... then, accordingly, thus, so	Suggests cause and effect
On the other hand, in contrast, conversely, pros and cons	Contrast words to discuss both sides of a controversy
More importantly, above all, remember	Emphasize important information
In other words, in the vernacular, it simply means, that is, briefly, in essence	Repeats the information presented in a simpler form

Streamline Your Notes

If you are taking handwritten notes (and most students do), use a shorthand style that includes only the essential elements and leaves out unnecessary words. Don't write in full sentences and forget grammar. Grammatical sentences require more time than you have while taking notes. Create your own abbreviations for common words used in class (just be sure to record what each abbreviation stands for). For example, as a student of developmental psychology, most of my notes referred to "dev" instead of development and "ψ" for psychology.

Use an outline or bullet point method to record a streamlined account of the main points of the lecture. As you take notes, indent your paragraphs and points deeply to help you note the organization of the lecture (like an informal outline) and to provide room for later notes and comments. If you find note-taking particularly difficult in a class, leave extra blank space at the end of each section or paragraph so that you can add more later after asking a question or reading the text. Focus on making legible rather than pretty handwriting. Some students write more sloppily as they plan to type their notes after class, but if they run out of time they might end up with notes they can't read.

Take Notes during Class Discussion

Discussion is not time to put your pen down and relax. Instructors use discussion to steer students toward grasping major points. It's not simply chatting. Listen actively during class discussions. The instructor will comment on important points and draw conclusions from the discussion. Record these.

Beware of PowerPoint

It can be deceptive. One bad habit that many students fall prey to is relying too heavily on a professor's PowerPoint slides. It is tempting to simply copy the information on the overhead slides, but professors require you to know much more than what is on the slides. Likewise, many professors make PowerPoint slides available for students to download. Some students print the slides as a substitute for taking notes in class. Printing the slides is an excellent idea but it's critical to remember that slides are not class notes. Downloading and printing a list of points and terms for the day's class is deceptively simple and can feel as if you already have recorded the content of the day's class. Professors explain much more than is on their slides. Use the slides as an outline of the professor's lecture and add information to support each bullet point. Consider what the bullet point is saying. Listen to the professor's explanation. Practice active listening and listen for information. Try to pull out what information supports or refutes this point. How does it relate to theory?

Organize Your Notes

Review your notes soon after class, making corrections or adding information as needed. Identify follow-up questions to ask your professor. Some students type their notes after class. Typing class notes can be a waste of time if you focus *only* on the typing. Typing your notes in order to organize and integrate them with prior lectures and readings is useful *if* you remember to focus on compiling information and creating links among sources of information rather than simply getting it into a typed form.

One of the challenges of handwritten notes is that they can be lost. Organize your notes in a loose-leaf binder so that you can't lose pages easily. A binder also lets you rearrange the pages as needed, add handouts from class, and remove pages neatly. Write notes on only one side of each loose-leaf page, so that you can see all the information at once and later add additional pages of notes easily. Or consider the digital route by saving your notes in an app such as an Endnote or OneNote notebook. Scan or take pictures of your notes and you'll have an easily accessible, portable, and searchable database of your notes.

Taking Notes on a Laptop or Tablet

Some students choose to take notes on a laptop or tablet. Check with your professor beforehand as some have policies prohibiting electronic devices in class. Students with excellent typing skills often prefer taking notes on their laptop as it's quick, editable, searchable, and can be easily linked to data management apps. On the other hand, professors and often other students find student use of laptops distracting because of the clicking of keys, digital displays that draw the eye, and the ability to view students' off-task activity (how easy is it to tear your eyes away from an unknown Facebook profile on a student's screen?). The concern about laptop use in class is not simply social—it's academic. Students who use a laptop take more notes, but those notes tend to be verbatim transcriptions of what the professor says. Students who take handwritten notes tend to show stronger conceptual understanding of the material and are more successful in applying and integrating material (Mueller & Oppenheimer, 2014). As we've discussed, learning is an active process: You need to manipulate material to learn it. Transcription is a passive process. Taking handwritten notes requires judging what material to record, finding ways to record it simply in ways that you understand—both lead to learning.

Note-taking is important not simply for recording information but for learning. Explaining ideas in your own words will ensure that you understand, recall, and apply it later to achieve your goals as a college student. The act of writing helps you retain material.

EXERCISE 4.7

Analyze Your Class Notes

How well do your notes capture what you learn in class? Analyze your class notes. Choose one class session.

1. What did you do in class? Did the professor lecture? Was there discussion? Group work? Note all of the activities that occurred that day. (If you can't recall, it suggests that you probably need to do a better job of taking notes.)
2. What did you record? In what form? Paragraphs? Lists of words? Phrases?
3. Do the detail and depth of your notes reflect the day's work?
4. How helpful are your resulting notes?
5. Identify challenges to taking useful notes. How can you overcome these challenges?

What If You Miss Class?

Regardless of how good a student you are, how detail-oriented, hardworking, or diligent, you can be certain that you will miss a class at some point in your academic career. What do you do after missing class? Do you just show up at the next class and start fresh? What about material that you've missed? How do you get the notes and find out what happened?

First, be aware of class attendance, late work, and makeup policies. This information is listed in your course syllabus. Some professors do not accept late work or offer makeup exams, regardless of the reason. Others offer opportunities to make up for lost work, but have very strict policies about when they will accept makeup work. Read the syllabus to ensure that you don't miss any opportunities.

If it is possible, e-mail your professor before missing class. Remember the tips for e-mail etiquette in Chapter 3. Understand that most faculty do not consider family vacations, flying home early for break, or work obligations appropriate reasons for missing class. If you're ill or have an emergency, try to send an e-mail to inform the professor that you cannot attend class and, if you wish, provide an excuse. Be professional—offer a concise explanation without going into personal details. If you cannot e-mail before class, do so afterward. If possible, hand in assignments beforehand, by e-mail (and offer to hand in a hard copy when you're back on campus, but an e-mailed assignment shows that it's completed on time).

Upon returning to class, never ask if you "missed anything important." Most professors feel that class time itself is important. This is a surefire way to make a professor's eyes roll (maybe inwardly, at least!). Also do not ask the professor to "go over what you missed." The professor lectured and discussed the material in class and likely will not run through an hour-long class for you now. Instead, demonstrate that you care and are willing to try by reading the course material and handouts, and then asking questions about specific material that you don't understand. This is a more productive use of your (and your professor's) time. It also demonstrates initiative.

Finally, turn to your classmates for information about what happened in class and ask whether they will share their notes. Be sure to read more than one student's notes because students have different perspectives and might miss some points. Read notes from several students and you're more likely to get a complete picture of what happened in class.

Test-Taking Tips

We've discussed habits of studying, reading, and note-taking that should keep you immersed in the subject matter of your courses. A test is on the horizon; how do you prepare?

Get the Lay of the Land

Well ahead of the test, conduct an overview of all work that needs to be done. Make a list of tasks, and allocate time to complete them. If you're behind on your reading, approach the unread material with a plan. What do you need to get from the readings? Decide how much time you have to catch up. Preview the reading, deciding which parts are most important to focus on and which can be omitted. Use the reading techniques described earlier in this chapter.

Space Study and Prep Time

Studying begins on day 1 of the course. If you follow the strategies for reading, class preparation, and note-taking described in this chapter, you will retain material as you learn it. To save more time and retain more, use cumulative review throughout the semester. Set aside a few minutes each week to review your notes—even if an exam is not on the horizon. This small step will help you learn more and you'll find that you have to devote less time to studying for exams.

The more often that you encounter material, the more likely you are to remember it. By distributing your learning sessions over the semester, you'll find that you learn more and don't need to cram.

When it comes time to study, ignore the advice of students who plan to devote an entire day cramming for an exam. Contrary to popular belief, long study periods (e.g., four or more hours) aren't effective. The best way to retain knowledge and prepare for exams is to squeeze in short review periods throughout the day. For example, distributing four thirty-minute sessions throughout the day is less fatiguing and more effective than a single two-hour session. In addition, try to recite the information at odd moments (say them in the shower or while walking to your car). By verbalizing the material you'll get an idea of how well you know it and where your weaknesses lie. Slow and steady really does win the race.

Anticipate Questions

Ask yourself, "If I were making up this test, given what we've focused on in class and the readings, I would probably ask my students. . . ," and then answer the questions. How do you anticipate questions? Think about how the various course topics relate to one another. Are there any repeated themes? Examine your notes and readings to determine how the course content supports the major themes of the course (you can often find these in the syllabus, first few lectures, and first chapter of the text).

Create Study Sheets

Create a series of study sheets that summarize important information for each major topic. A study sheet is a one-page synopsis of the relevant factual information, vocabulary, and theories relating to the topic. It requires you to identify, condense, and organize material from your text and the lectures. Preparing a study sheet requires actively processing all that you have learned and determining what you need to learn. The result is a comprehensive but condensed summary of a topic, much of which you might retain simply from engaging in the active processing required to prepare it. Create a study sheet for each major topic. Also, study sheets are excellent preparation for open-book exams.

EXERCISE 4.8

Create a Study Sheet

Choose a topic in one of your courses and create a study sheet to integrate all the information you have about it. Identify the main points and concepts. Compare your class notes with the textbook. Construct a study sheet that synthesizes all that you know about the topic. Identify any remaining questions. Based on your work, consider the following:

1. How might you use this technique in the future?
2. What are the advantages and disadvantages of creating and using study sheets?
3. Is this technique, creating study sheets, better suited to some kinds of information and topics than others?

An essential element to performing well on tests is preparation; however, preparation is not always enough to perform at your best. Test-taking skills also count. Students who excel understand *how* to take tests. They tailor their strategies to the type of test (e.g., multiple choice or essay) and know how to prepare themselves emotionally. Let's examine test taking.

Taking Tests

The first step after receiving any test is to read the directions carefully. This is true even if it is a multiple-choice test. For example, some instructors might require that you choose the *best* answer, while others might require you to mark *all* correct answers. If you are asked to choose the best answer and you mark more than one response, you'll lose credit. On the other hand, if you are asked to mark all correct answers, you may lose credit if you don't choose more than one answer. Read the directions carefully. If they are not clear, ask your instructor to explain them.

Once you have carefully read the directions, preview the entire test. Check to be sure that your test has no missing or duplicate pages. Read through the test and decide how to allocate your time. If your head is swimming with information that you're afraid that you'll forget, jot it down quickly. The following sections present strategies for taking multiple-choice tests and essay tests, as well as for test preparation in general.

Multiple-Choice Tests When answering a multiple-choice test, begin each item by reading the question. Then read all of the options. Don't rush, but take your time to read the question and each option completely. If the question is difficult, cross out any options that don't fit. In other words, eliminate distractors. If you can eliminate all of the distractors you'll have the correct answer. How do you identify distractors? Combine the question and each option into a complete statement. If the resulting statement is false, you've found a distractor. Stick with the subject matter of the course. If an option includes terms that seem out of place or that you don't recognize, it's probably a distracter (Pauk & Fiore, 2000). Here are some other tips:

- If one of the options is "all of the above," all that you need to do is determine whether two of the other options are correct. If so, then "all of the above" is your answer.
- Multiple-choice tests often include options that look alike; two options might be identical except for one or two words. It's logical to assume that one of the pair is correct (Pauk & Fiore, 2000).
- Note that correct answers are often longer and more inclusive than distracters.
- Tests often give away relevant information for one question in another question.
- After you have selected your answer, read the entire statement to be sure that it makes sense.
- Don't waste time on difficult questions. Eliminate as many distractors as possible. If you still don't know the answer, guess, mark the question, and return to it later.
- Don't leave any items blank.
- Sometimes questions are simple. Don't read into questions. Don't make the question more complex than it is intended to be.
- Students' first choices are usually correct. Unless you encounter specific material to change your mind or you are confident that your new answer is right, don't change your answers.
- Look for clues in other questions.

Essay Tests Your first step in taking an essay test is to read all of the questions thoroughly. Jot down any ideas and examples that come to you, so they don't clutter your mind. Consider the difficulty of each question, and answer them in a strategic order. Complete the easy questions first to reduce anxiety and facilitate clear thinking. After completing the easy questions, move on to those with the highest point value. The last questions you answer should be the most difficult, take the greatest amount of writing, or have the least point value.

As you consider each essay question, determine what is being asked. What do you know that is related to the question? Take a moment and organize your essay. Jot some notes or an outline of points that you want to make. Once you have a list of points or a basic structure, start writing. Don't meander, but get right to the point. Use your first paragraph to provide an overview of your essay. Be sure to state your main point within the first paragraph. Use the rest of your essay to discuss your points in more detail. Back up each point with specific information, examples, or quotations from the class readings and notes. Leave space at the end of each paragraph to allow you to add further information, if needed, as you proofread. Write on every other line and on just one side of the page, not only to allow space for adding information but also to make the answers easier for your instructor to read.

Budget your time for each essay question. When you reach the end of your allotted time for a given question, list your remaining points, leave extra space, and move on to the next item. Partially answering all questions (especially by listing all of the points that you want to make) is better than fully answering only a few questions and skipping others. You won't earn credit for the questions that you skip. After you've completed the rest of the test, return to items that are incomplete.

Once you're done with the test, proofread your answers. Modify them for clarity, adding details, if needed, to make your answer complete. Check for spelling, grammar, and punctuation errors. Students tend to lose points on essay tests because they fail to answer the question asked, don't provide examples or evidence to support their statements, don't write enough, are disorganized, or don't follow directions. Finally, avoid the "kitchen sink" method of answering essays—writing all that you know about a subject, hoping that the answer is somewhere in your essay.

Reduce the Stress That Accompanies Tests

Everyone finds taking exams at least a little bit stressful. Many students are surprised to find that they experience exams in some classes very stressful while exams in other classes are a breeze. Why? We are more likely to feel anxiety taking exams in classes that we feel are very important to our success or when taking "make it or break it" tests. We also feel more anxiety taking exams in subjects in which we feel less efficacious. Recall that self-efficacy refers to our feeling of competence in completing a task, such as an exam. Understanding why you might feel more anxiety in one class than another is an important step in approaching exams with more confidence and feeling less stressed.

Care for Your Physical Well-being Success on exams is not just about your mind—showing what you know—it also requires some physical preparation. Let your body and mind rest so that you are ready to work hard. Get a good night's sleep. Set your alarm a little bit early, and take the time to have breakfast. Arrive ten to fifteen minutes early for your test, allowing time to acclimate yourself, relax, and prepare. Bring all the materials you will need for the test, including pencils and pens, a calculator, and a watch. Having all the materials necessary and arriving early will help you focus on the task at hand.

Choose a seat that is well lit, located where you can't see many other students (and can't be easily distracted).

Don't Psych Yourself Out Try not to talk with other students just prior to the test, especially if they seem anxious. Anxiety can be highly contagious. Feeling stress is normal but you can control how you respond to that stress. Students who are anxious tend to engage in negative self-talk (e.g., "Everyone in this class is smarter than I am," "I always screw up on tests," and "If I don't do well on this exam, I'll flunk the course"). Negative self-talk just brings you down and increases your stress level. When you find yourself engaging in negative self-talk, catch it and stop. If you feel anxious, take some slow, deep breaths to relax; and use positive self-talk to raise your confidence. Try to encourage yourself as you would a friend. Repeat positive statements to yourself in place of the negative. Remind yourself that you are well prepared for the test, and believe that you are going to do well.

Reduce Anxiety during Your Exam If you find it hard to focus your eyes to read, use a physical object to help you focus. Place your pencil along the line you're reading or use a sheet of paper to focus your eyes. If you feel that your mind has gone blank, don't panic. Close your eyes, breathe, and return to the question. Try reading it "out loud" in your head—silently mouth the words to yourself. If you're stuck, mark the question and return to it later. If you find it hard to focus your concentration, draw your attention to the page. Circle or underline significant words to mark the page and draw your attention to the task at hand.

If you feel the tension rising, try using progressive relaxation techniques to help reduce your muscle tension. Breathe in deeply and flex your toes. Release and breathe out. Do the same for your calves, then your thighs, buttocks, stomach, chest, arms, shoulders, and neck. Repeatedly tense and release your major muscle groups; it takes only a moment and produces big results. You'll feel more relaxed and able to concentrate.

Learn from Returned Tests

Think that your learning is over once the test is? No! There's a lot you can learn from returned tests, so don't fall into the trap of checking your grade without reviewing the test. When you get a test back, you should examine it carefully and consider your errors. Why was the correct answer correct? Identify why you missed a question. Did you read it correctly? What do you need to learn to fill in these gaps in your knowledge?

Get clues for the next test. Look for the origin of each question (test, lectures, labs, supplementary readings, discussions). Check the level of detail and skill of the test. Were most of the questions about vocabulary, or did they ask for precise details and facts? Were the questions about main ideas, principles, applications, or all of these?

Decide which strategies worked and which didn't. Were you prepared for the test? Did you run out of time? How might you have better allocated your time? Identify those strategies that didn't work well and replace them. Use your tests to review when studying for final exams. Did you have any problems with anxiety or blocking during the test? Did you really know the answer to a question, but fail to read it carefully enough to recognize it?

Academic success requires work; it's an active process. Practice the tips in this chapter and refine them based on your needs. Not everyone studies in the same way. Be flexible in your study habits, and do what works for you. Above all, remember that a little work on getting organized, creating a schedule, and staying on top of your reading can save you from cramming later. Perhaps even better is knowing that you'll retain what you've learned well beyond the test, the course, and college.

Suggested Readings

Dweck, C. (2008). *Mindset: The new psychology of success*. New York: Ballentine.

Fry, R. (2012). *How to study*. Boston, MA: Course Technology.

Gardner, J. N., & Jewler, A. J. (2011). *Your college experience: Strategies for success*. New York: St. Martin's Press.

Newton, C. (2005). *How to win at college: Surprising secrets for success from the country's top students*. New York: Three Rivers Press.

Van Blerkom, D. L. (2012). *College study skills: Becoming a strategic learner*. Boston, CA: Wadsworth.

Wong, L. (2015). *Essential study skills*. Stamford, CT: Cengage.

Internet Resources (Available at http://www.tarakuther.com)

Interactive Study Tips

http://studytips.admsrv.ohio.edu/studytips/

Ohio University's Academic Advancement Center offers quizzes and interactive exercises on time management, memory, reading, notes, exam preparation, and more, making this site an essential stop on your next trip online.

How to Study

http://www.howtostudy.org/resources.php

This site organizes a collection of links for all aspects of study skills.

Learning Strategies: Maximizing Your Academic Experience

http://www.dartmouth.edu/~acskills/success/index.html

Dartmouth University's collection of assessments and resources for maximizing your academic experience.

Refection Prompts

I'm at My Best When . . .

When are you at your best? When do you find it easiest to concentrate on difficult tasks? Are you a morning person—someone who accomplishes the most in the early morning? Do you work better at night? Why do you think you have these working patterns? What are the implications for scheduling classes and studying? How can you use this knowledge to help yourself?

Making Time for Health

Usually when we talk about time management the emphasis is on ensuring that we get our work done. Good time management also ensures that we make time for our social life and for fun. Many students (and professors), however, prioritize work and friends over self-care. Ever notice how nearly everyone has a cold around exam time? Use your time management strategies to ensure that you make time to take care of yourself. Identify at least three times this week in which you will do something special for yourself to focus on your own health. It might be a yoga class, making a special meal, or doing an activity that you love. What are those times and what will you do?

Ideal Day

Suppose that you managed your time well. What would an ideal day look like? Write about realistically, as in how life is now, not as a fantasy. What would you do; how would you handle yourself in all situations? What two things could you do to bring yourself closer to that ideal?

Two Extra Hours

Suppose you suddenly had an extra two hours each day. How would you spend the time? Why? How does this proposed activity compare with the rest of your schedule? Is it more important than any of your current activities? If you believe it is, identify steps that you can take to make time for this activity.

Evaluating Time Management Strategies

After you've had a chance to try the time management strategies described in this chapter, write about your experience. Which strategies worked well? How might you modify them to fit your style and needs?

CHAPTER 5

Writing a Literature Review

Chapter Outline

It's the first day of class, and the professor has just handed out the course syllabus which includes a fifteen- to twenty-page paper on "*a topic of your choice*." "Fifteen pages! How am I supposed to know what I want to write fifteen pages about before taking the class? How can I write a paper on anything without knowing a little about it first?" Sound familiar? Don't know where to begin? The typical ambiguous term paper assignment can make even the best student feel queasy. Don't stress. Take control of your academic destiny by beginning your paper immediately. It's tempting to put off challenging or work-intensive assignments, but waiting until the last minute to write your paper will only increase your stress and make writing even more difficult. This chapter will walk you through the steps in writing a literature review, from selecting a topic to proofreading the final draft.

WHAT IS A LITERATURE REVIEW?

The term paper assigned by most professors usually is more appropriately called a *literature review* because it is intended to present and critically evaluate the literature on a given topic. The purpose is to present an organized discussion of current or historical research on a topic. Writing an effective review of the literature entails choosing a method to organize the studies that you will discuss in your paper (such as by thesis, methodology, or theoretical approach) and then identifying, synthesizing, and evaluating the published work relevant to your topic. Your paper should present the research in a way that tells a story about your topic, such as how theoretical perspectives on your topic or methods used to study your topic have changed over the decades. The studies you review should support your points and lead readers to draw conclusions regarding your argument. Another way of thinking about the literature review is that it answers a question. What's the question you'd like to answer? Pose your question and then synthesize an answer, using research to support the answer. Ultimately your paper will give readers a detailed summary of the existing knowledge base on your topic as well as your informed evaluation of the literature.

TABLE 5.1 **SKILLS ENTAILED IN WRITING A PSYCHOLOGY PAPER**

- ❑ Learning how to locate information about topics and subjects within psychology
- ❑ Collecting information
- ❑ Reading and understanding research articles in psychology
- ❑ Developing your own perspective on a topic
- ❑ Deciding what points and arguments are relevant
- ❑ Evaluating an author's claims
- ❑ Integrating ideas from multiple sources to support your ideas
- ❑ Developing writing skills and vocabulary
- ❑ Developing critical thinking skills
- ❑ Thinking and writing like a psychologist

At this point most students wonder, "Is my instructor a masochist? Why assign such a difficult project?" The answer is that writing is an integral part of learning psychology. It's an opportunity to learn about a topic of interest and acquire a host of skills, such as those in Table 5.1.

Perhaps the most important skills you'll rely on to complete your paper are information-seeking and critical thinking skills. Information-seeking skills enable you to find useful research articles and other materials and to scan the literature efficiently. Critical thinking skills entail applying principles of analysis to identify appropriate research studies, evaluating the literature, and organizing your review in sections that identify themes, major issues, or trends. These skills in defining questions, gathering information, and critically analyzing and synthesizing information are useful throughout life and valuable to employers. Your job in writing a literature review is not to list as many research articles as possible, but rather to carefully select those that support a comprehensive discussion about what has been published on your topic. A literature review should accomplish the following objectives:

1. Define the scope of the topic.
2. Discuss the major findings relating to your topic.
3. Summarize what is and is not known about the topic.
4. Evaluate the existing research, identifying controversy when it appears in the literature.
5. Discuss further questions for research. For example, identify gaps in the knowledge base. What questions remain? What direction should further research take?

As you might imagine, constructing a quality literature review takes work and insight. The degree of difficulty entailed in writing your paper is directly influenced by the topic you chose.

SELECT A TOPIC

Choosing a topic is one of the most important tasks in writing a paper, because "the paper can be no better than the topic" (Sternberg, 1993, p. 17). How can you choose a topic that is well researched and will sustain your (and your reader's) interest? Plan ahead and pay attention to the tips discussed in the following sections.

To write a good paper, you must begin to think about it early—when you receive the assignment. Don't underestimate the amount of time that it will take for you to decide on a topic for your paper. Choosing a topic obviously requires thinking, but students are sometimes surprised to discover that it also requires reading. How are you to decide what to write about without knowing a little about the course and the topic first? How can you choose a topic when you don't know much about the literature? You cannot. Scan the literature and learn a little bit about each topic to inform your decision.

Sources of Ideas for Paper Topics

It may not feel like it, but, believe it or not, you're surrounded by ideas for papers. Paper topics might come from reading magazines, books, and websites, watching television, observing people, or observing yourself. Pay attention to the social world around you, observe people's behavior and ask, "Why?" You'll never be at a loss for ideas. You may also find ideas by using the following resources, which are often overlooked.

Your Textbook Leaf through your class textbook and carefully scan the table of contents, which lists all of the topics covered in the text. Once you find a topic that sounds interesting, turn to that section of the text and skim through it. Textbook chapters usually provide short overviews of topics that condense broad areas of theory and research into a few pages. If you're still interested after reading more, you've found a potential paper topic. You may have to read several sections of the text to get to this point, so it's important to start early in the semester and try not to get discouraged. Once you've found a topic of interest, use the material in your text as a starting point to expand the topic into a paper. Read the appropriate sections of your text, and take note of any references that look promising. Although a textbook is a good source of ideas, you should not use it as a reference for your paper. Most professors require students to review original research from journal articles rather than rely on the broad summaries provided in textbooks.

Professors If your professor has provided a list of suggested topics, give them serious consideration. Recognize that professors can be an important source of information and ideas. However, professors are more likely to offer you help if you've done some work first. Approach your professor for feedback, but understand that you should come with several ideas and ask for advice. Don't expect your professor to provide you with a topic for your paper.

Print and Online Dictionaries and Encyclopedias Reading a short definition and overview of a topic can quickly tell you whether to pursue it. Reference tools such as encyclopedias and dictionaries were once found only in the reference section of libraries. While you can still locate these volumes in the library, many libraries also provide online access to these tools—and some are available to the public online and for free. Table 5.2 lists commonly

TABLE 5.2 **PSYCHOLOGY DICTIONARIES AND ENCYCLOPEDIAS**

Print

American Psychological Association. (2005). *The APA dictionary of psychology*. Washington DC: APA.

Colman, A. M. (2009). *A dictionary of psychology*. Cambridge, MA: Oxford University Press.

Hayes, N. & Stratton, P. (2012). *A student's dictionary of psychology*. New York: Hodder Education.

Matsumo, D. (2009). *The Cambridge dictionary of psychology*. Cambridge, MA: Cambridge University Press.

Reber, A. S. & Reber, E. S. (2009). *Penguin dictionary of psychology*. New York: Penguin.

Weiner, I. B. & Craighead, W. E. (2010). *The Corsini encyclopedia of psychology and behavioral science* Vols. 1–4. New York: John Wiley & Sons.

Online

All Psych Online Psychology Dictionary
http://allpsych.com/dictionary/

Psychology Dictionary
http://psychologydictionary.org/

Encyclopedia of Psychology
http://www.psychology.org/

PsychCentral
http://psychcentral.com/

AmeobaWeb
http://www.vanguard.edu/psychology/amoebaweb/

Encyclopedia of Psychology
http://www.psychology.org/

American Psychological Association
http://www.apa.org

American Psychological Society
http://www.psychologicalscience.org

available psychology reference books and websites. These resources can often help you in selecting and narrowing a topic, but remember that they are only a starting point. The short summaries characteristic of encyclopedia entries can help you to develop an initial understanding of the breadth and depth of the topic at hand. In most cases you will not cite the encyclopedia, reference book, or website in your paper. Instead your professor will expect you to use the journal articles in which the research is described as your references.

Media Television, magazines, and newspapers can offer ideas for papers. For example, each Tuesday, the *New York Times* newspaper includes a science section that usually has at least one article about health and psychology. These articles are a fantastic source of information and ideas. As you read or watch television, stop and consider the topic of the program or article. Why does the problem occur? How can it be prevented? What do we know about it? Ideas are everywhere; finding them requires an enquiring mind.

Internet The Internet is usually the first place students turn in searching for a topic. A quick Google or Yahoo search can be invaluable for identifying interesting topics, but treat information found on the Internet with caution. Unlike scholarly journals or books, anyone can post anything online, so it's up to you to think critically when evaluating the credibility of the source and determining how to use the content.

How do you evaluate a site's credibility? The URL can provide some information about a site's trustworthiness. Sites hosted by the government (.gov address for federal government and .us for state), universities (.edu address), and organizations (.org address) are often trustworthy sources of information. Professional organizations such as the American Psychological Association (APA) and Association for Psychological Science (APS) are also a good source of information about psychology. For example, APA and APS publish monthly magazines, *Monitor on Psychology* (http://www.apa.org/monitor/) and the *Observer* (http://www.psychologicalscience.org/index.php/publications/observer), that are excellent sources of paper ideas.

Wikipedia is another source of ideas as it is an online encyclopedia with short articles on a seemingly endless number of topics. Take great care, however, in considering information from Wikipedia articles because the entries vary widely in quality and reliability. Wikipedia articles are not reviewed for accuracy or quality. They are often modified by multiple contributors, but anyone with access to the Internet can contribute. Recently the Association for Psychological Science has begun to encourage psychologists and students to contribute to Wikipedia to share accurate information about psychological science. However, there is no way to tell which articles have been written by scholars. That said, perusing Wikipedia with a healthy dose of skepticism can lead to useful ideas for class papers. Similar to textbooks, however, websites can offer useful information to generate ideas but you will need to locate scholarly articles to actually write your paper.

EXERCISE 5.1

Criteria for Evaluating Internet Sources

Don't take what you read online at face value. Critically evaluate the source to determine the credibility of the information—and whether you should rely on it. Many university and library websites offer advice on how to evaluate Internet sources.

1. Locate and list three webpages hosted by .edu addresses that provide advice on evaluating Internet sources.
2. Discuss the advice offered by each site. Identify similarities and differences in the range of advice offered as well as specific tips.
3. Identify the three to five most important tips for evaluating Internet sources that you have learned from comparing these three resources.

EXERCISE 5.2

Practice Evaluating Internet Sources

1. Using the criteria identified in Exercise 5.1, list qualities that describe a trustworthy Internet source.
2. List qualities that signal an untrustworthy source to avoid.
3. Search Google for a topic of your choice. Peruse the results and choose an example of a trustworthy article. Explain why it is a credible source.
4. Provide an example of a poor, untrustworthy website or article. Explain why it is a poor source for a paper.

Psychology Journals Most professors require that students cite articles from psychology journals in their papers. Journals can be viewed as scientific magazines consisting of collections of articles written by scientists describing their research. Journals are published monthly or several times each year. Many psychology journals specialize in particular subfields, such as health psychology or cognitive psychology. As we will discuss later in this chapter, articles from psychology journals are radically different from magazine articles. For now, let's consider their value as sources of paper ideas.

For a paper in an Introductory Psychology course, look through general psychology journals that have articles spanning the fields within psychology.

This will help you to get a feel for the wide range of psychological topics that you have to choose from. For example, *Current Directions in Psychological Science* publishes short review-type articles (in a student-friendly writing style) that may spark some ideas. Also take a look at *American Psychologist* and the *Psi Chi Journal of Undergraduate Research.* If you're writing a paper for a class in a particular subfield, such as developmental psychology, look through more specialized psychology journals to find recent articles and get ideas. For example, if you're searching for a topic for your Adolescent Psychology paper, leaf through recent issues of journals specializing in adolescent development (e.g., *Journal of Research on Adolescence, Adolescence*). Once you find an article that's interesting, read it carefully and examine the reference section to find related articles.

Define and Narrow Your Topic: How to Locate Relevant Research

By now you should have one or two topics in mind. Your next step is to gather information to narrow your topic. Review the literature, specifically research articles from psychology journals, for each topic to determine if is appropriate for your paper assignment. Is the topic well researched? Is the topic narrow enough? Is the topic too narrow? You won't be able to determine the answers to these questions without searching and reading through some of the literature. How do you locate additional readings to narrow your topic and get started? While many of the resources that we have discussed are excellent sources of paper ideas, most instructors prefer (and often require) that students rely only on journal articles for writing papers. Consider the strengths and weakness of various sources of information and it is easy to see why professors prefer journal articles as references for student papers. Why are journal articles so special? Why do professors prefer them as references?

What Are Refereed Journal Articles? How are articles from psychology journals different from magazine articles? Magazines pay writers, whereas journals do not pay their authors. Magazine articles might be checked for accuracy, but they do not undergo peer review and are not scrutinized to the same extent as journal articles. Journal articles more extensively document the sources of ideas and evidence; magazines are rarely as extensively documented. Most importantly, journal articles in psychology are refereed, or published after a process of peer review, whereby several professionals review article submissions before an acceptance decision is made. When an author submits a manuscript to a journal, the editor sends copies of it out for review by the author's peers. This means that other psychologists are asked to read the article and determine whether it is suitable for publication. The peers who do the review are called *referees*. Sometimes peer-reviewed journals are referred to as *refereed journals*.

How do referees evaluate manuscripts? Although each reviewer may use slightly different criteria, manuscripts are reviewed based on scholarship. A publishable scholarly manuscript offers an important contribution to the field of psychology and includes a comprehensive review of the literature, concise writing, appropriate methodology and statistical analyses, and an understanding of the audience. Once the editor has received the reviews, a decision is made whether to reject the paper, accept it, or suggest that the author make some changes and resubmit. As you might imagine, this is a long and tedious process, but it ensures that the articles appearing in scholarly journals have scholarly merit.

Even those who are unfamiliar with journal articles quickly see that research articles have a specific format and layout. Understanding the layout will make articles more comprehensible. An empirical article consists of several sections: the abstract, introduction, method, results, discussion, and references. Each section has a specific purpose. The abstract (usually located underneath the article title and before the text of the article) briefly summarizes the study. The introduction is the first section of an article. It provides an overview of the research question, reviews the literature, and identifies the purpose of the study (the specific purpose and hypotheses are usually found at the very end of the introduction section). The method section explains how the research was conducted; it describes the participants, measures, instruments, and equipment, and procedure. The results section presents statistical analyses that address the research questions. Here, the studies findings are presented, with information displayed in graphs and tables. In the discussion section, the author examines the significance of the study's findings in light of prior research, discusses limitations of the study, and offers suggestions for further research. For more information about empirical articles, see Chapter 6. How do you find refereed articles for your paper? Follow these pointers.

Don't Rely on Google to Find References Many students are tempted to run a quick Google search to look for references, but search engines are not likely to yield the sources that you will need to write a decent paper. Remember that a literature review is a scholarly paper that integrates information from reputable sources, such as academic journals and scholarly texts, which are often not available through the Internet. In addition, most professors require that students only use scholarly sources and no Internet sources. Instead of searching Google, turn to your college library. College libraries subscribe to a number of electronic databases that index journal articles and books, permitting users to search by topic, author, title, and more. In addition to using your college's online databases, make a trip to the library. Walking the stacks, that is, browsing books on their shelves, can lead you to sources and help shape your paper. Another important reason to visit the library is to seek assistance from a reference librarian.

Consult the Reference Librarian for Help Your best source of information about the library resources and holdings is the reference librarian. Discuss your paper with him or her and explain what you're looking for (that's why it's important to have selected a preliminary topic beforehand). Ask the librarian to suggest sources of information. He or she can help you to devise specific search strategies to help you find what you need more quickly and efficiently; however you must approach him or her with a topic(s) in mind. Do not expect the reference librarian to give you a paper topic. The reference librarian can also assist you in using important reference tools, such as *PsychInfo*.

Use Psychology Databases: PsycInfo, PsychArticles The American Psychological Association publishes an important resource for locating journal articles: *PsychInfo*. *PsychInfo* is a Web database of abstracts from journal articles, book chapters, books, and dissertations published in psychology and the behavioral sciences. Each article entry includes bibliographic information (which helps you locate the article) and an abstract (which provides summary information to help you decide if the article is useful for your paper). *PsychInfo* is updated frequently and indexes articles from 1887 to the present, permitting a thorough search of the literature. Most institutions maintain a subscription to *PsychInfo* and some also have a subscription to *PsychArticles*, a service that provides full text articles from journals published by the American Psychological Association from 1894 to the present. Most institutions permit students to log into these databases off-campus and on their own computers making it possible to search the literature wherever and whenever they choose.

Entering a search term into *PsychInfo* usually will yield a long list of articles. You'll see the article title, authors, date, and journal. Click on a title and you will see the full bibliographic information for the article plus the abstract. An abstract is a short 150-word summary of the article. Read the abstract to decide whether it is worth reading the article itself. Note that the abstract is *not* the article—it's a very short summary. If you plan on using the article as a reference for your paper you must locate and read the entire article, not the abstract. Depending on your library's resources a pdf of the article may be linked to the entry, you may be able to obtain a copy from your library, or you may have to request it by interlibrary loan.

PsychInfo and other reference databases make it easy to conduct a thorough literature search, saving you lots of time in your research, *if* you know how to use them effectively. Skill, flexibility, and creativity are required to get the most from computerized reference databases. Sometimes the search for a topic yields few results because the wrong search words are used.

How do you determine the appropriate search terms? The *Thesaurus of Psychological Index Terms*, published by the American Psychological Association and linked to *PsychInfo* at http://help.psycnet.org/psycnet/

term-finder/, can help you select search terms as it lists all descriptors or index terms (called key terms) that appear in *PsychInfo*. Use the *Thesaurus* before beginning your search to brainstorm the most appropriate descriptors, and you'll save time and hassle. Also, after locating an article that is useful to your paper, look for the key terms under which the article is labeled. Use these key terms to find additional articles.

Additional features that make *PsychInfo* especially useful are the tools for refining searches; you can combine the results of several searches and limit the results of a search. Table 5.3 illustrates the steps in using an electronic

TABLE 5.3

CONDUCTING A LITERATURE SEARCH WITH *PSYCHINFO*

Before beginning your search, remember that you won't find everything in one pass. Instead, you'll need to refine your searching strategies and, depending on your topic, may conduct several searches. For example, consider a paper about risky behavior in adolescence.

1. Run the Initial Search: "Risky Behavior"

To gather articles about risky behavior, I typed in "risky behavior" as keywords and found that over 5,098 articles have "risky behavior" in their title, abstract, or subject.

2. Expand the Search with OR: "Risky Behavior OR Problem Behavior"

I remembered that "problem behavior" is a similar term. I searched for "problem behavior" and found 49,852 articles. I decided to see how many articles use both terms, so I entered in "risky behavior OR problem behavior" and found 54,580 references—clearly too many to use in my paper!

3. Narrow the Search with AND: "Risky Behavior AND Problem Behavior"

I decided to combine the terms to identify articles that address both risky behavior and problem behavior. I entered "risky behavior AND problem behavior" and found 370 articles.

4. Further Narrow the Search with AND: "Risky Behavior AND Problem Behavior AND Adolescents"

My paper is about risky behavior and problem behavior in adolescents, so I added the term "adolescents" to the search. I entered "risky behavior and problem behavior and adolescents" and found 230 articles.

5. Further Narrow the Search with AND: "(Risky Behavior AND Problem Behavior AND Adolescents) AND (Parents OR Peers)"

I'm particularly interested in parents and peers. I narrow the search to articles that examine parents or peers, since I'm interested in either. This is a more complicated search so I use parentheses to keep my terms separate. "(Risky behavior AND problem behavior AND adolescents)" searches for articles that meet all three criteria. I also use "(parents OR peers)" because I'm interested in articles that examine either parents or peers. I combine the two sets of terms to search for articles about risky and problem behavior in adolescence that examine both parents and peers: "(risky behavior and problem behavior and adolescents) AND (parents OR peers)" and found 189 articles.

6. Narrow by Year

There are still too many articles so I narrow my search to those published since 2010, using the year limiter in the left-hand column. After limiting my search to articles published after 2010, I find 25 articles, a manageable number.

database, including how to combine the results of several searches and how to limit the results of a search. Finally, note that if your institution does not subscribe to *PsychInfo*, you can access it online for free through the American Psychological Association website (http://www.apa.org). You'll have to obtain the articles through your school (or purchase them for a fee online), but this online resource permits you to do a great deal of research at home.

Real Tips for Real Students

Supplement Your Search with Google Scholar

Google Scholar (http://scholar.google,com) is a specialized Google search engine that filters only scholarly research articles, reports, and books. Google Scholar is not limited to psychology. It searches all fields. Your search may reveal many articles unrelated to psychology. Like *PsychInfo*, you can sort items by year. Perhaps what's best about Google Scholar is that pdf links are listed, if available online. Type in the title to an article that you are unable to access through your library and you might find that it's posted online (click "see all versions" to determine if pdf copies are available). Type an author's name and you'll see links to his or her work. While Google Scholar cannot replace specialized psychology databases such as *PsychInfo*, it is a useful supplement and can help you find needed articles.

Determine If There Is Enough Research Once you have an initial idea for a topic, you're not yet ready to begin writing your paper. Before committing yourself to a topic, be sure that there is adequate literature on it. Can you find articles that address your topic or do you find too many? The most common mistake that students make in choosing a paper topic is to choose one that is too broad. A literature review, by its very nature, provides comprehensive coverage of a topic. In order to provide comprehensive coverage, you'll need to choose a narrow topic (otherwise you're writing a book, not a class paper). Table 5.4 illustrates how to narrow and broaden your topic when searching *PsychInfo* and other computerized databases.

Narrowing your topic means that you'll target your paper to a specific line of research or aspect of your topic. Unless you are already knowledgeable about the research area, you can't preselect a topic that is narrow enough. This is another reason why you shouldn't procrastinate because choosing an appropriately narrow topic requires reading and getting a handle on the literature. Once you have tentatively chosen a topic, scan the literature (using the techniques described earlier in this chapter) to determine how well researched it is and to narrow your topic, if necessary. This is a good time to visit your professor or teaching assistant to get some feedback on your choice. Think you have a good understanding of how to use *PsychInfo* to locate articles as well as broaden and narrow searches? Try Exercise 5.3 to test your competence.

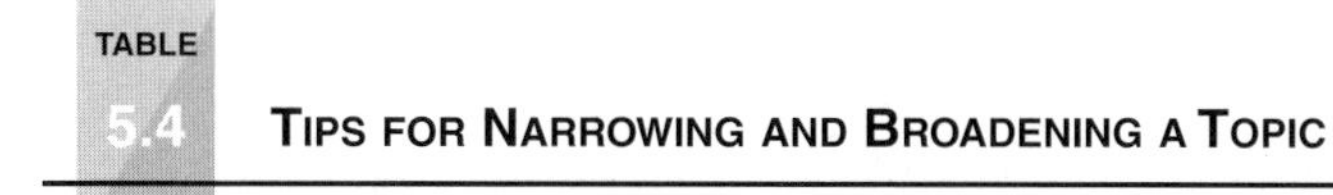

TIPS FOR NARROWING AND BROADENING A TOPIC

1. Initial Topic: "Abuse"

A search on *PsychInfo* revealed over 160,000 sources. This is way too broad a topic. Consider how to narrow it. Be more specific. What kind of abuse? Against whom?

2. Narrowed: "Child Abuse"

Even these topics are too broad for an assignment calling for a ten-page paper. For example, consider child abuse; it yielded over 30,000 sources on *PsychInfo*.

3. How to Narrow a Topic: Who? What? When? Where? How?

Consider the problem more specifically. Ask who, what, when, where, how? For example, consider child abuse.

Who?	What population are you researching?
What?	Are you interested in causes of abuse? Prevention? Treatment programs?
When?	Historical? Recent trends? Specific years?
Where?	The entire world? United States? Urban? Suburban?
How?	How does the abuse take place? What form of abuse? Physical? Sexual? Emotional? Neglect?

4. Sample Narrowed Topic: Child Abuse

Who?	Infants
What?	Causes
When?	2014
Where?	United States
How?	Physical abuse

After entering each of these terms (using AND) into *PsychInfo*, and limiting the year of publication to 2014, I have 0 results. The topic is too narrow!

5. Broaden the Topic

Broaden the topic by deleting some terms. When I include only: child abuse, causes, physical abuse (joined with AND), my search yields a dozen results. Next, I would further broaden my topic by looking only at child abuse, infants, causes (joined with AND) and so on until I find the articles that I need to write my paper.

EXERCISE 5.3
Using PsychInfo

Choose an area of research in which you are interested (e.g., the effects of child care on development). Be specific in order to narrow the results of your *PsychInfo* search to yield a manageable number of articles. For example, instead of examining child care on development, use more narrow terms such as child care in infancy; rather than development, use more narrow terms such as cognitive development, or social development.

(Continued)

EXERCISE 5.3 (Continued)

1. What is your research question?
2. Write the search terms that you will use.
3. Enter your search terms into *PsychInfo*. How many results did you get? Were your terms too narrow or too broad? Print out the first page of your results.
4. Try narrowing your topic. Write down the search terms used. How many results did you get? Print out the first page of your results.
5. Take a closer look at the results from the first page of your narrowed search. How do these results differ from those in your initial search? Discuss any patterns that you notice in article titles.
6. Try broadening your topic. Write down the search terms used. How many results did you get? Print out the first page of your results.
7. Take a closer look at the results from the first page of your broadened search. How do these results differ from those in your narrowed search? Discuss any patterns that you notice in article titles.
8. Return to the results page of your narrowed topic search. Choose one article that is particularly interesting. Retrieve the first page of that article using your library's full text and print resources. The reference librarian can assist you if you're experiencing difficulty. Print the first page of the article.

Choose an Appropriate Match to Your Abilities

Try not to choose a topic that is too easy or "safe" for you. The purpose of writing your paper is to learn something about a subject. Choose a topic that you're relatively unfamiliar with, to maximize the learning opportunity. Choosing a safe topic (e.g., one you've already written papers on) deprives you of the opportunity and challenge of gaining competence in a new area.

The opposite is also true; try not to choose a topic that is too difficult. Scan the abstracts of articles in your topic to be sure that you can understand the purposes and the underlying concepts and ideas. Avoid topics that you can't adequately present or evaluate from the information presented in articles. In other words, be "certain that the topic you choose does not require an understanding of concepts that your background does not permit you to grasp" (Sternberg, 1993, p. 18).

Begin considering your paper early so that you have time to select a topic that will maintain your interest. Allow yourself the opportunity to consider several topics and choose the one that appeals most to you. In other words, don't procrastinate. Too often, students wait until the last minute to select a topic.

Then they choose hastily and end up with a topic they are only marginally interested in. Be kind to yourself by taking the time to find an interesting topic. Few scholarly tasks are less fun than working on an uninteresting paper.

Read and Record Your Research Material

The primary sources that you will use in writing your paper will be published articles from psychology journals. Journal articles are the most important sources for current findings in psychology. Most professors prefer journal articles as sources over books because scholarly journals are published more frequently and have a more rigorous review and acceptance process than do books. As a psychology major, you will need to become familiar with journal articles, you aren't already.

How to Read Scholarly Articles

Thoroughly reading an article requires several passes. Your first pass should be an initial scan to determine whether the study is essential for your paper. Reading and taking notes is time-consuming; therefore, you want to be sure that the article will suit your needs before you spend a great deal of time on it. During your initial scan of the article, determine the research question, specific hypotheses, findings, and interpretation. After you've scanned for this material, stop and consider whether the article fits with the purpose of your paper. Is it relevant? How does the article apply to your paper? How will you use it?

If you've decided that the article is relevant to your paper, your next task is to read for depth. What is the problem or issue addressed? Discern the theories tested and the methods used. Who were the participants, and how were they tested? How were the findings interpreted? Consider the items in Table 5.5.

As you read, remember that journal articles can lead you to other articles and sources for your research. When you find a current article that is especially useful, examine the references and you'll find other sources that are relevant to your paper. If you examine the reference list for each article that you cite in your paper, you'll find that a great deal of your research is complete. However, it is important not to rely on this as your only strategy for locating articles because you may end up with a distorted view of the literature. Some authors may not cite other seminal works because of differences of opinion and bias. If you obtain all of your sources from the references of other articles, you might miss some important pieces of research, and you will certainly miss out on new research.

TABLE 5.5 **Guidelines for Reviewing Research Articles**

1. Is the author's hypothesis ambiguous or clearly articulated?
2. What is the author's research orientation and theoretical framework? What are the author's underlying assumptions? From what theoretical framework does the author address the problem? (You can find clues in the author's choice of citations and how often particular references are cited.)
3. Could the problem have been approached more effectively from another perspective?
4. Has the author evaluated the literature relevant to the issue? Were any areas of literature excluded from the author's review?
5. Does the author take a balanced perspective and include articles that take contrary positions?
6. Is the sample large and representative of the population the author wishes to address? How were participants selected?
7. What measures were used? Are the instruments' psychometric properties presented? How valid are the instruments? Do you think the instruments measure the intended constructs?
8. Were the data analyzed properly? What are the findings? Are the findings meaningful? Sometimes researchers find differences between variables that are statistically significant, but small; these differences may not be meaningful when applied.
9. How are the findings interpreted? Do you agree with the interpretation?
10. What are the strengths and weaknesses of the study? Every study has strengths and weaknesses.
11. Do the findings have applied or policy implications?

How to Read Scholarly Books

When you consider books as sources for your paper, remember that the more recently a book was published, the more likely it is to contain current theory and methodology. Edited books, which contain chapters written by many different authors, are often good sources of information. Because each chapter is written by a different author, it usually presents a different view of your topic.

Before you spend a great deal of time searching for books, be familiar with your professor's recommended and required resources. Some professors advise their students not to use books as sources because they're too long for student papers. Or simply that the material in books is older than what you'll find in journals. In addition, many books are not scholarly. Many popular self-help books, for example, are of questionable scientific value. Therefore, some professors discourage students from using books as sources because it can be difficult to evaluate their scholarly contribution.

If you decide to use books as source material for your paper, examine each one carefully. How do you determine the academic trustworthiness of a book?

- Examine the author's background. What are the author's academic credentials and experience?

- Examine the reference section, because the number and type of references can indicate how well the book has been researched. How many of the references are the author's?
- How sound are its facts, methodologies, and findings?
- Does the book have an index? As Scott, Koch, Scott, and Garrison (1999) explain, "in addition to making your search for relevant material easier, an index suggests a certain amount of professionalism on the part of the authors" (p. 109).
- Skim the introduction, preface, foreword, or first chapter to find clues about the book's purpose, intended audience, and scholarly quality.

Before beginning a scholarly book, preview it. It's easy to get lost in the prose within and later find that you cannot explain the author's perspective and supporting points. Savvy readers learn about the author's purpose and thesis *before* they read the book. It is counterintuitive but true: To get the most out of a book in the least amount of time, know what you're getting into and what you're looking for—before you begin.

What is the book about? Read the back cover and book jacket. More importantly, read the preface. Most students skip the preface; however, the preface contains essential information for understanding the book's thesis. The preface usually provides information about the author's objective, the organizational plan of the book, how the book is different from others on the market, and the author's background and qualifications (Pauk & Fiore, 2000). Once you know the author's objective or goal, it's easier to see relationships among the facts presented. The organizational plan is like a road map explaining where the author will take you. Reading the author's view of what the book contributes to the field and learning about his or her background and qualifications gives you more insight into his or her perspective, perhaps making it easier to comprehend the ideas that appear in the book.

In addition to (or sometimes in place of) a preface, most books begin with an introduction section or chapter. Read the introduction because it is a window into the book. It provides an overview to a text, making it easier to digest information in the subsequent chapters. The introduction usually is packed with facts and ideas so as to lay the foundation for the book (Pauk & Fiore, 2000).

As your mass of research sources grows, you may feel a sense of unease and wonder how you will sift through the pages and pages of information. Reading the articles and synthesizing the ideas into a cohesive paper may seem like a daunting task, but break it down into smaller pieces and it will seem more manageable. If you've taken your time in choosing a topic and narrowed it down appropriately, you've already begun reading some of the literature, or at least scanned some of it, and you probably have a better sense of how to organize your paper than you think.

Keep Your Purpose in Mind

Once you begin reading, it's easy to forget the purpose of your paper. Instead, you may find yourself describing every detail of each article. Stay focused. Before you begin reading and taking notes, clarify the purpose of your paper. Remain focused as you read and consider articles, and your paper will seem more manageable. Consider your thesis, problem, or research question. What is your angle? Are you considering issues of theory, methodology, or policy? What is the scope of the review? How have you limited the literature? For example, a student might limit the scope of a paper about conduct disorder to examining evaluations of behavioral interventions. Defining the scope of the review involves restating your narrow topic and setting rules for including or excluding articles. Write down your ideas about the purpose, angle, and scope of your paper. Write the purpose on a note card or sticky note and keep it near you. Refer to it often to remember and focus.

At first, concentrate on reading the abstracts for the articles that you've chosen. If you've defined your purpose well, you may find that after reading only the abstracts, you can eliminate some articles from consideration because they're not relevant to your paper. As you read, take occasional breaks to reread your stated purpose. Consider whether what you've read is within the scope that you delineated for your paper. Perhaps your reading has suggested that you change your focus or narrow your paper. Realize that your ideas about your paper will change and become more refined with your reading. Be open to change, and take notes on how you might refocus your paper.

The most important tip about reading is to begin early. Notice a trend? Lots of time and effort will be spent before you begin to write but ultimately you will write your paper more quickly. You'll need plenty of time to think about your paper, collect articles, and read them before any writing occurs. Reading for your paper is a process of information gathering and synthesis. As you read, you might encounter references that seem important. Return to the library to gather these new sources.

When do you stop reading? One clue that you have done a thorough review is when you notice that article authors cite studies that you have already reviewed. But this doesn't mean that you're ready to write the paper. Understand your sources, take notes, and think carefully about their implications before beginning to write. Consider how the articles fit together and how you might organize your review.

Take Notes

As you read, summarize the main findings and methods of each study that you think are important enough to include in your paper. If you consistently take the time to write a brief summary of each article that you plan to include, your literature review will be largely done by the time you sit down to formally write. Summarize each article in a page or less. Don't write down everything. Avoid copying word for word from a source because it makes it too easy to commit plagiarism without realizing it (we'll talk more about plagiarism later). Instead, explain the concept in your own words. If you must capture an author's exact language, perhaps because it isn't well understood, use quotation marks to indicate that the material is copied from the source. In addition to quotation marks, make note around the copied material to make it easy to see and remember that it isn't your own. Note-taking is a skill; it requires critical thinking and evaluation to record only the most essential features of a study (purpose, method, findings, and interpretation).

The method that you use to take notes is a personal choice. Traditionally, experts advocated using an analog (hard copy) note-card system comprised of five- by eight-inch cards, organized by topic. This system requires that you use a separate card for each article. Write the APA style reference on the back of the card and notes on the front (if you're not sure what an APA style reference is, see Chapter 6 for a discussion of APA style). Note cards allow you to physically organize information and sort it into topical categories that will help you to organize the outline of your paper. Note cards travel well and offer a handy way of arranging and rearranging information.

A variety of apps, websites, and computer programs can be used to simulate the note-card system—and offer many advantages. Apps such as Google Keep, Evernote, and Onenote are platforms that can simulate note cards (plus they're automatically backed up). Consider each page or note in these programs as an individual note card to take notes on a specific study. If you take digital notes, clearly mark each reference and backup all of your work each day. E-mail it to yourself, save it on a cloud drive, or print a hard copy to ensure that none of your work is lost. Digital note-taking offers several advantages over the old note-card system: search, portability, and pretyped notes. You may find that most of the notes that will become the prose of your first draft are already typed. Import (or cut and paste) your notes into a word processing program to write your paper. You can cut and paste the material to organize it, then edit, and add transitions, analysis, and interpretation. Always backup your work and make a "safe copy" to edit during each writing session.

Remember that good notes concisely and accurately summarize the main points of a source. Be precise in indicating paraphrases and direct quotes. Take the time to record the reference, using correct APA style. Take it from my own experience, hunting for an unrecorded reference is very frustrating! It can sometimes take an hour to locate a source once you've begun writing whereas it takes only a few minutes to record the information properly while you're taking notes. Also, take great care to ensure that any direct quotations you copy from a source are indicated as such. This is especially important if you choose to keep digital notes. I find it helpful to highlight direct quotes in a bright color as a precaution. Sometimes students forget that a sentence or two was copied from a source—and is not their own summary—and inadvertently commit plagiarism. Regardless of whether intended, plagiarism is a serious breach of academic honesty.

Avoid Plagiarism

Plagiarism means using another person's work (i.e., ideas, research, writing, websites, charts, data, or other original work) without giving credit and without clearly acknowledging its source. The rules of plagiarism apply to all sources, both published (books, magazines, newspapers, websites, and textbooks) and unpublished (class lectures, notes, handouts, speeches, and student papers). To avoid plagiarizing, writers must give credit anytime they use information from a source. Citations giving the source of information must accompany: (1) discussions of another person's ideas, arguments, or theory; (2) facts that are not common knowledge; (3) quotations of a person's spoken or written words; and (4) paraphrases of another person's spoken or written words.

How can you avoid plagiarism? By using your own words to express the ideas of others, and then giving credit to the originators of those ideas. Try to convey the author's main idea without using his or her words or sentence structure. Always cite information and ideas that are learned through your research, no matter where you find them (even if it is on the Internet or in an encyclopedia). Common knowledge is not cited, but be careful of what you consider to be common knowledge. Examples of common knowledge are well-known dates and familiar sayings. Generally, information that could be found in a number of general sources (e.g., popular magazines) may not have to be cited. Whenever in doubt, cite. It is better to be safe and overcite your sources than to accidentally plagiarize.

Appropriate Use of Quotations When you repeat an author's exact words, you must indicate that the material is a direct quote and give its source. APA style requires that you enclose the material in quotation marks and cite the author's last name, year, and the page number for the quote (American Psychological Association, 2010). Here is an example of a short quotation, given in text:

> Bornstein and Arterberry (1999) argued that "perception begins our experience and interpretation of the world, and is crucial to the growth of thought" (p. 231).

If the quotation contains forty or more words, it should be displayed as a freestanding block, with the quotation marks omitted:

> Bornstein and Arterberry (1999) argued that
>
> Perception begins our experience and interpretation of the world, and is crucial to the growth of thought, to the regulation of emotions, to interaction in social

> relationships, and to progress in most aspects of our development. The input, translation, and encoding of sensory information in perception is requisite to reflection and action (p. 231).

In summary, it is permissible to include a direct quote in your paper as long as it is appropriately documented. Enclose the material in quotation marks, and cite the authors, year of publication, and page numbers. Quoting a source without providing documentation is plagiarism. That said, check with your instructor as some professors prefer that students not use direct quotations in their papers.

Now that you've reviewed the appropriate use of quotes, be aware that it's best not to use too many of them in your paper. A paper represents the synthesis and analysis of what you've read. When you use direct quotes too often, the resulting paper is just a string of other people's words, rather than your own analysis, interpretation, and expression of their ideas. Be careful not to quote because of laziness; it is much easier to use direct quotes than it is to paraphrase. Quote directly from a source only when you cannot capture the original ideas in your own words. Use quotes only when the author's language is distinctive and enhances your argument. In other words, record quotations only when "(1) the language of the original was especially important or vivid and therefore worth preserving, and (2) when you wanted to invoke the authority of your source" (Meyer, 1985, p. 78).

Real Tips for Real Students

Cited = Read

Cite only papers that you have read. When you cite an article in your paper, it means that you have read and used the article to write your paper. Any article cited in your paper should appear in your reference list at the end of your paper. Your professor will expect you to have the article and be able to explain its findings and how you used it in your paper. Citing articles that you have not read is a form of academic dishonesty. However, it occasionally is appropriate to use the phrase "as cited in" to refer to a source that you have found in another source but have not read. For example, "Allport's thesis (as cited in Smith, 2015)" indicates that the writer has not read Allport's thesis, but instead learned about it Smith's article. Take care in using "as cited in" as student papers should be based on materials that they have read. Also, some instructors do not permit students to reference sources that they haven't read. Ask your instructor before using "as cited in."

Appropriate Paraphrasing Like any paper, yours will discuss a great deal of research conducted by other people—and you must give appropriate credit to the authors you have read. How do you relay the sources of ideas and give credit? Enter paraphrasing. Paraphrasing refers to restating an author's ideas or information in your own words. Even though you are using your own words, you must cite the source of your information. The American

Psychological Association (2010) has published a style book describing the nuts and bolts of writing papers. According to APA style, appropriate citation of paraphrases includes the author's last name and year of publication; you are encouraged but not required to provide a page number. Note that you are to provide the page number only when quoting directly from a source. For example, a paraphrase of the text quoted earlier might read as follows:

> Perception is essential to cognitive, emotional, and social development because it determines how we interpret and react to the sensory world around us (Bornstein & Arterberry, 1999, p. 170).

As you can see, the paraphrase concisely restates the main idea of the passage, using different words and sentence structure.

How do you paraphrase? First, be sure that you understand the information you wish to paraphrase. Your goal is to restate the idea and convey the same meaning, so it is essential that you understand the original passage before trying to paraphrase it. Realize that you may have to edit your paraphrase several times. Write your paraphrase; then reread the original passage to check for accuracy and to be sure that you haven't borrowed language or structure. Revise your paraphrase as needed. Remember to use your own grammatical structure, restate the material in your own words, and cite the source (the page number is preferred, but not required). Pretend to explain the idea to a friend—then write what you say. Practice is important because appropriate paraphrasing is difficult. Paraphrasing allows you to summarize an author's main points concisely in your own writing style, contributing to the "flow" of your paper. Test your ability to quote and paraphrase as well as learn about how your institution views plagiarism and its consequences by completing Exercise 5.4.

EXERCISE 5.4

Understanding and Avoiding Plagiarism

1. Identify an interesting passage from your textbook. Write a short paragraph about the topic, including a quotation, using appropriate APA style to indicate that it is a quotation and not your own words.
2. Now write a short paragraph paraphrasing, instead of quoting the passage. Note that paraphrasing entails more than using a thesaurus to replace a few words. Appropriate paraphrasing requires conveying the ideas in an entirely new set of words and sentence structure from the original.
3. Reflect on the process of paraphrasing. Was it challenging? Why? How might you gain experience and become more comfortable with this new skill?
4. Identify reasons why students might plagiarize.
5. Look up your institution's definitions and policies about plagiarism. What are the consequences of plagiarism at your institution?

Frequently students commit plagiarism without realizing it, by incorrectly quoting and paraphrasing material. Remember that ignorance of the rules—or laziness—is no excuse for plagiarism. Many professors don't provide a "get out of jail free card." In other words, if you inadvertently plagiarize, you might find yourself with an F or a zero on an assignment and no way to make it up. Do you want to be marked as a dishonest, lazy student? A cheat? A liar? This is not an exaggeration. Plagiarism is a serious offence that marks offenders as unethical. For more information and resources to help you understand the scope or plagiarism as well as quizzes to determine if you really understand acceptable use of information and how to appropriately cite material, see the websites at the end of this chapter.

Exercise 5.5
Academic Honesty Policy

Locate your college's academic honesty policy. Conduct a quick search of your institution's website to locate the policy.

1. Provide a link to the page.
2. Summarize the policy.
3. What behaviors and activities are listed?
4. What is the process for addressing cases of academic dishonesty?
5. What is the range of consequences for academic dishonesty?
6. What does the policy imply about the importance of academic honesty? What do you think?

Real Tips for Real Students
Avoid Dishonest Shortcuts

Writing papers is difficult. It is tempting to take short cuts. Some of these short cuts may seem harmless, but all are forms of academic dishonesty:

- Recycling an old paper used in a prior class
- Buying a paper online
- Downloading a paper online
- Cutting and pasting from Internet pages
- Using a service that writes papers for students
- Asking someone else to write a paper
- Using a sibling, parent, or friend's paper

Recognize that these are dishonest and unethical ways of completing paper assignments. You'll cheat yourself of the learning and skills that are developed by researching and writing papers. Professors also have ways of discovering the use of these techniques, so success with these devious methods is unlikely.

WRITE YOUR PAPER

Now that you've read your articles, taken notes, and spent time thinking about the articles, it is time to organize and write your paper. Where do you begin?

Prepare an Outline

Before you begin writing, prepare an outline. It's much easier to prepare an outline once you've read and taken notes, so save this step until you have a set of notes from your reading, have had time to think about the reading, and have made lists of the material that you think is important to include in your paper. Consider the theme, issue, or research question that you plan to explore in your paper. What have you learned so far? Outlining helps you to get a better understanding of your paper because it forces you to list your ideas and to arrange them logically. Perhaps most important, an outline is a concrete plan for your writing. It will not only help you to stay on track (i.e., keep you from introducing irrelevant topics) but also keep you from leaving important material out of your paper. You'll find that you can write your paper more quickly because you'll know exactly what to put in each section. An outline doesn't have to be fancy. Just jot down the points you want to make and then order them so that they make sense. It's easier to do this using a word processing program to cut and paste your ideas as you wish.

Some students and professors dislike using outlines and think they are a waste of time. Typically, if you are experiencing difficulty structuring your outline, it means that your ideas are too vague and fuzzy. Read and think about your project, and organizational themes will emerge. Outlining is a valuable skill; but if you really can't write an outline, then just begin writing. Some authors prefer to write a rough draft of their paper, allowing thoughts and creativity to flow freely. Once you've written a rough draft, read through it and outline what you've written. This is called *reverse outlining* and it will help you to see the structure of your argument. You can then reorder the outline as needed to make sense and present your argument skillfully.

All good literature reviews can be outlined easily. The first sentence of each paragraph should provide an overview of the paragraph. Therefore, by examining the first sentence of each paragraph, one can compile an outline of the structure of the paper. Once you have done so, examine the structure. First, ask yourself whether each paragraph has a purpose. Then examine the ordering of paragraphs. What idea is expressed in each paragraph? Are the ideas ordered in a logical fashion? Reorder as needed.

Write

Students often worry about how to start writing, and then don't begin. A simple list of points to address helps prevent writer's block. Once you have an outline, your paper is organized, and you can work on filling in the outline. Don't worry about starting at the beginning. Don't get stuck on a first sentence or paragraph. Just start anywhere. Write directly in a word processing program so you can cut and paste sentences in paragraphs into endless patterns. Take advantage of this technological capability and begin writing whatever part of your paper flows most naturally. You can arrange and rearrange your writing later.

Real Tips for Real Students
Referring to Specific Articles

In scholarly writing articles are referred by their author's last names. Do not introduce an article by writing out its title. Do not type the title. Refer to articles by the author's last name and year. Likewise, refer to authors only by their last names. Full names and first names are generally not used nor are institutional affiliations. For example, instead of, "In an article entitled Psychology is for the Birds, John T. Smith of New York College found ..." write "Smith (2014) found ..."

Ultimately your paper will be organized into several sections. The first section of your paper, the introduction, explains the research question and explains why it is worth examining. The last paragraph of the introduction section should outline the organization of the paper. In the body of the paper you will present evidence from research studies to support your points. Describe and evaluate each study, and make comparisons among the studies. Compare studies based on assumptions, theories tested, hypotheses, research designs, methods, findings, and interpretations. How do the studies support the theme of your paper? In the final section of the paper, draw conclusions, discuss implications, and suggest avenues for further research. Based on the studies reviewed and the comparisons and evaluations made, what conclusions do you draw? What research is left to be done? Recommend future studies. By now you should have a list of all the important ideas you hope to convey in your paper.

As you begin to write, remember that this is only your first draft. Not every word will stay, and not every word has to be perfect. Don't worry about errors. Just get the ideas out; you'll catch the errors later as you edit. Write anything that appears relevant, and think about where to put it and how to reorganize it later. Regularly save your work on your computer and on a cloud drive or flash drive so that your work is protected in the event of a computer catastrophe. Print a hard copy at the end of each writing session, and preferably more often (e.g., after completing two or three pages).

Begin working early, to give yourself time to write and rewrite. Time is essential to writing a comprehensive review of the literature; time to read, let ideas simmer, write, gain perspective on what you've written, and revise. As you write, you may find that some elements of your research are incomplete. Go back to the library and gather additional resources to fill in any gaps in your research or argument.

Revise

The most important part of writing is rewriting, so be prepared for lots of editing and rewrites. Many students neglect this part of the writing process and instead print out a paper and submit it right away. The best papers ferment over time. Once you have a draft, spend at least twenty-four hours away from it. Let it sit for a day or two, and you'll be able to approach it with fresh eyes. With time, you'll find it easier to separate yourself from your work and become more objective.

Before you begin the editing and revising process, make a "safe" copy of your paper in case you decide to undo some of your revisions. Read through your draft and note what needs to be done. Is the organization consistent with your outline? Are you happy with the outline, or should it be modified based on the paper you have written? As you read, you might want to list gaps in the paper's organization that need to be filled, missing details to provide, and other tasks to complete, such as checking spelling and grammar or tracking down an errant reference. Recognize that you will revise the paper several times; don't feel the need to complete the final draft right away.

Read your paper aloud. Reorganize sections, edit them, or even delete them if you deem them unnecessary. Examine the order of sentences and paragraphs. Sometimes moving a sentence up in a paragraph (or even deleting it) makes a world of difference. As you revise your paper, consider whether you've left anything out. Can anything be deleted? Are there extraneous details or sections? Are the paragraphs and sections coherent and logical? Have you used transitions between paragraphs and sections so that the paper flows? Have you used consistent style throughout? Have you used the proper guidelines, as stipulated by your instructor or APA style? (See Chapter 6 for more on APA style.)

Think you're done? Print out your final draft and proofread it aloud. Check for the placement of commas and your use of grammar. You might be surprised by the errors that you find. Take your final draft to the writing center at your college or university. You'll get an extra pair of eyes to read your work and some helpful feedback on how to improve your paper. Now make your corrections and print out your final draft.

Remember that good writing is the result of practice. The process gets easier with experience, but we all begin a paper with at least a little trepidation. Start early and take time to read and mull over your articles. Revise your paper several times, waiting a day or two between each draft, to gain distance. Use the literature review checklist in Checklist 5.1 as a guide to writing your literature review. Finally, don't let procrastination or fear stop you from writing.

CHECKLIST 5.1

Literature Review Checklist

- ❑ Is the topic appropriate (e.g., is it a topic within the field of psychology)?
- ❑ Does the title of your paper describe the topic of your review?
- ❑ Does your review include an introduction section that defines the purpose of the review and its significance?
- ❑ Does the introduction section explain the organization of the literature review?
- ❑ Are journal articles included as sources?
- ❑ Do you include current (and appropriate) articles as sources?
- ❑ Does your review discuss the major findings relating to your topic?
- ❑ Do you evaluate existing research?
- ❑ Have you explained why particular studies and sets of findings are strong?
- ❑ Have you explained why particular studies and sets of findings are weak?
- ❑ Have you included enough detail about each study to help the reader determine the significance of each article?
- ❑ Have you described relationships between studies?
- ❑ Have gaps in the literature been noted and explained?
- ❑ Have any controversies in the field been described?
- ❑ Have you chosen a method of organizing the literature reviewed in your paper?
- ❑ Have you outlined your paper after writing it to examine its organization?
- ❑ Does your literature review answer an identifiable question?
- ❑ Does each study you reviewed correspond with a specific part of your topic outline?
- ❑ Have you deleted studies that do not relate to your purpose or argument?
- ❑ Does each part of your review flow logically from the preceding part?
- ❑ Do you use transitions between paragraphs to indicate the flow of major points in your outline?
- ❑ Does your review include a conclusion section?

(Continued)

CHECKLIST 5.1 (Continued)

- ❑ Does your review discuss further questions for research?
- ❑ Does your conclusion address the purpose identified in the introduction?
- ❑ Did you revise your manuscript several times?
- ❑ Did you spell check the manuscript?
- ❑ Are quotations used only when needed?
- ❑ Are quotations appropriately cited? Can any quotations be paraphrased?
- ❑ Are all paraphrases appropriately cited?
- ❑ Have you avoided the use of slang, abbreviations, and contractions?
- ❑ Have you used the past tense to refer to research studies?

SUGGESTED READINGS

Beins, B. & Beins, A. (2012). *Effective writing in psychology: Papers, posters, and presentations.* Hoboken, NJ: Wiley.

Rosnow, R. L. & Rosnow, M. (2011). *Writing papers in psychology.* Belmont, CA: Wadsworth.

Mitchell, H. L. & Jolley, J. M. (2013). *Writing for psychology*. Belmont, CA: Wadsworth.

Kail, R. V. (2015). *Scientific writing for psychology: Lessons in clarity and style*. Thousand Oaks, CA: Sage.

Meyer, M. (1985). *The little, brown guide to writing research papers*. Glenville, IL: Scott, Foresman and Company.

INTERNET RESOURCES (Available at http://www.tarakuther.com)

Writing in Psychology

http://psychology.gmu.edu/writing/

Purdue University's OWL is the go-to source for writing advice.

A Brief Guide To Writing a Psychology Paper

http://writingproject.fas.harvard.edu/files/hwp/files/bg_psychology.pdf

Harvard College's guide offers excellent advice.

Writing a Psychology Literature Review

http://web.psych.washington.edu/writingcenter/writingguides/pdf/litrev.pdf

University of Washington Psychology Writing Center's take on writing literature reviews.

PsychInfo Guide

http://www.library.auckland.ac.nz/docs/helpsheets/psycinfoguide.pdf

Everything you need to know about using *PsychInfo* in this handy guide. A must-read that will make finding relevant articles much easier.

Plagiarism Tutorial

http://www.lib.usm.edu/legacy/plag/plagiarismtutorial.php

Excellent site with several lessons and two quizzes to assess your understanding of plagiarism.

PsychInfo

http://help.psycnet.org/psycnet/term-finder/

APA's online *PsychInfo* site

Google Scholar

http://scholar.google.com

Google Keep

https://keep.google.com/

Evernote

http://evernote.com

Onenote

http://www.onenote.com/

Reflection Prompts

How I Feel about Writing

How do you feel about writing? Imagine receiving a paper assignment in class. What are your initial thoughts and emotions? Would you like to change any of these reactions? Which ones? How would you prefer to react? What small steps can you take to make it easier to react in a more satisfactory way?

My Writing Interests

Which writing experiences do you find fun? Do you prefer free writing, or do you like writing papers, essays, or creative pieces? How are these different for you, and what do you prefer about each? What topics do you most prefer writing about? Why?

My Writing Habits

What are your habits and typical ways of completing a writing assignment? Do you find that you procrastinate? How? Is there any way that you can prevent this? How can using some of the techniques described in this chapter make completing writing assignments and other tasks quicker and easier?

CHAPTER

6

WRITING AN EMPIRICAL PAPER

CHAPTER OUTLINE

The ability to write literature review papers is a critical skill for success as a psychology major. Unlike many other majors, psychology students must learn how to write a second kind of paper. They must learn how to report the reports of empirical work, that is, research studies. Psychology is a science and, as a major, you learn how to read and understand scientific literature, and contribute to the literature by writing empirical papers and lab reports. All colleges and universities require psychology majors to complete courses in research methodology in which students must conduct research studies and write empirical papers to describe their research. An empirical paper discusses the question under study, the methodology used to gather information about the question, and the findings and their implications. Understanding how to write an empirical paper is essential to your academic success. In this chapter we discuss the mechanics of the empirical paper. After a brief discussion of the *Publication Manual of the American Psychological Association* (2010), we will examine each section of an empirical paper. The chapter closes with a sample template for your empirical paper.

APA Style: The *Publication Manual of the American Psychological Association*

While reading journal articles, you've probably noticed the distinct style of scientific writing. Why is the style so structured? Consider the purpose of written reports—communication—to tell readers about your research and explain what you did and what you found. Excellent scientific communication provides readers with enough information to enable them to critically evaluate the procedures, judge the quality of the research, and replicate (or reproduce) the results. Scientific writing is filled with facts that are appropriately paraphrased and documented. Because publication space in scholarly journals is limited, authors attempt to provide complete information in as few words as possible. Each word is carefully chosen for its precision. Scientific writing promotes clear communication, but it is very different from other types of writing and often requires more practice to master.

In psychology, authors are expected to follow the standard format specified by the sixth edition of the *Publication Manual of the American Psychological Association* (2010). Although learning the format known as APA style is challenging, ultimately a standard style of scientific communication makes it easier for researchers to report findings and for readers to comprehend them. This chapter provides a brief overview of APA style and the structure of research reports. Remember that this presentation is brief and cannot replace the *Publication Manual*, which is over 250 pages long. If you have questions about specific issues, consult the *Publication Manual* and your professor.

STRUCTURE OF THE EMPIRICAL PAPER

An empirical paper or research article is a highly structured, concise, professional way of communicating the results of a research study. It consists of several sections, each with a specific purpose. The *title page* communicates the title, the authors, and the authors' institutional affiliations. The *abstract* provides a brief summary of the study. The *introduction* is the first section of an article. It gives an overview of the research question, discusses the relevant literature, and identifies the purpose of the study. The *method* section explains how the research was conducted; it includes a description of the participants, measures, instruments and equipment, and procedure. The *results* section presents statistical analyses that address the research questions, with information displayed in graphs and tables. The *discussion* section explores the significance of the study's findings in light of prior research, limitations of the study, and suggestions for further research. Last but not least is the *reference* section, which provides accurate references for all material that was cited in the paper. Now let's examine each section of the empirical paper.

Title Page

Don't underestimate the importance of a title. The title gives readers a mini-introduction to your paper and helps them to decide if they want to read the abstract and paper. The title should offer a concise summary of the paper—the topic, variables, and theoretical issue under study—all in no more than twelve words. According the *Publication Manual*, "a title should be fully explanatory when standing alone" (APA, 2010, p. 23). A good title is hard to write; plan to spend some time on it. It's often easier to write the title once the paper is complete.

- The paper title is written in uppercase and lowercase letters, positioned in the upper half of the first page, and centered between the right and left margin.
- Center the author's name, written in uppercase and lowercase letters, on the line below the title.
- The institutional affiliation appears in uppercase and lowercase letters, centered on the line below the author(s).
- The running head is a short version of your title that appears at the top of the pages of a paper or published article. The running head is typed flush left (all uppercase) following "Running head:" on the first page, then appears on its own (without the "Running head" label on all subsequent pages). The running head should not exceed fifty characters, including punctuation and spacing. Using most word processors, the running head and page number can be inserted into a header, which then automatically appears on all pages.

- The page number appears in the top right hand corner.
- Similar to the entire paper, the title page is double spaced, in twelve-point font, with one-inch margins.
- The title is not in bold type, italics, or underlined.
- For a sample title page, see the sample template at the end of this chapter.
- Note that you may decide to change your title as you complete your research study. Your title is not set in stone; revise it, if needed, to reflect the findings and the content of your paper.

Abstract

Like the title, the abstract gives readers a glimpse into your paper. The abstract provides a brief comprehensive overview of your study, providing enough information for readers to determine if they want to read the article itself (that is, determine if the article is likely to provide information to address their questions). Write the abstract after you've completed your paper and have a firm perspective of the findings and their importance. Describe the problem under investigation, presenting the major hypotheses, participants, materials, and procedure. Summarize the results and conclusions, indicating the implications or applications. A good abstract interests readers and convinces them that the study is worth reading. An abstract should be self-explanatory and range from 150 to 250 words. Sticking to the word count is very difficult, but well-written shorter abstracts are best. Most writers begin by composing a longer summary and slowly pare down unneeded words. The abstract appears on the second page of your paper. The word "Abstract" should appear centered at the top of the page. The abstract appears on the second line, left justification, with no indentation.

Introduction

The title of the paper appears on the first line of page 3, centered and capitalized. The introduction begins on line 2, flush with the left margin and indented. The introduction is your opportunity to introduce readers to your research question, what is known about the topic, why the topic is important, and how your study contributes to what is already known. Consider the introduction as three separate sections. The first section, a paragraph or two in length, introduces the problem: What is the topic under study, and how will it be approached? Why is it important? The second section of the introduction provides a review of relevant literature to explain what is known about the specific question under study (review Chapter 5 for suggestions on how to conduct a literature review). Be specific and present only research that is directly relevant to the research question. What has prior research shown? What are limitations in prior research? How is your study an extension of prior research? The third section of the introduction states the purpose and rationale of the research study, and provides a brief overview of your study. Now, let's consider each part of the introduction in more depth.

The first paragraphs are introductory paragraphs and act to lure readers into your paper. These paragraphs often are the most difficult to write, so consider saving them for later, after you've written the rest of the paper. Use the funnel approach to structure the introduction. Begin with a general statement (the wide opening of the funnel) and get more specific (narrow the funnel) with each sentence, until the final sentence introduces the purpose of your study. An additional introductory paragraph may explain why the research question addressed by your study is important. Your goal is to make readers see the point of your study and to convince them that your project tackles an important question or issue.

The next section of the introduction reviews the literature relevant to your study. It typically is several pages long, and cites theory and research that expand and support the rationale for your study. The literature searching and summarizing strategies discussed in Chapter 5 illustrate how to search the literature, take notes, and organize a literature review. Your goal is to inform readers of the published literature on your problem, demonstrate the importance of the question, and justify the rationale for your methods. As you review the literature, it is important to remain focused on your research topic. Discuss only research that is pertinent to your project. The review is selective and should "avoid nonessential details; instead emphasize pertinent findings, relevant methodological issues, and major conclusions" (American Psychological Association, 2010, p. 28). Refer readers to published reviews that examine more general issues, so that they can obtain additional information, if desired.

An effective review of the literature orients readers to what is known and answers several questions:

- What is the purpose of the study?
- What do we know about this area of research?
- How does the study relate to prior research? How does it draw upon and extend prior work? What is the nature of your contribution?
- Why is the study important or interesting?
- What rationale links the research questions and research design? How did you choose the research design, and how does the design address the question?

It is vital that you demonstrate the logical continuity between prior research, your research question, and your research design. Unquestionably, this is the most difficult part of writing the introduction. As you write, keep your purpose in mind: Your goal is to interest readers, explain why your study is relevant, and motivate them to continue (Sternberg, 1993). Finally, be very careful to appropriately cite the sources of information in your literature review. If you are unsure of the overall use of citations or how to appropriately quote or paraphrase sources, see the section on plagiarism in Chapter 5 and the *Publication Manual*.

The final component of the introduction section explains the purpose and rationale for your study. Explain your hypotheses (your specific predictions about the research results) and provide a brief overview of your study. How does your research design relate to the theoretical issue that you wish to address? This is particularly important if you are employing an unusual design.

Real Tips for Real Students
Reference Managers

Writing a paper requires a great deal of organization. One way to keep track of the articles you read and make parenthetical citation easier is to use a reference manager. A reference manager is a program that allows you to include full citation information for an article as well as your own notes. The best part of using a reference manager is that it syncs with your word processing program to organize your citations. For example, when you discuss an article by Smith, the reference manager will insert the parenthetical citation. Even better is that the program can automatically generate your reference list. There are a variety of reference managers to consider. Two free popular reference managers are Mendeley (http://www.mendeley.com) and Zotero (http://www.zotero.org). Start using a reference manager early in your academic career and you'll build an easily accessible library that can help you throughout college and beyond.

Method

The introduction answers the questions, "What?" and, "Why?" The method section explains, "How." The purpose of the method section is to clearly explain how you conducted your study. The method section should provide enough pertinent details so that readers can replicate your research. Typically the methods section contains several sections—participants, apparatus materials or measures, and procedures. Begin the method section, titled "Methods" on a new line, bolded and centered between the right and left margin.

Participants On a separate line, flush with the left margin, list "Participants" in bold. The next line, indented, begins the participants section, which answers the questions, "Who participated in the study?" "How many participated?" and, "How were they selected?" In this section, describe the demographic characteristics of the participants. Explain any demographic details that might affect your study, including age, sex, ethnicity, geographic location, and number of participants assigned to each treatment group. Explain how participants were selected and how they were assigned to groups. What were the circumstances in which they participated, and were any inducements offered (e.g., extra credit)?

Apparatus, Materials, or Measures Depending on your study, this section might be entitled apparatus, materials, or measures. Similar to the participants section, this section begins on a new line with the bold label "Apparatus," "Materials," or "Measures," listed. Indent the next line and describe the equipment or instruments used to conduct the study. If you used specialized equipment to conduct the research, describe it and explain how it was used. If the equipment is a manufactured item, include information on the manufacturer and the model number. If you developed an apparatus or any materials for your study, describe them in enough detail so that readers could reproduce them (including exact dimensions and physical properties of any apparatus that you construct). If standardized tests or measures were used, describe them, include their psychometric properties (e.g., reliability and validity), and explain how they were coded or scored. As you write this section, remember that your goal is to describe how you measured your variables and what methods you used to collect data.

Procedure On a new line, flush left and bold, type "Procedure." This section describes the steps you took in conducting your research. Tell readers what was done, how, and in what order. Clearly describe what happened to participants from the time they walked into the lab until the time they left the lab—the beginning to the end of their experience. If you administered surveys to participants, describe the survey conditions and instructions provided. If your research was experimental, describe how participants were exposed to the independent variable; include a description of any instructions that participants received. Describe your methodology and any control features of the design, such as counterbalancing or the use of control groups. Again, your goal is to provide sufficient detail so that a reader can replicate your study.

Results

The heading for the "Results" section appears centered and bold between the right and left margin. On the following left-justified line, begin your results section. Ask yourself, "What did I find? How can I say what I found in a careful, detailed way? Is what I am planning to say precise and to the point? Have I left out anything of importance?" (Rosnow & Rosnow, 2001, p. 58). Report the most interesting results first, or those that are most relevant to the hypotheses tested. Save results that are less interesting and relevant for later in the results section. In other words, think about the importance of your findings and present them accordingly. Don't just give your readers a laundry list of findings. Instead, carefully consider how to present the results, including the order and style of presentation.

The results section provides answers to your research questions in the form of reports of descriptive and inferential statistics. Descriptive statistics summarize the data. Inferential statistics examine your hypotheses and test the likelihood that the results are not due to chance. As you report tests of statistical significance, the *Publication Manual* recommends that you include the name of the test, obtained value, degrees of freedom, significance level, and effect size. Note that these guidelines are intended for publication in scholarly journals; your professor may modify these guidelines for your class. Tables are an effective way of concisely conveying a great deal of information. The *Publication Manual* recommends including tables to list means, medians, standard deviations, and confidence intervals. Any tables that you use must be self-explanatory (e.g., with titles and fully labeled) and should not repeat information that is presented in the text. Review the *Publication Manual* for detailed explanations of how to construct tables to represent your data.

Discussion

The discussion section begins with the word "Discussion" bolded and centered. The text on the following line is flush left and indented. Here you will describe the significance of your findings, place them in context, and discuss their implications. In other words, the discussion takes a big picture, bird's eye view perspective. As you structure the discussion section, ask yourself: What did I set out to learn, what was the purpose of the study and what did I find? Also consider: "Were there any serendipitous findings of interest? How valid and generalizable are my findings? Are there larger implications of these findings? Is there an alternative way to interpret my results?" (Rosnow & Rosnow, 2008, p. 53).

Begin the discussion section by reminding readers of the purpose of your study. Then consider your data. Was there support for your hypotheses? Explain. If the data do not support your hypotheses, can you provide another interpretation? If so, clearly state that your interpretation is speculative and that further research is needed to confirm it. Now, discuss your findings within the context of prior research. How do your findings compare with those of other researchers? Does your work extend prior findings? If your findings do not replicate prior work or do not make sense given the literature you have reviewed, you might explore methodological differences or other factors that may account for the disparate findings. What are the theoretical and practical implications of your findings? As you write this section, remember that your goal is to connect your findings with prior research. Do not present new statistical analyses not included in the results section. Instead, the discussion section is a place for you to explain the value of your findings, and not the data itself.

The discussion section should also explore limitations or shortcomings of your study (every study has weaknesses). What factors might limit the extent to which you can generalize your results? Try to think of objections someone might make to the conclusions that you draw (whether the objections are correct or not), and either answer them or qualify your conclusions to take them into account. If you think that possible objections are weak, explain why. Help readers to understand exactly what can and cannot be concluded from your study. Finally, consider avenues for future research. Do not end your discussion section, and therefore article, with the sentence, "More research is needed." Be specific. What are the remaining unanswered research questions? Given what you have learned, what research is the next step? Provide specific questions and topics for further research.

Exercise 6.1
Test Your Understanding of Journal Articles

Using *PsychInfo*, locate an empirical journal article in an area of interest. Retrieve the article using your library's full text and in print resources. The reference librarian can offer assistance if you experience difficulty. Read the article and complete the following:

1. Write the article's citation in APA style.
2. Examine the abstract of the article. Based on the abstract, what do you expect to learn in this article?
3. What is the purpose of the study? Where did you find that information?
4. How was the study conducted? Describe the methodology? Where did you locate that information?
5. What were the findings of the study? Where did you look to learn about the findings?
6. What were the author's conclusions? How did the results of this study compare with prior research? Where did you look to learn about the findings?
7. Reflect back on the abstract. How well did it reflect the content of the article? Did you learn what you thought you would?

Exercise 6.2
Write an Abstract

Choose an empirical article. *Do not read the abstract.* Read the article very carefully.

1. Once you feel that you grasp the article well, write an abstract describing the research study.
2. Compare your abstract to the published abstract. How well do they match?
3. What details should you have included? Any that were unnecessary?

References

The reference section begins on a new page with the word "References" centered and bolded. The reference section lists all articles or books that you cited in your paper, including enough information so that an interested reader can locate them. If a source is listed in the reference section, it must be cited within the paper. List only the sources that you used. The most common sources of reference material in student papers are journal articles, books, and perhaps material from reputable sources on the Internet. The *Publication Manual* lists slightly different formats for journal articles, books, and Internet sources, as well as slight differences depending on the number of authors. Table 6.1 illustrates how to cite journal articles, books, and Internet sources. Let's examine each type of citation.

TABLE 6.1 **APA STYLE REFERENCES**

Journal Articles

One Author:

Torraco, R. J. (2005). Writing integrative literature reviews: Guidelines and examples. *Human Resource Development Review, 4*(3), 356–367. doi:10.1177/1534484305278283.

Two Authors:

Dearnley, C. & Matthew, B. (2007). Factors that contribute to undergraduate success. *Teaching in Higher Education, 12*(3), 377–391. doi: 10.1080/13562510701278740

Three Authors:

Cooley, E. L., Garcia, A. L., & Hughes, J. L. (2008). Undergraduate research in liberal arts colleges: Reflections on mutual benefits for faculty and students. *North American Journal of Psychology, 10*(3), 463–471.

Books

One Author:

Palladino Schulthesiss, D. E. (2008). *Psychology as a major: Is it right for me and what can I do with my degree.* Washington, DC: APA.

Two Authors:

Landrum, R. E. & Davis, S. F. (2010). *The psychology major: Career options and strategies for success.* Upper Saddle River, NJ: Prentice Hall.

Three Authors:

Silvia, P. J., Delaney, P. F., & Marcovitch, S. (2009). *What psychology majors could (and should) be doing: An informal guide to research experience and professional skills.* Washington, DC: APA.

Chapters in Edited Books

One Author:

Handlesman, M. M. (2001). Learning to become ethical. In S. Walfish & B. Tolan (Eds). *Succeeding in graduate school: The career guide for psychology students* (pp. 189–202). Mahwah, NJ: Erlbaum.

Two Authors:

Campbell, C. & Anderson, T. L. (2010). Mentoring in professional psychology. In M. B. Kenkel & R. L. Peterson (Eds.). *Competency-based training for professional psychology* (pp. 237–247). Washington, DC: APA.

Three Authors:

Wasik, B. H., Song, S., & Knotek, S. Preparing for careers in school psychology. In S. F. Davis, P. J. Giordano, & C. A. Licht (Eds). *Your career in psychology: Putting your graduate degree to work* (pp. 231–244). Hoboken, NJ: Wiley-Blackwell.

Internet

Lloyd, M. M. (2004). *Marky Lloyd's careers in psychology page.* Retrieved January 8, 2015 from http://www.psychwww.com/careers/index.htm

List journal articles in the following way:

- List the author's last name and first initial.
- The year of publication follows, in parentheses, with a period.
- The article title comes next. Don't capitalize each word of the title; only the first word of the article title is capitalized. If the article title contains a colon, the first word after the colon is capitalized as well. Follow the article title with a period.
- The title of the journal and volume number come next and are italicized. Capitalize each word of the journal title. Place a comma after the journal title and after the volume number. Note that only the number is used to indicate volume; don't use "V," "Volume," or "Vol."
- Last are the page numbers, followed by a period. Again, note that only the numbers themselves are used to indicate pages; don't use "page," "p," or "pg."
- Following the page number is the digital object identifier (DOI). References that are obtained online, such as through subscription services such as *PsychInfo*, are labeled with a DOI that is a unique strong of numbers and letters that labels an article for database searches. The DOI usually appears on the first page of an article, near the copyright notice. Older articles may not list DOIs. If you include a DOI, it appears after the period following the page numbers as "doi:" and list the numbers without a space after the colon. Check with your professor.

Including the DOI is a recent addition to the *Publication Manual* and some instructors may not require their students to include them.
- The first journal article example in Table 6.1 illustrates an article by one author, the second example illustrates two authors, and the third illustrates three authors.

List books as follows:

- Books are listed by the author's last name and first initial.
- The year of publication follows, in parentheses, with a period.
- Next comes the book title, italicized. Like the journal article title, only the first word of the book title is capitalized. If the book title contains a colon, the first word after the colon is capitalized as well.
- Finally, list the place of publication, a colon, and the publisher.
- The first book example in Table 6.1 illustrates a book by one author, the second example illustrates two authors, and the third illustrates three authors.

List edited books as follows:

- List the chapter author's last name and first initial.
- The year of publication follows, in parentheses, with a period.
- The title of the chapter follows, with only the first word capitalized, ending with a period.
- Next indicate the editors and book by writing, "In" and listing the editors by first initial and last name, followed by "Ed." in parentheses, with a comma. Then list the title of the book, capitalizing only the first word.
- Provide the page numbers in parentheses, signified by "pp." Note that this is the only time that "pp" is used in APA style.
- Finally, provide the place of publication, followed by a colon, and the publisher.
- Electronic books include a DOI, which should be listed after the period following publisher, with "doi" and a colon listed in lowercase letters.
- The first example in Table 6.1 lists a sole authored chapter in a book edited by two people. The second example illustrates two authors and two editors, and the third example lists three authors and two editors.

List Internet sources as follows:

- Cite Internet sources by the author's last name (if no author appears, then cite the organization; if there is no author or organization, the article title moves to the position of author).
- Indicate the year of publication (if listed) in parentheses. If the year of publication is not listed, then use "n.d." to indicate no date, in parentheses.
- The title of the page appears next, in italics (with only the first word capitalized).

- Next, list the date that you retrieved the information and the Internet address (and don't use a period after the Internet address).
- Note that the *Publication Manual* includes different reference styles for blog posts, online forum/discussion group posts, and messages according on electronic mailing lists. Learn more by perusing the *Publication Manual* or ask your instructor for assistance.

Exercise 6.3
Practice Preparing Reference Lists

1. Conduct a *PsychInfo* search on the topic of your choice. Identify five publications including at least one article and one book chapter.
2. Construct a reference list.
3. Compare reference lists with another student. Do they differ in style? Together, review the guidelines for APA style and correct your reference lists.
4. Seek feedback from your professor.
5. APA style is challenging and most beginning writers make errors. What kinds of errors did you make? Correct your reference list.
6. Locate three more publications and try again.

Real Tips for Real Students
Verify APA Style in Downloaded Citations

Many students quickly realize that article entries in library databases such as *PsychInfo* are often accompanied by a link listing the article citation in various formats, such as APA or MLA. Likewise, Google Scholar also includes a citation link for each article. These citations are valuable information for your records but take care in using these citations. Do not trust them. Check auto generated citations carefully as they are often incorrect. Don't lose points on your paper to careless errors.

Writing an empirical paper entails using a highly structured, scientific style. The sample paper at the end of this chapter illustrates how to format your empirical paper and provides additional information about formatting. Use Checklist 6.1 to help you determine whether your paper meets the major guidelines set by APA style. At first the elements of an empirical paper—and the formal style of writing—may seem foreign. The sample APA style paper at the end of this chapter illustrates the sections as well as describes the content of each section. With practice you will find that writing comes more easily and perhaps you will come to see the value in clear concise scientific communication. It likely will not be as easy as the other forms of writing you have undertaken to date, but the ability to write in a formal style and with precision will suit you well in your career.

EXERCISE 6.4

APA Style Template

Choose an empirical article and create your own APA style template that summarizes the information in the article.

1. Prepare a title page for the article.
2. Prepare an abstract in which you briefly describe the study.
3. Prepare an introduction section in which you summarize the literature review and purpose within two to three paragraphs.
4. Prepare the APA style methods section including participants, method, and procedure. Summarize each.
5. Prepare the APA style results section. Summarize their findings.
6. Prepare the APA style discussion section. Describe the findings and implications in two paragraphs.

CHECKLIST 6.1

APA Style Checklist

Page Formatting

- ❑ Have you used one-inch margins?
- ❑ Have you double spaced the document?
- ❑ Have you used a running head and number on every page?
- ❑ Have you checked for typos?
- ❑ Have you used five- to seven-space paragraph indents?

Title Page

- ❑ Is your title no longer than twelve words?
- ❑ Is the running head no longer than fifty characters and placed as a header at the top of each page?
- ❑ Did you include your name and affiliation below the title and centered on the page and line?

Abstract

- ❑ Does the abstract appear on a new page, without indentation, headed by the word "Abstract" centered?
- ❑ Is the abstract a minimum of 150 and no longer than 250 words?

Introduction

- ❑ Does the introduction begin on a new page, headed by the paper's title?
- ❑ Have you included all authors' names in the first in-text citation?

- ❑ Have you used “and” to link authors names in text?
- ❑ Have you used “&” to link authors names in parenthetical citations?
- ❑ Did you include the year in parenthetical citations?

Method

- ❑ Does the method section begin immediately after the introduction, with no page break?
- ❑ Does the method section begin on a new line, with “Method” centered, and bolded?
- ❑ Is the method section written in the past tense?
- ❑ Is the method section broken into participant and materials/apparatus, and procedure subsections?

Results

- ❑ Does the results section begin immediately after the introduction, with no page break?
- ❑ Does the results section begin on a new line, with “Results” centered, and bolded?
- ❑ Is the results section written in the past tense?
- ❑ Have you reported the effect size?
- ❑ Have you organized the results into paragraphs and subsections?
- ❑ Did you italicize mathematical symbols, use numbers rather than words, and capitalize the names of independent variables?
- ❑ Did you report the value for nonsignificant results without interpreting them?
- ❑ Did you interpret all significant results?
- ❑ Did you explain interactions?
- ❑ Did you create tables to summarize all data?
- ❑ Did you create figures to illustrate interactions?

Discussion

- ❑ Does the discussion section begin immediately after the introduction, with no page break?
- ❑ Does the discussion section begin on a new line, with “Discussion” centered, and bolded?
- ❑ Did you use the past tense to describe results and refer to prior findings?
- ❑ Did you use the present tense to discuss theories and conclusions?

References

- ❑ Did you begin the reference list on a new page, headed by the word “References” centered?
- ❑ Are the references listed in alphabetical order?
- ❑ Is the first line of each reference flush with the left margin and the subsequent lines tab-indented?
- ❑ Have you cited only work that you have read?

Suggested Readings

American Psychological Association. (2010). *Publication manual of the American Psychological Association*. Washington, DC: Author.

American Psychological Association. (2009). *Mastering APA style: Student's workbook and training guide*. Washington, DC: Author.

Beins, B. & Beins, A. (2012). *Effective writing in psychology: Papers, posters, and presentations*. Hoboken, NJ: Wiley.

Landrum, R E. (2012). *Undergraduate writing in psychology: Learning to tell the scientific story*. Washington DC: APA.

Miller, R. A. (2013). *Writing in psychology*. London: Routledge.

Mitchell, H. L. & Jolley, J. M. (2013). *Writing for psychology*. Belmont, CA: Wadsworth.

Schwartz, M. A. & Landrum, R. E. (2013). *An easy guide to APA style*. New York: Sage.

Internet Resources (Available at http://www.tarakuther.com)

APA Style Online

http://www.apastyle.org

This site from the American Psychological Association presents an overview of APA style, along with answers to frequently asked questions.

The Elements of Style

http://www.bartleby.com/141/index.html

This website gives you access to Strunk and White's classic volume on how to write clearly and concisely.

How to Write a Research Report in Psychology

http://www.psych.upenn.edu/~baron/labrep.html

At this site you'll find an overview of the sections in an empirical paper, with additional advice on grammar.

Writing an Empirical Paper in APA Style

http://web.psych.washington.edu/writingcenter/writingguides/pdf/APApaper.pdf

University of Washington Psychology Writing Center's guide.

Writing Empirical Psychology Papers (for Beginners)

http://www.muhlenberg.edu/depts/psychology/EmpiricalPrimer.htm

Concrete tips to help you improve your paper.

Mendeley

http://www.mendeley.com

Free online and off-line reference manager.

Zotero

http://www.zotero.org

Free online and off-line reference manager.

Reflection Prompts

My Research Question

What's your research project? Don't use your notes or readings, but write as much as you can about your project. What is your research question? How did it evolve? Where did you get the idea? How is your study an improvement over prior studies? Why is your study important? How well can you remember your points? How can you immerse yourself more fully in your project?

My Findings

Tell a story about your research project. What did you set out to do, and what did you find? Try to explain what your statistical analyses tested. Pretend that you're explaining your project to a friend or a high school student. How would you explain your results in a way that a student could understand?

Implications

Answer the question: So what? You don't need to have completed your research to consider this question. In fact, thinking about how your study matters, what's its contribution, can help you refine your question. Be grandiose and try to think about far-reaching implications for laws, social policy, regulations, education, and so on.

If I Could Do It All Over

Pretend that you are going to revise your study and start from the beginning. What would you do differently? Why?

Appendix I: Sample Paper

My Paper: A Template

Jane J. Smith

Your State University

TEMPLATE PAPER 2

Abstract

The abstract should be self-explanatory, self-contained, and should not exceed 250 words. Describe the problem under investigation, the major hypotheses, participants, materials, and procedure. Summarize the results and conclusions, indicating the implications or applications. A good abstract interests readers and convinces them that the study is worth reading.

1 inch ←→

1 inch ←→

My Paper: A Template from Which to Work

Begin the introduction with a general statement about your topic area. Consider your readers and attempt to peak their interest. Use the funnel effect in the first paragraph of your introduction so that you begin with general statements, each one becoming more narrowly focused, until you end with a statement of the problem under study.

A second paragraph of the introduction might explain the importance of the research question. What is its theoretical or applied relevance?

After introducing the problem, the second component of the introduction section provides a literature review of what is known about the topic. What has prior research shown? What are limitations in prior research? How is your study an extension of prior research? As you write the literature review, cite only those studies that are most pertinent to your research question (and use appropriate documentation, as described in Chapter 5). The literature review is typically several pages long.

End the introductory section with a clear statement of the purpose and rationale of your study. Discuss hypotheses and set the stage for the method section.

Method

The method section explains how the study was conducted. Provide enough detail so that a reader could replicate your research. Typically the methods section contains several sections: participants, apparatus materials or measures, and procedure.

TEMPLATE PAPER 4

Notice that three levels of headings are used. The first is written in upper and lower case, centered. The second level of headings is written in upper and lower case letters, flush left, and italicized. The third level of headings is indented and italicized, with only the first letter of the first word italicized, and is followed by a period. Headings may be used to organize your introduction section. Review the *Publication Manual* to learn more about the use of headings.

Participants

The participants section describes the characteristics of the participants and explains how they were selected. Explain any demographic details that might affect your study, including age, sex, ethnicity, geographic location, and number of participants assigned to each treatment group. Report any inducements to participate (e.g., money, extra credit).

Apparatus/Measures

Depending on your study, this section might be entitled apparatus, materials, or measures. Briefly describe the equipment or instruments used in the study. If the equipment is a manufactured item, include information on the manufacturer and the model number. If you developed an apparatus or materials for your study, describe them in enough detail so that a reader could reproduce them. If standardized tests or measures were used, describe them, their psychometric properties (e.g., reliability and validity), and how they were coded or scored.

Procedure

Describe each step in conducting the study. Clearly describe what happened to participants from the time they walked into the lab to when they left, the beginning to the end of the study. Describe your methodology and any control features of the design such as counterbalancing or the use of control groups. What instructions were provided to participants? How were participants debriefed at the end of the study.

Results

Begin your results section by explaining the main findings. Follow up by explaining the analyses in detail. Report all relevant results, even those that are counter to your hypothesis. As you report tests of statistical significance, include the name of the test, degrees of freedom, and significance level. Provide enough detail to justify the conclusions that you will make in the discussion section. Provide tables to display complex sets of data (e.g., means and standard deviations, the results of complex analyses). For information on how to construct tables, see the *Publication Manual*.

Discussion

Begin the discussion section by reiterating the purpose of the study. Provide a statement on the support of your original hypotheses. Next, examine your findings. Explain what the results mean, consider them in the context of the literature, and discuss their implications. Identify possible limitations of your study. Close with a discussion of avenues for future research.

TEMPLATE PAPER 6

References

Note that the reference section includes only articles that were cited in your study. List the references in alphabetical order. See Table 6.1 for sample article, book, and Internet references. Further examples of references appear in the *Publication Manual*.

What Can I Do With a Bachelor's Degree in Psychology?

CHAPTER 7

Chapter Outline

If you've decided to major in psychology you're in good company because psychology is consistently among the top five most popular bachelor's degrees awarded each year. In the 2010–11 academic year, 101,000 students earned bachelor's degrees in psychology (National Center for Education Statistics, 2013). Why are so many students attracted to psychology? Psychology courses cover a range of fascinating topics, such as how we think, learn, use our memory, feel emotions, cope with adversity, and change throughout our lives. Much of what we study in psychology is directly relevant to our everyday life. We all seek to understand human behavior and the environment around us.

Many undergraduate students choose psychology because of their desire to become psychologists or to work with people. However, a bachelor's degree in psychology will not qualify you to be a psychologist. Becoming a psychologist requires a doctoral degree, which entails several years of education, training, and supervision beyond the bachelor's degree.

So why major in psychology? Although a baccalaureate in psychology won't qualify you to formally practice psychology, you'll learn skills that are applicable to a variety of jobs, including many that entail helping other people. This chapter describes the skills that employers seek, the kinds of jobs that bachelor's degree graduates in psychology hold, and how you can cultivate useful skills and enhance your employability.

SKILLS AND ABILITIES SOUGHT BY EMPLOYERS

A bachelor's degree in psychology cultivates skills that are the foundation for a variety of career paths in the mental health professions, science, and business. When considering careers, evaluate and think carefully about the skills and knowledge that you've acquired over the college years. It may help for you to reconsider your answers to the exercises about your interests and competencies in Chapter 2. A thorough understanding of your talents and proficiencies is particularly important because most job advertisements are not organized by college major and, therefore, it is unlikely that you will see classified ads listing "Psychology Majors Wanted." While it is rare to see classified ads explicitly recruiting psychology majors, don't be fooled. Your major has helped you to develop a host of skills that employers want. It's up to you to identify those skills and educate employers.

What do employers look for in a new hire? Table 7.1 lists the most desirable qualities in prospective employees, according to surveys of a broad sample of employers (National Association of Colleges and Employers, 2014a). Carefully examine the list, and you'll quickly notice that interpersonal skills—including the abilities to communicate, influence others, and work in groups—are highly valued. These results indicate that "people skills," typical

TABLE 7.1 **Top Ten Qualities Employers Seek in Prospective Employees, in Order of Importance**

1. Teamwork skills
2. Decision-making and problem-solving skills
3. Planning and organizational skills
4. Verbal communication skills
5. Ability to obtain and process information
6. Quantitative skills
7. Job-related knowledge
8. Proficiency with computer software programs
9. Writing ability
10. Persuasion skills

National Association of Colleges and Employers (2014a)

of psychology majors, honed through course work, practica, and extracurricular activities, provide an upper hand in the job market.

Let's take a closer look at the competencies that employers seek.

- **Interpersonal and Teamwork Skills.** Listening skills and the ability to verbally communicate clearly and concisely. Group skills, the ability to share responsibility with others, conflict management, and an appreciation of individual differences are desired by employers.
- **Thinking and Problem-Solving Skills.** Successful employees have good judgment and decision-making skills. They can apply information to solve problems and analyze problems on the basis of personal experience and psychological principles. Analytical and decision-making skills are important because many of today's jobs require higher levels of complex, critical thinking than ever before.
- **Information Acquisition and Synthesis Skills.** Successful employees understand how they absorb and retain information. They know how to learn, where to find information, and how to evaluate and use it. A commitment to learning is essential in today's marketplace.
- **Reading and Writing Skills**. The abilities to extract important ideas from reading and to document them are valued by employers. Strong writing skills, such as the ability to write reports, proposals, and summaries, are desirable.
- **Career-Related Work Experience.** Successful job applicants have obtained hands-on, practical experience through cooperative education, internships, practica, part-time jobs, or summer work experience. They can apply their school-based knowledge in practical settings.

- **Data Analysis Skills.** Employers seek prospective employees with quantitative skills, the ability to reason numerically, and the ability to identify and solve problems in data. Graduates who can collect, record, and report statistical information will find success.
- **Computer Literacy.** Knowledge of computer applications—including word processing, spreadsheet, and database software—and familiarity with the Internet and e-mail are essential.
- **Self-Management and Adaptability.** Employers desire self-management skills such as the ability to set and pursue goals, tolerate stress, control one's emotions, and engage in appropriate behavior. Employers seek employees who are adaptable, flexible, and capable of handling multiple tasks. The ability to utilize resources in order to effectively complete tasks (e.g., creating a schedule, writing a budget, assigning space, and managing others) is essential. Employers also value the ability to tolerate ambiguity—the fact there often is no clear right or wrong answer or approach to a problem. Instead, successful employees adapt to the situation and carefully evaluate options to determine the best approach for a given situation.

EXERCISE 7.1
Developing Skills

Consider how psychology majors can develop the eight competencies listed in Table 7.1. For each competency, discuss at least two courses or experiences that can aid its development.

Psychology students have the opportunity to acquire these desirable skills as well as specific, useful, knowledge about psychology, such as how attitudes are formed and changed, or how people think, solve problems, and process information. An understanding of group dynamics and knowing how people perceive and sense their environment is also helpful. The goals of undergraduate education in psychology match employers' expectations well. There are two competencies that set psychology graduates apart from other majors: people skills and research skills. People skills include knowledge and an understanding of psychological principles and group dynamics, as well as interpersonal skills—self-management skills. Employers also value research skills such as report writing, the ability to carry out a research project, and the ability to conduct statistical analyses. The blend of liberal arts and science is what makes the psychology major unique, and it's what makes you very employable.

Jobs for Psychology Majors

The majority of students who graduate with a bachelor's degree in psychology do not go to graduate school. It is estimated that about one-quarter of psychology undergraduate degree recipients attend graduate school immediately after graduation (Goldstein, 2010). Instead, psychology baccalaureates head into the job market and find success. A recent study of bachelor's degree recipients found that about 9% of psychology recent bachelor's degree recipients were unemployed in 2011 and about 6.5% of graduates with experience were unemployed (Carnevale & Cheah, 2013), as compared with the 2011 national average of 14.5% of recent bachelor's degree graduates (Bureau of Labor Statistics, 2013). Unemployment rates ranged from about 5% in nursing to about 15% in information systems management.

About one-half of psychology bachelor's degree recipients work in business settings. They are also employed in education, government, and nonprofit settings. Table 7.2 lists common job titles psychology majors have obtained after graduation. It is not a complete list; many other opportunities are out there waiting for you.

TABLE 7.2 Positions Obtained by Psychology Majors

Business and Academic Settings	Social and Human Service Settings
Administration	Activities coordinator
Administrative assistant	Administration
Advertising trainee	Behavioral specialist
Affirmative action officer	Career counselor
Benefits manager	Case worker
Claims specialist	Child care worker/supervisor
Community relations officer	Child care provider
Customer relations	Child protection worker
Data management	Clinical coordinator
Employee counselor	Community outreach worker
Employee recruitment	Corrections officer
Human resources coordinator /manager/specialist	Counselor assistant
Lab coordinator	Crisis intervention counselor
Labor relations manager/specialist	Data management
Laboratory assistant	Employment counselor
Loan officer	Group home attendant

Management trainee	Mental health assistant
Marketing	Occupational therapist
Personnel manager/officer	Parent/family education
Product and services research	Preschool teacher
Programs/events coordination	Probation officer
Public opinion surveyor	Program manager
Public relations	Rehabilitation counselor
Research assistant	Residence counselor
Retail sales management	Social service assistant
Sales representative	Social worker
Special features writing/reporting	Social worker assistant
Staff training and development	Substance abuse counselor
Teaching assistant	Youth counselor
Trainer/training officer	

Adapted from: Appleby, Millspaugh, & Hammersley, 2011; DeGalan & Lambert, 1995; Rajecki 2012; Lloyd, 1997

Real Tip for Real Students
Job Titles Are Misleading

Many students find that one of the most overwhelming aspects of job searching is deciphering job titles. Students often pass over job titles that sound too complicated—or too simple. Try to look beyond the job title and instead focus on the duties and skills required because a given set of duties can be labeled with a great many different job titles. Don't skim job listings by title—take the time to read the duties and you may find that you're qualified for some positions you didn't expect.

Psychology majors obtain jobs that require human service skills (also known as people skills, the ability to communicate effectively with others) and research and information skills (the ability to identify problems and locate, analyze, and apply information to solve problems). All jobs entail both types of skills but in differing degrees. Your career options are varied if you think creatively and focus on your skills. As you look for a position, remember that many people do not understand psychology. It is your responsibility to educate employers about how your degree has prepared you for a position with their organization or company. Next are some of the settings that employ psychology majors, organized by the degree they emphasize research skills and human service skills, but remember that all jobs tap both sets of competencies.

Job Settings That Emphasize Research and Information Management Skills

The particular research-oriented skills valued by employers vary by setting, employer, and experience level. Research and information-related tasks include administrative work and data collection, entry, analysis, interpretation and dissemination. Conceptualize the term *data*, broadly as it includes more than the quantitative data you might enter into a statistics program like SPSS. Data refers to information. Employers look for employees who can manipulate, interpret, and apply information. Many employment settings emphasize research and information management skills and employers tend to view liberal arts majors, and especially psychology majors, favorably (McGovern & Carr, 1989). Graduates who obtain positions in business work in human resources departments, public relations, retail, advertising, and other positions.

Public Relations Public relations professionals work in businesses, government, universities, hospitals, schools, and other organizations to build and maintain positive relationships with the public. An entry-level position usually entails assisting a public relations professional work to improve their organization's communication with the community; with consumer, employee, and public interest groups; and with the media. Part of the job entails informing the community and media about an organization's policies, activities, and accomplishments; but public relations specialists also must keep an organization's management and administrative personnel aware of the attitudes and concerns of the public and special interest groups. Public relations work is information-laden in the sense that it entails gathering information about how a client, organization, or product is perceived, using it to craft a message, and then gather data to determine the effectiveness of the communication. Public relations activities include setting up speaking engagements for management, helping to prepare speeches, and assisting in planning conferences and presentations. Titles include public relations specialist, information officer, press secretary, communications specialist, public affairs specialist, and others. Entry-level titles are often labeled as *assistant*.

Advertising and Marketing There are many different kinds of entry-level positions in advertising. Assistant account coordinators work in the account management department, which identifies and solicits new clients, and ensures that clients' advertising needs are met. Assistant media planners work in the media department, which places ads; they study what people read and watch in order to determine where to place advertising, and then attempt to place the right ad at the right time to reach the intended audience. Assistant media buyers help media buyers secure ad time and space and ensure that the advertisements appear as planned and in line with the intended budget. There are also many administrative positions within advertising firms. Market research assistants work on teams to collect data about a product in order to advertise it more effectively.

Administrative Assistant Administrative assistants engage in office management functions and support executive staff in a variety of ways. Activities include word processing, scheduling meetings and appointments, maintaining files, and sitting in on meetings. They may conduct research to support a particular project, manage databases, create reports, and oversee projects. In addition to coordinating administrative and information management activities within an office, many administrative assistants train and orient new staff. The responsibilities vary with the employer, setting, and employee competencies. Employees who are capable, motivated, and take initiative are likely to be awarded greater responsibility and challenge.

Computer Support and Information Technology A computer support specialist provides technical assistance to users of hardware, software, and computer systems, acting as a troubleshooter who interprets problems and provides technical support for hardware, software, and systems. Technical support specialists are employed by companies to help employees solve computer-related problems. They respond to inquiries from users, diagnose and solve problems, and may install, modify, clean, and repair computer hardware and software. Help desk technicians answer telephone calls and e-mail inquiries from customers seeking technical assistance for a given hardware or software product. They help users by listening, asking questions to diagnose the problem, and walking the user through steps to solve the problem. Many companies consult help desk technicians about customers' experiences with the product, what gives them the most trouble, and other customer concerns.

Job Settings That Emphasize Human Service Skills

Make no mistake, people skills are a part of every job. That said, some jobs require more contact with people and more interpersonal skills than others.

Retail Management The retail sector is a large and important part of the U.S. economy. Retail sales workers sell goods, provide customer service, and help buyers make informed purchases. Bachelor's degree holders are often hired as managers (often first as assistant managers). For example, many large retail stores have management training programs in which a worker learns about all aspects of the business and is then placed as an assistant manager or store manager. An understanding of consumer behavior is important in order to deliver the appropriate sale techniques to achieve success. Managers are responsible for managing the activity of part or all of a store, including managing staff, tracking inventory, marketing products, devising techniques to attract customers, and promoting sales and good customer relations.

Human Resources Careers in human resources focus on helping employers work with their employees. Human resources positions encompass many titles (personnel administrator, employment specialist, human resources coordinator/specialist/manager, affirmative action coordinator, employee relations manager) and serve various functions: employment and placement, wage and salary administration, training and development, benefits administration, research and information management. For example, human resources personnel work to attract the most qualified employees, match them to the jobs for which they are best suited, and help them to succeed in their jobs. Activities include recruiting and interviewing potential employees, training and development of workers to help them develop and enhance their morale and performance, organization development (helping companies and businesses deal with change), and career development (helping employees manage their careers). Human resources personnel often collect applications and resumes for jobs, assemble applicant files, perform background checks, orient new employees, educate employees about salary and benefits, and assess departmental needs for staffing. Entry-level positions often include the title *assistant* and the duties typically involve assisting a more senior human resources professional. Human resources positions involve not only working with people but also a great deal of paperwork and information management; accurate record keeping about employment salary and benefits is essential to the work of human resources personnel.

Human Services This category of positions includes various job titles, such as social services worker, program coordinator, case management worker, social work assistant, community support worker, alcohol and substance abuse counselor, mental health worker, community outreach worker, life skill counselor, child care worker, and gerontology aide. Each of these positions entails working closely with clients and providing direct and indirect services to clients. Typical duties include assessing clients' needs and eligibility for services, helping clients obtain services (such as food stamps, Medicaid, and other human services programs), and providing emotional support. Some prepare and conduct lessons and educational programs to teach about risks to health. In communities, group homes, or government-supported housing programs, human services workers assist clients in need of counseling, assist adults with daily living skills, and organize group activities. Advancement, additional opportunities, and pay raises come with experience and/or a master's degree.

Law Enforcement Psychology majors may work in law enforcement settings in administrative roles. They also work in direct contact with law offenders. Parole officer, probation officer, juvenile correctional officer, and correctional casework specialist are examples of titles for workers who provide services to offenders in custody or on probation or parole. Entry-level positions might carry the term *assistant*. These workers make recommendations and work with others to carry out release plans and monitor educational and employment stipulations. Police officers have lots of contact with the public—people skills are an essential part of a successful officer's tool box. Typical activities of police officers include: maintaining regular patrols, responding to calls for service, directing traffic as needed, investigating a crime scene, or providing first aid to an accident victim. As an officer is promoted through the ranks he or she takes on more leadership responsibilities, for example, to a position as detective with a primary responsibility of investigating crime scenes. Skills in observation, attention to detail, and critical thinking—all part of the psychology major's repertoire make for successful police officers.

Each of the careers we have discussed requires both research and people skills, to varying degrees. Each entails a different set of duties that tap competences that psychology majors develop. What can you expect to earn with your bachelor's degree? In 2012 the median of salary earnings of all bachelor's degree holders, regardless of experience was about $58,000 (National Center for Education Statistics, 2014). The average starting salary for bachelor's degree recipients in 2013 was $45,000 (National Association of Colleges and Employers, 2014b). The average starting salaries for psychology majors of the class 2013 was $38,000 (National Association of Colleges and Employers, 2014b). Salaries vary by occupation, region, and experience. Generally speaking, graduates employed in business settings, including human resources, advertising, and marketing, tend to earn higher median entry-level salaries than do graduates employed in human service settings. According to Salary.com, the highest median 2014 entry-level salaries were in retail management ($48,000), law enforcement (parole officer: $49,000 and police officer: $46,000), human resources ($47,000), and public relations ($43,000), followed by administrative assistant ($36,000), case worker ($36,000), community outreach worker ($32,000), and human services worker ($25,000).

Learning about Careers

The U.S. federal government recognizes nearly 1,000 different occupations. How many can you name? How do you learn about these opportunities? Your first stop is the *Occupational Outlook Handbook*, published by U.S. Department of Labor and available online as a searchable database: http://www.bls.gov/ooh/. The *Occupational Outlook Handbook* provides information about hundreds of careers. Details include training, job outlook, wages, related careers, and websites to help you explore further. The *Occupational Outlook Handbook* can help you identify job titles that you can Google to learn more about.

The U.S. Department of Labor also sponsors a search tool for career exploration and job analysis: O*NET OnLine (http://www.onetonline.org/). O*NET includes much of the information from the *Occupational Outlook Handbook* as well as information on key attributes of workers. Most notably, job seekers can search for jobs by skills, interests, knowledge, and other factors. Finally, America's Career InfoNet is the place to look for occupation and industry information, such as industry profiles and labor market data by state. It also includes career exploration tools, career videos, education resources, self-assessment tools, career exploration assistance, and more.

EXERCISE 7.2

*Using O*NET and the* Occupational Outlook Handbook *to Identify Careers*

This exercise requires that you run several O*NET searches to identify jobs that match your interests and capabilities. Specifically:

1. Search by interest. Use the advanced tab on O*NET to search by interests. Note that the interests listed are Holland Codes (see your responses in Chapter 2 to view your specific interests). List two occupations that you find interesting.
2. Search by skills: Use the advanced tab to search by skills. List two occupations that you find interesting.
3. Search by another criterion: Use another search option under the advanced tab (e.g., abilities, knowledge, work activities). Discuss the option you chose and list two resulting occupations.
4. Choose two of the six occupations that you have identified in this exercise. Look up the two occupations in the *Occupational Outlook Handbook*. For each, answer:
   a. What duties are performed in this occupation?
   b. What education or training is needed?
   c. What is the typical salary?
   d. What is the projected job outlook for this occupation?

There is a great deal of information about careers and career exploration on the Internet. Googling specific job titles can help you learn about employers who hire workers, required education or experience needed, and even information about typical salaries. Exercise 7.3 prompts you to use the Internet to locate information about a career of interest.

EXERCISE 7.3
Career Research

Choose a career that you would like to learn more about. This exercise helps you to take a very close look at an occupation.

1. What career did you choose?
2. Describe the nature of the work.
   a. List at least three job duties or work tasks performed in this occupation.
   b. What kind of work would someone be doing if he or she was hired as a college graduate with no prior experience in this field?
   c. What other occupations are related to this job?
3. Training/licensing/certification and other qualifications
   a. What is the lowest level of education needed for entry into this occupation?
   b. What is the most desirable education level?
   c. Is special licensing or certification required? If so, please explain.
   d. Which major(s) courses of study or training are most desirable?
   e. What kinds of skills are needed? Please be as specific as possible.
   f. Does this occupation have specific physical requirements and/or desirable personal traits (friendliness, patience, etc.)? If so, please describe them.
4. Advancement and job outlook
   a. What are the opportunities for advancement in this job?
   b. What is the turnover rate for employees in this occupation?
   c. List at least three kinds of organizations that employ people in this occupation.
   d. What is the projected employment outlook for this occupation?
5. Salary benefits
   a. What is the potential salary range for this occupation?
   b. What other benefits are generally associated with this job?

ACQUIRE USEFUL SKILLS

As you've seen, the psychology major is quite useful with its blend of liberal arts and science, but you cannot rest on your laurels. Regardless of your major, obtaining a job and entering a career requires preparation and planning, and this is especially true in difficult economies. To enhance your marketability and help your psychology education work for you, you must plan your career goals. Thinking ahead can be difficult but try to imagine your ideal self a few years from now. The counseling center or career development center at your school can help you to select your goals through personality, ability, and vocational interest assessments and counseling. The career development center may also offer alumni contacts who can tell you about their experiences and offer advice. As you consider career paths, complete Exercise 7.4 to learn more about your fit to careers and to plan your education.

Real Tips for Real Students
Put Your Electives to Good Use

Elective courses are a way to help you to develop the knowledge and skills that you will need to succeed in your chosen career. Choose your elective courses wisely to demonstrate that you are a person who knows what you want to do and who has made wise choices in preparation of that goal. For example, if you were considering a career working with juvenile offenders, appropriate electives might include classes in the departments of criminal justice, sociology, social work, public policy, communications, human development, anthropology (e.g., ethnic identity, social and cultural behavior, urban anthropology), and English (e.g., literature for adolescents).

Exercise 7.4
Good Preparation Takes Planning

1. Identify one (or two) specific occupations for which you are preparing.
   a. What is the work environment of a person employed in this area (e.g., workload, hours, deadlines, travel)?
   b. Why is this occupation a good fit for you in terms of your characteristics, skills, interests, abilities, and values (refer back to Chapter 2)?
   c. How much and what kind of education will you need for this career?
2. Examine the university course catalog and the materials that the psychology department provides to its majors at your school. What skills can you develop if you take full advantage of these opportunities during your undergraduate years?
3. What electives should you choose to prepare yourself for your chosen career?
4. Identify opportunities for outside-of-class experience, through research, internships, or work experience. The psychology department course catalog and website, your advisor, and the career services office at your school can provide assistance with this task.

a. Describe the activity.
b. When do you make contact and who do you contact?
c. How will this experience enhance your education? What will you learn? What skills will you gain? What are the outcomes of this experience?

After you've considered where you'd like to be, that is, your ultimate career goal, take a few elective courses outside of psychology that are specific to your goals. For example, if you plan to enter the business world, a course in management or accounting certainly wouldn't hurt. If you would like a job in human services, take courses in social work, communication, criminal justice, sociology, or anthropology. Regardless of your career plans, classes and experiences that enhance your communications skills (e.g., courses in writing, speech, and communications; writing for the campus newspaper) are a good investment because employers view communication skills favorably (National Association of Colleges and Employers, 2014a). Consider learning a language; Spanish is useful in all settings. Depending on your career goals, a minor or even double major can offer additional preparation. For example, students interested in human resource careers might consider a business minor while those interested in law enforcement might consider a minor in justice and law administration. One survey of graduates with bachelor's degrees in psychology found that the happiest and most successful graduates took coursework in a field related to their career—especially a minor or double major (Landrum, 2009). However, weigh the costs and benefits of a double major or minor given your situation. If it delays your graduation, can you afford the additional time and money to complete a double major?

Seek research experience by assisting professors with their research or by developing an independent research project. Research experience demonstrates your ability to work independently and sharpens your analytic and critical thinking skills. It also provides employers with evidence of your motivation, initiative, and willingness to go beyond basic requirements.

Secure an internship or practicum for hands-on experience. Internships provide wonderful opportunities for learning and training that you can use later. Another advantage of an internship is that it lets you sample a potential career. Do you really want to work with people? Your internship experiences may surprise you. The career center at your school can place you with an internship that provides valuable hands-on experience. In addition, internships can lead to contacts in the field, a possible offer for paid employment after graduation, and someone who can provide a reference or recommendation based on your ability to apply your knowledge of psychology in a real-world setting. In addition to, or in place of, an internship, seek work experience. There are plenty of part-time and summer jobs that allow you to hone your interpersonal skills and try out potential careers.

Extracurricular activities can help you develop useful skills and enhance your marketability. Similar to internships and work experience, extracurricular activities can give you opportunities to test career paths, develop contacts, and work on your communication skills. In addition, employers value volunteer work for campus and community organizations because it shows that you're a good citizen. Extracurricular participation gives employers evidence about your leadership skills, your ability to work effectively in a group, and your initiative and motivation. Finally, be open to new possibilities. Flexibility is an important life skill; it is critical to coping and optimal development throughout adulthood. Employers also rate adaptability as highly desired in new employees (National Association of Colleges and Employers, 2000). Keep an open mind and explore multiple possibilities to find a job that you'll love.

Suggested Readings

Appleby, D. C., Millspaugh, B. S., & Hammersley, M. J. (2011). *An online resource to enable undergraduate psychology majors to identify and investigate 172 psychology and psychology-related careers.* Office of Teaching Resources in Psychology. http://teachpsych.org/Resources/Documents/otrp/resources/appleby14.pdf

Landrum, R. E. & Davis, S. F. (2013). *The psychology major: Career options and strategies for success.* New York: Pearson.

Kuther, T. L. & Morgan, R. D. (2010). *Careers in psychology: Opportunities in a changing world*. Belmont, CA: Wadsworth.

Morgan, B. L. & Korschgen, A. J. (2009). *Majoring in psych? Career options for psychology undergraduates.* Needham Heights, MA: Allyn and Bacon.

Rajecki, D. W. (2012). Psychology baccalaureates at work: Major area subspecializations, earnings, and occupations. *Teaching of Psychology*, 39(3), 185–189.

Internet Resources (Available at http://www.tarakuther.com)

Occupational Outlook Handbook

http://www.bls.gov/OCO/

Provides national data on a variety of careers in order to assist individuals making decisions about their careers. It is revised every two years.

Occupational Information Network Resource Center

http://www.onetcenter.org/

Administered and sponsored by the U.S. Department of Labor's Employment and Training Administration, this site contains career exploration tools, testing and assessment guides, occupational listings, and more.

Careers in Psychology

http://www.psywww.com/careers/index.htm

Dr. Margaret Lloyd's website discusses entry-level and graduate-level careers in psychology, as well as how to prepare for them.

Pursuing Psychology Career Page

http://www.uni.edu/walsh/linda1.html

Dr. Linda Weber provides a list of links to excellent materials on career development and resources for psychology majors.

Descriptions of Occupations of Interest to Psychology Majors from the Dictionary of Occupational Titles

http://www.uni.edu/walsh/DOTdescrips.htm

Dr. Drew Appleby's list of over 100 occupations that psychology majors can pursue and links to the descriptions of these occupations U.S. Department of Labor's *Dictionary of Occupational Titles (DOT).*

Salary.com

Salary information for all fields, searchable by education and experience. Relevant job ads accompany each search.

Reflection Prompts

Part-Time Jobs

When considering their experience, all too often students dismiss their part-time jobs. What jobs have you had? What duties did each entail? What did you do? What skills did you use to complete the job? What did you like about it? Dislike? What did you learn from each job?

What's Not for You?

Part of figuring out a career path is figuring out what you don't want to do. Describe one or two careers that you know are not for you. What are they? What do they do? Why aren't they for you? How do you know?

My Strengths and Weaknesses

Consider the skills that a liberal arts degree builds as well as the skills employers seek. Identify your strengths. What do you do well? What do you enjoy? What are your weaknesses? How do you feel about your weaknesses? How might you strengthen these areas?

Considering Life after College

Taking classes, studying for exams, writing papers—sometimes students forget to think about the big picture. By now you likely have thought about what you would like to do after graduation. Now consider how your postgraduation life will differ from your present experience. How will you spend your time? Is there anything about college that you will miss? What won't you miss? Transitions from one phase of life to another, like from college to work, are exciting but also stressful. What can you do now to prepare? What types of activities might ease your transition to work?

Finding a Job with Your Bachelor's Degree

Chapter 8

Chapter Outline

As the saying goes, "time flies when you're having fun." Before you know it, graduation will be here. If you've decided to seek employment with your bachelor's degree, start planning early and hone your job seeking skills. This chapter discusses how to find a job with your bachelor's degree, including where to look, how to construct a résumé, the importance of cover letters, interviewing, and more.

Applying for Jobs

The first stop on your job search should be the career services office at your college, where you'll find skilled professionals who can help you with all aspects of the job search. Career services offices have a variety of resources for locating available positions, including books, databases, and lists of employers who have contacted them seeking to employ college students and recent graduates.

Where to Look for Jobs

There are several places to look for job advertisements. Job ads are often posted in local newspapers; most maintain searchable online databases of job ads. Job search sites permit job hunters to comprehensively search the job market. Some examples of job search sites include:

- Careerbuilder.com
- Idealist.org (for nonprofit jobs and volunteer opportunities)
- Indeed.com
- Monster.com
- Simplyhired.com
- USAJobs.gov (for government jobs)

Contact the human resources department of major businesses, corporations, and agencies in your area to inquire about job openings. Many businesses and organizations advertise jobs on their webpages, typically linked from the Human Resources webpage.

Use Your Network

Remember the most important job-hunting resource of all: You! Applicants commonly overlook their own personal networks when scouting for available positions. Through school, friends (and their parents), part-time jobs, and internships, you've already made many connections. Tap into these professional connections. If you've completed an internship or practicum, you may already have a foot in the door and a potential employer has already had a peek at your work habits. Even if the organization where you did your internship is not hiring additional staff, your supervisor probably has outside contacts. Tap into your personal connections to locate job openings because most jobs are not advertised in newspapers or other ads. You can learn about these unadvertised positions only by word of mouth. Networking—establishing connections—will help you to become more knowledgeable about positions within the hidden job market.

Job Applications

As you apply for jobs you'll find that many employers require applicants to complete a job application form or even a large packet of forms. Take care in completing job applications because they reveal a great deal about you. Your job application tells potential employers about your work habits, your ability to follow instructions, your personality and character, your personal achievements and job performance, and your potential to succeed (Landrum, 2009). Neatness, spelling, and grammar count, regardless of the position to which you apply. A sloppy application tells employers that they can expect carelessness and sloppiness from you. Be honest and accurate, and remember to ask the people you plan to list as references beforehand (notify them each time they are listed and, if you begin a second job search in the future, ask again). You may find that some applications include personality inventories and other kinds of psychological assessments. Be truthful. Finally, many job applications do not instruct applicants to include a résumé but you should always supplement your application with a copy of your résumé because it lists all of your relevant experiences and highlights your strengths.

EXERCISE 8.1

Deconstructing Job Ads

Conduct a search on a job search website, such as those listed at the end of this chapter. Locate one or two job ads that appeal to you.

1. What is the job?
2. What are the demographic details, such as location?
3. What are the education or experience requirements listed?
4. What skills are needed to succeed in the job? If the ad does not list them (and it likely will not), brainstorm what skills would be coveted by the employer.
5. Consider the assessments that you conducted throughout this book. What is your skill set? How does it compare with that needed for the job?
6. What skills might you improve to enhance your fit to the job?
7. How would you sell yourself to the employer?

SOCIAL MEDIA AND YOUR JOB HUNT

The last decade has witnessed a major shift in how people interact with each other. Social media sites, such as Facebook, Twitter, Instagram, Pinterest, and Vine, have made it possible to share your experiences and thoughts with others with one text or status update. Social media makes it possible to quickly connect with everyone you know, but, often, also with people you don't know, such as potential employers. Your activities on social media can help you find and win jobs—but it can also cost you jobs. Social media is particularly valuable when it comes to meeting people.

Use LinkedIn to Expand Your Professional Network

It is never too early to work on developing a professional network. The Internet makes it easier than ever to create a professional persona and develop useful contacts that will influence your career. The largest and most popular social networking site for professionals is Linkedin.com. A basic account is free and permits you to access a great deal of information to aid your job hunt and professional development. You can search for companies, research professionals in companies, make contact with and ask professionals relevant questions, and find communities of students and professionals who share your interests in psychology.

To establish a presence on LinkedIn you must create a concise, professional profile. It should state your skills, accomplishments, education, and career goals. Use the information in your résumé to prepare your LinkedIn profile (more on the résumé later in this chapter). Unlike your résumé, a LinkedIn profile contains a headshot photo. Most people prefer to connect with a face and so a photo is an important addition to your profile. However be sure that it is appropriate and professional.

After you have created your profile, proofread it carefully, and when ready for the world to see it, adjust the privacy settings to "Public" on your profile. Now your profile will show up in search results. Take great care in preparing your profile as employers will see this before they see you. A poor profile can hurt your search more than a good profile can help.

You're not taking full advantage of LinkedIn if all you do is post a profile. The purpose of LinkedIn is to establish connections or links with others—especially people at companies where you want to work. When you view a profile you can determine if you know any people in common or if you are connected through second degree relationships (such as you share a friend of a friend in common). Make the most out of LinkedIn by joining LinkedIn groups or communities. There are more than 200,000 groups. Consider joining college and alumni groups and search for psychology-related groups. Examples of psychology-related groups include: The Psychology Network (141,000 members), Psychology Students Network (41,000 members), and Psi Chi (8,200 members).

Employers Will Google You

Not all employers Google potential employees, but you can never be sure. No way to tell whether an employer will run your name through an Internet search engine—and no way to know if he or she has. Why Google applicants? Hiring an employee is a big deal. Employers invest money and time into the process and expect to hire an employee who is mature, responsible, and reliable. Applicants must be deemed trustworthy and capable of handling an employer's valuable business. In prior decades, employers relied only on interviews and references. Today, applicants freely share much about themselves online that can influence an employer's hiring decision. A quick Internet search can reveal posts and photos on social media sites that can sway an employer against an applicant. Social media profiles and posts likely won't boost your application, unprofessional profiles that suggest poor judgment can send an employer packing. Table 8.1 illustrates what might turn off employers.

TABLE 8.1

Social Media Mistakes

Information on a social media profile that can prompt an employer to eliminate a candidate:

- ❑ Provocative or inappropriate photographs or information
- ❑ Information about them drinking or drug use
- ❑ Bad-mouthing employers or colleagues
- ❑ Poor grammar, poor spelling, and texting/illiterate language
- ❑ Discriminatory comments related to race, gender, religion, etc.
- ❑ Lying about qualifications
- ❑ Sharing confidential information from previous employers
- ❑ Criminal behavior
- ❑ Unprofessional screen name

Source: Career Builder, 2014

Exercise 8.2

Become Aware of Your Digital Footprint

It is in your best interest to review your online presence and determine if you are portrayed well.

1. Google yourself. Then use Bing and Yahoo. Enter the search terms you used. Try enclosing your name in quotation marks to search your exact name.
2. How many results did you find? Do they refer to you?
3. Is the first page of results flattering? Is it the message that you want to send?
4. What, if anything, would you like to change? How might you go about changing the information?

Exercise 8.3

Analyze Your Social Media Accounts

Take a critical look at your Facebook profile from the perspective of an employer. Consider:

- Are there any photos that might be interpreted poorly?
- Are your posts grammatically correct?
- Is the content of your posts neutral or positive?
- Do you avoid commenting about drugs or alcohol?
- Do you know all of your Facebook friends?
- Are your privacy settings private? Can only friends view your material? Is your profile set to private? But remember that nothing is every truly private on the Internet. Don't rest on your laurels.

1. Discuss your observations. What changes will you make to improve your profile?
2. Review your Twitter account. Discuss the results.
3. Review your Instagram account. Discuss the results.
4. Review your Pinterest account. Discuss the results.
5. Do you have other social media accounts? Try this exercise again and discuss your findings.

Scrub Your Social Media Accounts

Untag or, preferably, remove drunken party photos and any other photos that portray you in a negative light. As you review photos think about whether an employer would want the person in the photo as an employee. Look at the content of your wall on Facebook and messages on Twitter. Any particularly negative status updates? Do you trash any faculty or schools? Any comments that might be construed as racist, sexist, homophobic? Profanity? Sarcastic comments and jokes that your friends know are flippant remarks likely won't be taken as such by employers.

Maintain an Appropriate Profile Photo. Even if you set your privacy settings high your name and profile photo may still be visible. Make sure that your profile photo is what you want professors and admissions committees to see.

Filter your Friends. It's not uncommon for individuals to have 1,000 or more "friends." Consider restricting your friends to people you actually know.

Restrict Public Search. Make it difficult for people to find your Facebook profile by going private and making their profiles visible to "friends only." Some applicants change their profile name (such as by using their middle name as last name). Others deactivate their accounts altogether. I don't think it's necessary to deactivate your account as there is no need for paranoia, but restricting public search is a good idea. However, remember that setting a profile to private is not a guarantee. Students sometimes worry that employers will think that an applicant has something to hide when his or her Facebook or other profile is private. On the contrary, a private profile is a sign of maturity. It shows that you recognize a separation between your professional and private life. Moreover, be cautious about what you post online and recognize that even the tightest privacy settings can fail. Make sure that your online profiles reflect you as you'd like admissions committees to see you. Then try these other tips for managing your digital footprint as you apply to grad school.

Prepare to Be Googled: Create Your Ideal Self

Rather than focus only on cleaning up your social media profiles, be proactive. Create the digital profile that depicts the ideal you—how you want to be portrayed. Use your social media presence to show your expertise in a given subject. Tailor your profile to demonstrate your passion. LinkedIn is particularly useful for self-promotion as it is essentially a social résumé. Unlike other social media, keep your LinkedIn profile visible to the public. If you use Twitter, post professional tweets about your interests. Likewise for Instagram and Pinterest. Your profiles don't have to be limited to professorial interactions—they're personal accounts—but before posting personal material, consider how a potential employer might interpret it.

Your online reputation follows you and is hard to erase. Control what you put online to ensure that the best possible—most professional—self is portrayed. You can never be sure whether an employer will review your digital reputation, but always a good idea to put your best foot forward.

PREPARE YOUR RÉSUMÉ

A résumé is a summary of your educational history, work experience, and career objectives. Employers always expect to see a résumé (even if it isn't stated in the advertisement). As you prepare your résumé, remember that it often is the only impression that an employer has of you. It is a chance to present your strengths, to communicate that you have valuable skills, and to emphasize the aspects of your educational and employment background that make you unique. A résumé is your ticket through the door; its purpose is to convince an employer to interview you, but most employers glance at a résumé for only twenty to thirty seconds (Krannich, 2005). If the initial scan of your résumé doesn't catch the employer's attention, the opportunity is lost. How do you make it past the twenty-second test?

Consider the main question that employers ask themselves as they read résumés: Why should I learn more about this applicant? Keep this question in mind as you prepare your résumé, answer it, and you'll have a unique résumé that will get you to the next stage of the job hunt. Before you write, reevaluate your skills and abilities in light of employer preferences. Review the top qualities employers prefer in Chapter 7 as well as your responses to the self-assessments in Chapter 2. Outline your skills and abilities as well as your work experience and extracurricular activities to make it easier to prepare a thorough résumé. Highlight your strengths. Writing a résumé may seem overwhelming, but you'll soon see that it is a simple matter of showcasing your skills.

Parts of the Résumé

There are several ways of formatting résumés but all include the same type of information: contact, education, and experience (and related skills). In recent years, a qualifications summary statement has become an important part of the résumé.

Heading/Contact Information All of your contact information should go at the top of your résumé. Include your name, permanent address (this is particularly important if you live on campus and are moving home after graduation), phone (with area code), and e-mail. If you're graduating college soon think twice about using your university e-mail as some graduates lose access to university e-mail soon after graduating. Use a professional e-mail address rather than a fun, personal e-mail address (silly usernames such as "Butterfly-girl," "Temptress," or "JediMaster," are unprofessional and send the message that you are not ready for hiring). If possible, use your name as your e-mail address and choose a provider that will be around for years to come, such as Gmail, Yahoo, or Outlook. Include your website or blog only if the content reflects your professional ambitions.

Education Report the name of the degree that you received or will receive (AS, BS, BA, etc.), institution name and address, month and year of graduation, major, minor/concentration, grade point average (only if it is higher than 3.0), and academic honors, if applicable.

Experience Discuss your work experience. List your most recent job first and work your way backward. For each job, indicate the position title, company or organization name, address, and dates of employment. Include all relevant employment experiences: part-time, internships, cooperative education, or self-employment. Recruiters are interested in the skills that you've developed, not whether or how much you were paid. Experiences also include activities that are relevant to the objective stated on your résumé. Include activities and awards only if they are significant experiences that speak to your capacities as an employee (such as leadership experience). If you can draw a valid connection between your professional goal and the activity, keep it in. If not, take it out. For each position, briefly describe your duties and responsibilities as they relate to the position you are seeking, and emphasize specific skills and achievements. Use active words to describe your duties and the results that you produced. Table 8.2 provides a list of action verbs to help you construct this section of your résumé.

Summary of Qualifications The qualifications summary is an important contribution to a résumé. It contains an overview of your major qualifications—what you want the employer to remember about you. Remember the thirty-second rule: Your résumé often has only thirty seconds to get noticed. Place the most important and relevant information first. State your best qualifications simply and concisely. A sample chronological résumé appears in Table 8.2.

TABLE 8.2

ACTION VERBS TO SPICE UP YOUR RÉSUMÉ

Achieved	Conducted	Financed	Marketed	Reinforced
Acquired	Consolidated	Formulated	Measured	Repaired
Acted	Constructed	Gathered	Met	Represented
Adapted	Consulted	Generated	Modified	Researched
Administered	Contributed	Guided	Monitored	Resolved
Advised	Controlled	Handled	Motivated	Reviewed
Allocated	Counseled	Headed	Obtained	Revised
Analyzed	Created	Helped	Operated	Scheduled
Applied	Coordinated	Identified	Organized	Served
Arranged	Decided	Illustrated	Oversaw	Showed
Assembled	Decreased	Implemented	Planned	Simplified
Assessed	Defined	Improved	Predicted	Sketched
Assisted	Demonstrated	Improvised	Prepared	Sold
Attained	Designed	Increased	Presented	Solved
Averted	Determined	Increased	Processed	Staffed
Balanced	Developed	Informed	Produced	Streamlined
Briefed	Directed	Initiated	Devised	Studied
Budgeted	Discovered	Innovated	Diagnosed	Submitted
Built	Documented	Installed	Negotiated	Summarized
Calculated	Drafted	Instituted	Observed	Supervised
Clarified	Earned	Instructed	Participated	Supported
Classified	Edited	Integrated	Performed	Synthesized
Coached	Eliminated	Converted	Persuaded	Systematized
Collaborated	Empowered	Integrated	Planned	Tabulated
Collected	Encouraged	Interpreted	Projected	Taught
Communicated	Enforced	Introduced	Proposed	Tested
Compared	Ensured	Invented	Qualified	Trained
Compiled	Established	Investigated	Quantified	Translated
Completed	Estimated	Learned	Questioned	Undertook
Composed	Evaluated	Lectured	Realized	Updated
Computed	Examined	Led	Received	Utilized
Conceptualized	Expanded	Maintained	Recommended	Verified
Condensed	Expedited	Managed	Recorded	Wrote
Conducted	Facilitated	Mapped	Reduced	

Adapted from: Appleby, 1997; DeGalan & Lambert, 1995; Lock, 1988

Types of Résumés

Résumés can be categorized into at least two types. The *chronological résumé* is organized by position or job. All jobs are listed in reverse chronological order starting with the most recent. Duties and skills are highlighted within each work experience. Table 8.3 illustrates the chronological résumé. Chronological résumés are challenging when a job seeker has little experience. The *functional résumé* is a good option for recent graduates as it is organized by skills and competencies, regardless of when they were obtained. Each skill is listed and the work experience and duties are discussed within. The material that appears first in a résumé tends to get the most attention. Consider that an employer may review a résumé for only about thirty seconds and a functional résumé makes sense. Table 8.4 illustrates a functional résumé.

TABLE 8.3

Chronological Résumé

Christine L. Pimentel

9713 Union • Street San Francisco, California 94109 • (415) 714-8642 • pime14@yahoo.com

Personal Profile

Motivated, high-energy CAL Berkeley graduate desires opportunity to affiliate with firm that can benefit from demonstrated success providing *administrative, research*, and *marketing* support within client-focused organizations. Especially competent in settings requiring *strong project coordination, presentation*, and *communication skills*. Considered by former employers as *self-managed, well-organized*, and *detail-oriented* with an *effective balance of task - and people-oriented skills*.

Education

Bachelor of Arts Degree in Psychology (GPA 3.3) **2008**
UNIVERSITY OF CALIFORNIA, BERKELEY

Activities:

- "Service for Sight" and "Foundation Fighting Blindness," Volunteer
- "Sports for Kids," Volunteer engaged in tutoring elementary students
- Member, Delta Gamma Fraternity – Vice President and Director of Alumni Relations

Honors:

- Recipient, California Alumni Scholarship Award for Excellence in Leadership

Experience

RESEARCH/PROJECT COORDINATION: Utilized analytical and critical thinking abilities while supporting and working collaboratively with consulting firm's legal team and financial analysis.

- Performed detailed research required in massive corporate (PG&E) bankruptcy case while employed by San Francisco consulting firm.
- Analyzed databases, files, and coded maps for California counties while collaborating with former PG&E engineers to ensure all debts have been cleared prior to PG&E emerging from bankruptcy.

INTERPERSONAL/COMMUNICATION: Effectively communicated with managers, decision-makers, and clients in sales and support roles.

- Participated in developing marketing strategies, including redefining image and promotion of special events for newly renovated on-campus restaurant.
- Assisted manager in preparing regional sales presentations and worked cohesively with commission on sales team for major fashion retailer.

ORGANIZATION/ADMINISTRATION: Good writing, editing, and proofreading skills for accurate business correspondence, proposals, and reports.

- Performed administrative responsibilities and prepared claims for Central California insurance firm.

TECHNICAL SKILLS: Proficient in Microsoft Word, Excel, PowerPoint, and Access; spreadsheet development and industry-specific database software experience.

Employment summary

Administrative Assistant, Gonzales Consulting, San Francisco, California **10/07 – 2/08**
Customer Service/Server, Bears Lair Restaurant, University of California, Berkeley **4/06 – 6/07**
Sales Associate, Nordstrom, Walnut Creek, California **5/05 – 7/06**
Assistant Claims Examiner, Grover Insurance Company, Clovis, California **Summer, 2004**

Source: From Eischen, C. W. & Eischen, L. A. (2010). *Résumés, cover letters, networking, and interviewing*, 3rd ed. Belmont, CA: Cengage.

TABLE 8.4 **Functional Résumé**

PHILLIP H. MOSS

75 Bernard Drive West
Santa Cruz, California 93710
(831) 831-3333

COMMUNITY ACTIVIST • PROJECT MANAGER • TECHNOLOGY COORDINATOR

Talented, bilingual young professional with BA Degree in Economics and Latin America/ Latino Studies, plus experience organizing and coordinating UFW research projects in Central California. Seeking career opportunity where skills and dedication can promote social change and enhance individuals' lives. Possess experience in project organization and coordination, grant writing, developing multimedia presentations, research, and writing using advanced technology and Internet resources, network administration, and web design.

Community Activism/Project Management

- Coordinated UCSC Global Information Internship Program (GIIP), placing university students (35) in community service organizations domestically and internationally. Designed curriculum and taught information technology to GIIP interns.
- Devised, researched, and implemented program to provide technology to enhance the research and networking capabilities of the UFW offices in the Watsonville, Delano, and other California sites. This entailed training staff on software and hardware applications. Placed 6 interns with UFW.
- Organized successful food drive at University of California, Santa Cruz, which produced in excess of 1,000 food items for unemployed migrant workers in the Central Coast area.
- Presently place interns with Pacific Community Advocacy Group – program is dedicated to improving housing, health, and community services for the low-income residents within the Monterey and Salinas region.

Technology Coordinator Activities

- Provided technical knowledge in setting up multi-station network for several UFW offices within Central California. In addition, provided software instruction for administrative staff.
- Member and Activist for Computer Professionals for Social Responsibility – a group taking an active role in refurbishing older technology to benefit community service, (not-for-profit) organizations.
- Conducted substantial research regarding technology's impetus for economic development in third-world countries. Research focused on momentum technology provides to developing economies and the institutions within these countries.
- Organized successful food drive at University of California, Santa Cruz, which produced in excess of 1,000 food items for unemployed migrant workers in the Central Coast area.

PROFESSIONAL EXPERIENCE

Technology Coordinator, UFW, Watsonville, California — **2007 & 2008**
Instructor, Center for Global, International & Regional Studies, UCSC — **2006 – 2007**
Counselor/Technology Coordinator, Society & Technology Institute, UCSC — **Summer, 2005**

EDUCATION/HONORS

Bachelor of Arts Degree in Psychology **6/2008**
University of California at Santa Cruz

Highlights: Honors Graduate and Recipient of Merrill Scholars Award Recipient of "Outstanding UCSC Student Employee of the Year" award for 2007

Source: Eischen, C. W. & Eischen, L. A. (2010). *Résumés, cover letters, networking, and interviewing*, 3rd ed. Belmont, CA: Cengage.

Exercise 8.4

Write the Experience Section for Your Chronological Résumé

This exercise will walk you through the most challenging part of the résumé: writing the experience section.

1. List all of the jobs that you have had, along with the dates of employment.
2. What did each job entail? Freewrite about your activities, responsibilities, and everything you did. What were you particularly good at? Identify achievements.
3. Condense each description into one to two sentences.
4. Identify action words to describe each job and further condense each job description into one sentence.
5. Format the experience section of your résumé.

Exercise 8.5

Write the Skill Section for Your Functional Résumé

A functional résumé is useful as it presents your skills in light of your experience. This exercise will help you to translate your experiences into skills.

Preparation

1. List skills that employers value (see Chapter 7).
2. Gather the results of Exercise 8.2, your list of jobs and duties.

Brainstorm

3. Brainstorm the skills that you used to complete the duties for each job.
4. Link each skill to one or more trait the employers value (review Table 7.1 for skills employers value).
5. Choose a main skill to describe each job.

(Continued)

EXERCISE 8.5 (Continued)

Write the Skills Section

6. Organize your skills by importance.
7. List each skill, then the place you developed it and your duties (how you developed and demonstrated it).

Real Tips for Real Students

Create a Text Résumé

Sometimes an online application will require that you cut and paste your résumé into a form or e-mail rather than attach a file. Create an electronic copy of your résumé in plain text. Remove all formatting: bold, tabs, centering, and bullets. Include straight text that will not confuse the scanner. Instead of bullet points use asterisks (*). Save your résumé as a plain text file (.txt) and cut and paste as needed.

Make your résumé as professional looking as possible. Be concise; a new graduate's résumé should be no more than one page in length. Carefully proofread your résumé, because typographical, spelling, and grammar errors are unacceptable and will cost you an interview. Print your résumé on white or off-white paper, using a laser printer. Review Table 8.5 for more résumé tips. Also note that many employers request that applicants upload electronic résumés to their website or e-mail them to the human resources department. Convert your résumé to a .pdf file so that the formatting is retained regardless of what computer system the employer uses. Appearances count, so check your résumé pdf file for errors in formatting even if the version saved in your word processing file is flawless.

TABLE 8.5 RÉSUMÉ CHECKLIST

- ❑ Clearly communicate your purpose and value.
- ❑ Communicate your strongest points first.
- ❑ Don't make statements that you can't document.
- ❑ Be direct, succinct, and expressive with language.
- ❑ Don't use lengthy sentences and descriptions; this is the only time that sentence fragments are acceptable, but use them judiciously.
- ❑ Don't use the passive voice.
- ❑ Don't change the tense of verbs throughout the résumé.

- ❑ Confine your information to one page.
- ❑ Use space to organize your résumé; it should not appear cramped.
- ❑ Aim for overall visual balance on the page.
- ❑ Use a font size of ten to fourteen points.
- ❑ Choose a simple typeface and stick to it (i.e., don't change fonts).
- ❑ Use spacing and bold for emphasis.
- ❑ Don't fold or staple your résumé.
- ❑ Check spelling, grammar, and punctuation.
- ❑ Proofread.
- ❑ Ask someone else to proofread.
- ❑ Get outside help. Get feedback from two or three people, including someone who regularly evaluates résumés and hires employees.
- ❑ Do not include your reference information on your résumé (see sample).
- ❑ Before giving their names to a potential employer, ask your references if they are willing to serve as references.

Adapted from: Appleby, 1997; DeGalan & Lambert, 1995; Krannich, 2005

EXERCISE 8.6

Construct a LinkedIn Profile

Use the information in your résumé to construct a LinkedIn profile. Specifically, create your profile on paper, first, in order to seek feedback and edit it prior to posting it. Compose text for each of the following sections:

1. Headline: Your headline is a short, memorable professional slogan.
2. Education: Include all your schools, major(s) and minor(s), courses, and study abroad or summer programs.
3. Experience: List the jobs you held, even if they were part-time, along with what you accomplished at each.
4. Organizations: List any clubs you've joined at school or outside. Describe what you did with each organization.
5. Skills and expertise: List at least five key skills.
6. Volunteer experience: Even if you weren't paid for a job, be sure to list it.
7. Honors and awards: List them.
8. Courses: List the classes that show off the skills and interests you're most excited about.
9. Summary: Concise and confident statement about your qualifications and goals, as well as aspirations.
10. Recommendations: Brainstorm who you might ask to write a recommendation.

The Cover Letter

The cover letter is an introduction to your résumé that enables you to tailor your application to the prospective employer. Your cover letter must be concise and explain what you can offer an employer. An employer might spend ten seconds scanning your cover letter—get your message out quickly and efficiently. In no more than three paragraphs, explain your interest in the position and how you can contribute to the organization. Highlight the most important aspects of your background that are relevant to the position and/or organization. Finally provide contact information (a phone number and e-mail address), thank the reader, and reiterate your interest in the position.

Remember that the cover letter is an introduction that should motivate the reader to examine your résumé. An effective cover letter is written with the needs of the audience (i.e., prospective employer) in mind. Before writing a cover letter, ask yourself, "What is the purpose of this letter? What are the needs of the reader? What benefits will an employer gain from me? How can I maintain the reader's interest? How can I end the letter persuasively, so that the reader will want to examine my résumé and contact me?" Be explicit and communicate what you can do for the employer, not what the job will do for you. Remember that this is a "free sample" of your work and indicates what the employer can expect of you. Checklist 8.2 provides tips for writing your cover letter. If you are submitting your résumé by e-mail, shorten your cover letter to simply identify the position to which you are applying and why you are a good fit (in about two to three sentences).

Real Tips for Real Students
Research Employers

As you prepare a job application do your homework to know exactly why you want to work for the employer. Tailor your materials to each employer. Employers want to hire people who are interested in them—not just those who want a job. Convey your interest in your cover letter and what you can contribute.

CHECKLIST 8.2
Cover Letter Checklist

- ❑ Address the letter to an individual, using the person's name and title. If answering a blind advertisement, use the following address: "To Whom It May Concern."
- ❑ Indicate the position for which you are applying and explain why you are qualified to fill it.

- ❑ Include a phone number and e-mail where you can be reached.
- ❑ Ask someone to proofread your letter for spelling, grammar, and punctuation errors.
- ❑ Indicate how your education and work skills are transferable and relevant to the position for which you are applying.
- ❑ Keep a copy of each cover letter for your records; write notes from any phone conversations that might occur on your copy of the cover letter.
- ❑ Make a connection with the company through a person you know, some information you've researched, or a specific interest.

Adapted from Appleby, 1997; DeGalan & Lambert, 1995; Krannich, 2005

Interview

Congratulations! If you have been asked to come for an interview, you have made it past the first round of reviews and have an opportunity to land the position. The interview is the most important criterion for hiring; it beats out grades, related work experience, and recommendations. Often second, and even third, interviews occur. The interview is your one chance to impress the prospective employer. How do you do it? Display good communication skills, clearly defined professional goals, and an honest, outgoing personality (Appleby, 1999). Interviews are stressful, but you can increase your confidence by being thoroughly prepared.

Prepare

Understand the purpose of the interview, and keep the interviewer's objectives in mind. From your perspective, the purpose of the job interview is to get a second interview or job offer; but for employers, the purpose of the job interview is to whittle down the list of applicants to one or two finalists. The interviewer is interested in answering several questions:

- Why does this person want to work for us?
- What position is this person suited for?
- What are his or her qualifications?
- Why should I hire him or her?
- Does this person meet my employment needs?
- Is he or she trustworthy?

Because many applicants apply for each position, the interviewer often looks for reasons why you should not be hired. Interviewers are interested in identifying your weaknesses. Your job is to communicate your strengths. This means that you must understand yourself, but you also must understand the company or organization to which you are applying in order to determine how to package your strengths in order to appeal to the interviewer.

Research the company. Learn as much as you can about the company and the people with whom you'll interview. What is the relative size and growth of the industry? What product lines or services are offered? Where is the headquarters? Identify the competition. Be familiar with any recent items in the news. Try to predict what will be asked during the interview, and prepare answers. Expect to be asked to identify a challenge you faced and how you overcame it. It's a difficult, but predictable, question. Think about it now and you'll be better equipped to respond during your interview. Be ready to show that you are interested and enthusiastic in the company. Exercise 8.7 presents common questions asked during interviews. You also will be judged on the questions that you ask. Ask thoughtful and intelligent questions about the company and position. Exercise 8.8 provides sample questions that an applicant might ask on an interview.

EXERCISE 8.7
Common Interview Questions

What do you hope to be doing five or ten years from now?
Why did you apply for this job?
Tell me about yourself.
What are your strengths and weaknesses?
What can you offer to us and what can we offer to you?
What are the two or three accomplishments in your life that have given you the greatest satisfaction?
Do you work well under pressure?
Have you ever held any supervisory or leadership roles?
What do you like to do in your spare time?
What other jobs are you applying for?
Is there anything else we should know about you?
Why do you feel that you will be successful in this position?
What courses did you like best? Least? Why?
What did you learn or gain from your part-time and summer job experience?
What are your plans for graduate study?
Why did you choose your major?
What can a psychology major do for this organization?
If you could do it all again, what would you change about your education?
Did you do the best you could in school? Why or why not?
Why did you leave your last employer?

What job did you like the most? The least? Why?
Have you ever been fired?
Why do you want to join our organization?
Why should we hire you?
When will you be ready to work?
What do you want to do with your life?
Do you have any actual work experience?
How would you describe your ideal job?
Are you a team player? Explain.
What motivates you?
Tell me about some of your recent goals and what you did to achieve them.
Have you ever had a conflict with a boss or professor? How did you resolve it?
If I were to ask one of your professors to describe you, what would he or she say?
Why did you choose to attend your college?
What qualities do you feel a successful manager should have?
What do you know about our company?
What kind of salary are you looking for?

Prompt:

1. Which of these questions do you find most challenging? Select three.
2. Why are they challenging?
3. Discuss how you might answer each of the questions you have identified.

Adapted from: Appleby 1997; DeGalan & Lambert, 1995; Krannich, 2005; Landrum, 2009

EXERCISE 8.8

Questions to Ask during an Interview

Tell me about the duties and responsibilities of this job.
How long has this position been in the company?
What would be the ideal type of person for this position?
What kinds of skills or personality characteristics are ideal for this position?
Whom would I be working with?
What am I expected to accomplish during the first year?
How will I be evaluated?
Are promotions and raises tied to performance criteria?
What is unique about working for this company?
What does the future look like for this company?

(Continued)

EXERCISE 8.8 (Continued)

Prompt:

1. Which of these questions is most important to you?
2. Identify two other questions that you might ask potential employers.
3. Discuss why you have selected each question.

Adapted from: Appleby, 1997; DeGalan & Lambert, 1995; Krannich, 2005

What to Wear

It may not be nice, but we are judged on our appearance. Dress appropriately for your interview because your appearance communicates messages about your level of seriousness and professionalism. During the first five minutes of an interview, interviewers make initial judgments or create expectations about your professionalism and "fit" for a position based on your appearance and demeanor. Use this to your advantage by dressing appropriately. Even if you are applying to a company with a casual dress code, dress up for the interview to communicate your enthusiasm for the position.

Whether you're a man or a woman, you can't go wrong with a basic dark suit. Some fields are more dressy than others but a simple suit and subtle accessories always work. Men should wear a white or blue oxford shirt with an understated tie. Women should wear a modest blouse, with understated hair and makeup. Keep jewelry to a minimum. Consider removing facial piercings. Err toward the side of conservative as you want to be remembered for what you say and not what you're wearing. Remember that these are merely general rules. You might want to see how others in your field dress for appropriate cues. Aim to dress for the position, wearing attire that you might wear to work, but a little bit dressier.

During the Interview

Be enthusiastic. Remember that your interviewer is committed to his or her position and the company, and wants to hire someone who is similarly committed. Demonstrate your enthusiasm by discussing what you've learned from your research and preparation. Ask questions to fill in any gaps in your understanding. Convey a sense of long-term interest by asking about opportunities for further professional education and advancement.

Throughout the interview, be aware of your body language and keep fidgeting to a minimum. Lean very slightly toward the interviewer to communicate your interest in what he or she is saying (Krannich, 2005). Maintain eye contact to convey interest and trustworthiness. Smile to convey your positive attitude. Don't forget that your tone of voice can indicate how interested you are in the interview and the organization. Here are some other helpful tips for acing interviews:

- Bring a copy of your résumé. It comes in handy if you have to fill in applications and provides initial information for your interviewer.
- Allow the interviewer to direct the conversation.
- Answer questions in a clear and positive manner.
- Never speak negatively about former employers or colleagues, no matter what.
- Let the interviewer lead the conversation toward salary and benefits. Try not to focus your interest on these issues (at least not during the initial interview).
- When discussing salary, be flexible.
- If the employer doesn't say when you'll hear about their decision, ask when you can call to follow up.
- Thank the employer for the interview.

Above all remember that employers anticipate applicants to be on their best behavior during an interview. They recognize that any perceived flaws, such as arrogance, impoliteness, or poor listening skills, will likely be more apparent when the applicant becomes an employee. Be self-aware because any negative interactions or ambivalent signals can stop your application in its tracks.

Thank-You Note

Immediately after your interview, e-mail a thank-you note and follow it up with a mailed note. Few applicants do, so you'll stand out (Appleby, 1997; Krannich, 2005). A mailed note signifies extra effort and is especially memorable. Express your appreciation for the opportunity to meet the employer and his or her time and consideration. Restate your interest, and highlight any noteworthy points made in your conversation. Be brief.

The Job Offer

Usually job offers are made over the phone or in person; however, it may also be delivered by e-mail. No matter how the offer is delivered, you're likely to be surprised. The most appropriate response to an offer in person or by phone is to ask any questions that come to mind, and then request time (a day or two) to think about the offer.

Before accepting an offer, be sure that you understand the conditions and elements of the job. In many cases, salaries for entry-level positions leave little room for negotiation. Take your lead from the employer as to whether the salary is negotiable. If the salary is lower than you hoped and it isn't negotiable, you must decide whether you're still willing to accept the position, and what, if anything, would make it more attractive. As you think about whether to accept the job offer, consider the scope of the position, how it fits your career goals, opportunities for professional growth, and pragmatics (geographic location, benefits, salary, work hours, etc.). If you decide to accept the offer, be sure to inform any employers still actively considering you. Also contact your references to inform them of your new job as well as to thank them for their assistance.

If you decide not to accept the job, notify the employer as soon as possible, by telephone. Timeliness is important because other applicants also are waiting for a response. Be polite, thank the employer for the offer, and wish him or her success. Follow up with a polite e-mail as well, which ensures that your reply is recorded.

Suggested Readings

Bolles, R .N. (2015). *What color is your parachute? A practical manual for job-hunters and career-changers.* Berkeley, CA: Ten Speed Press.

Cano, L. X. (2014). *Resumes that stand out!: Tips for college students and recent grads for writing a superior resume and securing an interview*. Chester Publishing.

Heinzel, K. A. (2013). *Private notes of a headhunter: Proven job search and interviewing techniques for college students and recent grads*. Santa Rosa, CA: Pythian House Publishing.

Landrum, R. E. (2009). *Finding jobs with a psychology bachelor's degree: Expert advice for launching your career.* Washington DC: APA.

Pollak, L. (2012). *Getting from college to career: Your essential guide to succeeding in the real world*. New York: HarperCollins.

Internet Resources (Available at http://www.tarakuther.com)

Job Hunter's Bible

http://www.jobhuntersbible.com/

Richard Bolles, author of *What Color Is Your Parachute? A Practical Manual for Job-Hunters and Career-Changers,* maintains this site of job hunting and career development resources.

Quintessential Careers

http://www.quintcareers.com

Offers an extensive online guide to job hunting and career exploration, complete with resources on résumés, cover letters, interviewing, and more.

MonsterCollege.com

http://college.monster.com/

Network for college students and recent graduates. Includes job search tools, articles, a salary search center, and more.

JobSearch.About.com

http://jobsearch.about.com/

Thorough site covering all aspects of the job search for applicants in all fields and at all levels of experience.

Career Services

http://portal.utpa.edu/utpa_main/dsa_home/career_home/cs_alumni/jobsearching

This page from the University of Texas—Pan American includes links to an excellent assortment of job search and career preparation articles.

Youtern

http://www.youtern.com/thesavvyintern/

Links to internships, mentors, and outstanding career advice for college students.

Reflection Prompts

Think Ahead

Try to imagine your ideal life five years from now. What are you doing? Where do you live? How do you spend your days? What steps should you take now to get there?

What Are My Priorities?

What is important to you in a career and job? For example, is geography important to you? Are you willing to move anywhere a job will take you?

What do you value? Proximity to family and friends, time off, fascinating work? What are the things that matter to you? How can these inform your job hunt?

Social Media

What role does social media play in your life? Pay attention—how often do you find yourself checking your phone? How do you use social media in your everyday life? How might your use of social media influence your job search? How might you minimize negative effects and maximize opportunities?

What Can I Do with a Graduate Degree in Psychology?

CHAPTER 9

Chapter Outline

In 2012, about 110,000 bachelor's degrees were awarded in psychology, as compared with about 27,000 master's and 6,000 doctoral degrees (National Center for Education Statistics, 2013). Armed with a blend of liberal arts skills, the majority of psychology majors successfully enter the workforce following graduation. About one-quarter of graduates, however, choose to pursue graduate study. In this chapter we discuss some of the reasons psychology majors pursue graduate study and the opportunities that accompany graduate study.

Why Go to Graduate School?

There are a variety of reasons to consider attending graduate school. First and foremost is a deep-seated interest in understanding human behavior. Successful graduate students love to learn, they thirst for knowledge, and thrive on discovery. Some pursue graduate study in order to work closely with others in need and improve others' quality of life. As we discussed, graduate study isn't necessary to find a career in a helping field, but it can open doors to additional opportunities to supervise, administrate, and conduct research. A graduate degree affords opportunities for research careers in and out of academia.

Specialized Knowledge

Graduate education imparts specialized knowledge for students who have already obtained bachelor's degrees. During college, psychology majors are exposed to all subfields of psychology and obtain a broad knowledge of the field. Graduate study, in contrast, entails specializing in one subfield of psychology, such as experimental psychology, for example. Graduate education provides depth of knowledge in a specialized area of psychology. Graduate students become experts in specific fields such as cognitive psychology, clinical psychology, or developmental psychology. All graduate students gain advanced knowledge. Doctoral students become psychologists.

Generalizable Skills

As you are aware, undergraduate training in psychology provides students with opportunities to learn many valuable skills. Graduate education further hones these skills and provides other opportunities for personal and professional development. Although the particular set of skills developed varies depending on the student, program, advisor, and experiences, generally speaking, graduate training in psychology gives students the opportunity to develop and master the abilities and competencies shown in Table 9.1 (McGovern et al., 1991; APA, 2013).

TABLE 9.1 Skills Honed in Graduate School

Problem Finding, Definition, and Solving Skills	Training in research design and methodology offers graduate students valuable experience in identifying, defining, and solving problems, honing their critical thinking skills. Given limited or ambiguous information, graduate degree holders learn to identify central issues and extrapolate the most important problems to be addressed. They learn that there is often more than one acceptable way to solve a problem.
Information Acquisition, Management, and Synthesis	Some of the most highly valued skills obtained in graduate school include the ability to gather, summarize, synthesize, and draw conclusions from information. Students develop the cognitive tools needed to deal with inconsistent and uncertain information, extract key ideas from information rapidly, impose structure on ambiguous or messy data, and translate information into meaningful conclusions and recommendations.
Methodological and Quantitative Skills	Graduate students in psychology develop inferential skills, statistical reasoning, and analysis skills. Students become able to draw appropriate inferences from numerical data, and learn how to present data to a nontechnical audience. They learn to not only conceptualize phenomena based on cause and effect but also understand the limitations of conclusions given by particular methodological approaches.
Planning and Leadership Skills	Conducting therapy and engaging in long-term research projects encourage graduate students to develop planning skills. Students learn how to identify the steps needed to complete a given project, from beginning to end, and gain expertise in identifying and anticipating problems.
Interpersonal and Intrapersonal Awareness and Agility	Working closely with others in research contexts provides valuable opportunities for learning how to be a team player. Training in psychology offers an understanding and appreciation of the capabilities and limitations of people from cognitive, perceptual, physical, motivational, and developmental as well as other perspectives. Graduate students often learn how to become more self-observant and aware of their abilities and limitations, as well as understand how to motivate themselves.
Reading, Writing, and Communication Skills	Graduate students learn how to structure and evaluate written and oral arguments, as well as how to write concisely in a professional style. Research presentations and teaching assistantships give students opportunities to learn how to communicate research and theoretical concepts to professional and lay audiences.
Application	Graduate education provides opportunities to learn how to apply research-based knowledge to solve real-life problems, and to use psychological principles and methods to change behaviors and mental processes in clinical and organizational settings. These are important skills that place advanced degree holders at an advantage in a variety of career settings.
Adaptability	Graduate education trains students to think flexibly and accept some ambiguity. Students learn to become action-oriented and develop the ability to work on and consider several problems at once.

Financial Considerations

Many students pursue graduate degrees because education pays. Not only does it provide personal enrichment and knowledge, but it enables graduates to increase their salaries substantially. Entry-level salaries vary widely by degree. According to the National Science Foundation (2012), the median entry-level salary for recent bachelor's degree recipients in 2010 was $30,000; recent master's degree recipients earned a median salary of $42,000. Recent doctoral recipients with less than five years of experience earned a median salary of $90,000 in 2013 (National Science Foundation, 2014). Salaries vary by geographic location, field, and experience. Your salary will increase as you accumulate experience. However, the increase in salary that typically accompanies a graduate degree comes at a price: Graduate degrees are expensive. In 2013, the median annual graduate school tuition was about $16,500 ($10,500 for public institutions and $22,000 for private institutions) (National Center for Education Statistics, 2013). Note that these numbers do not include books, equipment, room and board, or additional living expenses. The financial considerations of graduate study are important as the loss of income and potential increase in debt can have lifelong consequences.

Real Tips for Real Students
Consider the Financial Side of Graduate Study

As you consider graduate study keep in mind that the costs are greater than just tuition. Consider the years in which you will not earn a salary and the benefits, such as health insurance, that you might miss. What will it mean to enter the work world several years later than your friends? What might this late entry, coupled with possibly hefty education loans, mean for your ability to buy a house or start a family? Keep these in mind. Lots of people go to graduate school without thinking about the future beyond having a shiny new degree. Make an informed decision.

GRADUATE DEGREES

There are two types of graduate degrees: master's and doctoral. Both offer specialized training in psychology but they differ in the quantity of training, length of study, and specific requirements. Let's consider the more popular of the two degrees: the master's degree.

The Master's Degree

Master's degrees comprise the vast majority of graduate degrees awarded each year.

What Can You Do with a Master's Degree? Depending on the program and curriculum, a master's degree enables graduates to: (a) teach psychology in high school (other certification may be needed); (b) become more competitive for management, leadership, and consulting positions in government and industry; (c) practice counseling (credentials vary by state); (d) practice school psychology (certification/licensure requirements vary by state); and (e) obtain data management and analysis positions in government, industry (e.g., insurance, pharmaceutical, and manufacturing companies), and nonprofit organizations.

Master's level professionals in psychology are employed in a variety of settings (all of which also employ doctoral-level psychologists), such as (Singleton, Tate, & Kohout, 2003):

- Educational settings: elementary or secondary school, school system district offices, special education, and vocational or adult education
- Human services settings: counseling and guidance centers, student counseling centers, nursing homes, substance abuse treatment centers and other community social services agencies that help people with developmental disabilities as well as other needs.
- Business and government: consulting firms, private research organizations, government research, corporations, small business, criminal justice system, military, government agencies, and nonprofit organizations
- Hospitals and clinics: outpatient mental health clinics, community mental health centers, and HMO and other managed care settings

Why Choose a Master's Degree? Master's degrees offer several advantages over doctoral degrees:

Earning a master's degree typically requires two years as compared with the five to eight years entailed by a doctoral degree. Length of time to degree is an important consideration for all students but especially for those with families. Consider how the length of graduate study will affect the family unit. Doctoral programs place students under great stress for an extended period of time. Students with families may not be able or willing to place long-term stress on their families.

Master's degrees are more inexpensive than doctoral degrees. However, master's degrees aren't cheap once you factor in tuition as well as any salary lost while attending school. But because master's degrees typically take about two years of study, they will nearly always be less expensive than doctoral degrees.

Master's programs are more readily available and flexible. Many more colleges offer master's programs than doctoral programs. A doctoral program may not be available in a given geographical location, and students may not be able or willing to relocate to attend graduate school. Master's programs are more likely to offer part-time study, which allows time for employment and family responsibilities. In addition, most doctoral programs allow for entry only in the fall semester, whereas master's programs sometimes allow spring admissions.

Master's often programs have lower admissions requirements. Some students choose a master's degree as a stepping stone to a doctoral degree. Students whose credentials do not permit them immediate entry to graduate school often consider this route.

Master's programs provide sufficient training and credentials for a variety of careers. A master's degree will not permit you to use the term *psychologist* because this term is regulated by state licensing boards and requires a doctoral degree, supervised experience, and passing an exam. However, master's-level professionals may conduct individual counseling and therapy by obtaining certification appropriate to their level of education and experience. Specifically, master's level professionals in psychology can be licensed in all states as marriage and family therapists and/or licensed professional counselors and sometimes as clinical social workers. They provide assessment and intervention services in community-based programs, public and private institutions, and programs dealing with special problems such as substance abuse, spouse abuse, crisis intervention, and vocational rehabilitation (Himelein, 1999). In institutional settings, master's degree holders may work as behavior change specialists who design and implement programs to serve special populations. States differ in regulations and requirements, so learn about the requirements in your state to ensure that you obtain any needed experiences while in school. A variety of related fields permit graduates to work in a helping capacity with people. Consider the careers in Table 9.2.

TABLE 9.2 MASTER'S DEGREES IN OTHER HELPING FIELDS

	Activities	Education
Social Work	As a profession, social work is dedicated to helping people to adapt and function as best they can in their environment. Social workers provide direct services or therapy, serving individuals, families, and communities. They work in hospitals, clinics, schools, correction facilities, specialized programs, and private practice. Social workers assist clients in identifying problems, issues, and concerns, help them to consider and implement effective solutions, and guide them in locating reliable resources.	The master of social work (MSW) enables degree holders to practice therapy independently, because they are eligible for licensure in all states. The MSW requires two to three years of study, depending on the program and when the supervised internship (of 900 hours for licensure) is scheduled.

TABLE 9.2 Master's Degrees in Other Helping Fields

	Activities	Education
Counseling	There are many different types of counselors, but all help people who are experiencing personal, family, or mental health problems. Counselors also help people make educational and career decisions. Counselors work in schools, colleges, health care facilities, job training, career development centers, social agencies, correctional institutions, residential care centers, drug and alcohol rehabilitation programs, state and government agencies, group practice, and private practice.	Typically, a master's degree in counseling requires two years of course work including 600 hours of supervised clinical experience. Master's degree holders in counseling may conduct therapy independently and may seek licensure or certification.
Occupational Therapy	Occupational therapists work with clients who are experiencing disabilities (emotional, mental, physical, and developmental) that influence their occupational performance or well-being. Occupational therapists assess physical, mental, and emotional deficiencies, and counsel patients to help them improve their ability to function in their daily environments. For example, an occupational therapist might help a client to improve basic motor functions or reasoning abilities, as well as helping him or her to compensate for permanent loss of function. Occupational therapists obtain positions in hospitals, offices and clinics of occupational therapists and other health practitioners, school systems, home health agencies, nursing homes, community mental health centers, adult day care programs, job training services, and residential care facilities.	Since 2007, the minimum educational requirement for entry into this field is a master's degree in occupational therapy. All fifty states in the United States regulate occupational therapy, meaning that graduates must obtain licensure.
Speech Pathology	Speech pathologists assess, diagnose, and treat communication disabilities such as stuttering, or impaired language. They work with clients who have difficulty understanding and producing language, including clients with cognitive communication impairments such as attention and memory disorders. Speech pathologists help clients to develop and regain language (e.g., assist with making speech sounds). Their work also involves counseling clients and families to help them to better understand the disorder and treatment. Speech pathologists provide direct clinical services in schools, nursing homes, mental health centers, private practices, and medical settings, often as part of a team of allied health professionals.	A master's degree in speech pathology (approximately two years of course work) is required for entry into the profession. Nearly all states require speech pathologists to be licensed, with 300–375 hours of supervised clinical experience required for licensure (varying by state).

If you choose a master's degree in psychology, expect to complete two years of full-time graduate study. Requirements for service-oriented subfields such as clinical, counseling, and school psychology usually include experience in an applied setting. Research-oriented subfields such as experimental or developmental psychology usually require a master's thesis based on a research project. Some programs require students to pass a comprehensive exam that evaluates students' knowledge and reasoning.

The Doctoral Degree

A master's degree may allow you to work directly with people, but if you're planning on conducting research or teaching at the college level, a doctoral degree is essential. A doctoral degree provides a greater range of flexibility and autonomy, but it requires a great commitment of time and expense. Most students earn doctoral degrees after five and as much as eight years of study. In clinical or counseling psychology, the requirement for the doctoral degree generally includes a year or more of internship or supervised experience.

Why do students seek doctoral degrees? Generally students pursue doctoral degrees for any of the following reasons: (a) to teach college; (b) to conduct research in a university or private organization in industry or business; (c) to be licensed as a psychologist and practice psychology independently; or (d) to engage in a variety of consulting roles allowing autonomy. Many psychologists engage in more than one of these roles. For example, a college professor might consult to a pharmaceutical company or a practicing psychologist might also teach a few college courses.

As you consider pursuing a doctoral degree in psychology, the first and most important decisions to make is whether to pursue a PhD or PsyD, the two doctoral degrees that a psychology student may pursue. Your choice will determine your career and the degree of research training you obtain.

The PhD refers to the doctor of philosophy. Like the master's degree, the PhD is awarded in many fields. It is a research degree that culminates in an original contribution to the research literature, a dissertation. Writing a dissertation typically entails conducting an original research study that contributes new knowledge to the field and writing a book that discusses the research literature in the field, your particular study and its contributions. If you're considering pursing a PhD in psychology, note that courses in quantitative research methods and statistics, including the use of statistical software, are an integral part of graduate study and are needed to complete the dissertation. Earning a PhD in practice areas of psychology, such as clinical, counseling, or school psychology, also requires obtaining clinical experience, usually a year-long internship in addition to coursework and the dissertation. The PhD in clinical or counseling psychology is a flexible degree—it trains people for research, teaching, writing, and clinical practice.

The PsyD refers to the doctor of psychology. It is offered only in clinical and counseling psychology and is considered a professional degree, much like a JD (doctor of jurisprudence, a lawyer's degree). How is the PsyD different from the PhD? The main difference is that the PsyD emphasizes practice, whereas the PhD emphasizes research, with more required courses in methodology and statistics. The PhD degree prepares graduates for both research and practice, while the PsyD prepares graduates to be consumers of research, to understand, interpret, and apply it. The PsyD is usually based on practical and applied work, as well as on examinations. The dissertation is usually a theoretical paper. The PsyD degree is for those who aim to engage in clinical practice rather than conduct research.

Graduate-Level Careers in Psychology

Graduate education opens the door to many opportunities. What follows are a sampling of possible careers, but note that no one program will prepare you for all of these careers. Before you decide on a graduate degree and program, it's important to consider all the types of careers that you might enjoy and choose a degree and program that will not limit your options.

Teaching Careers

Many students seek a graduate degree in order to teach at a high school, two-year, or four-year college. Master's degree holders may teach psychology in a high school (although additional certification may be necessary, depending on the state) or community college setting. In recent years, faculty positions at two-year and community colleges have become more competitive; many are held by doctoral degree holders. Similarly, although master's degree holders may be hired to teach at four-year colleges on a part-time basis, they are unlikely to be hired for full-time positions (Peters, 1992).

If your goal is to teach at the college level, it's in your best interest to pursue a doctoral degree, which will provide you with the most opportunities for employment, mobility, and advancement as a faculty member (Actkinson, 2000; Lloyd, 2000). Graduates with doctoral degrees may teach undergraduate, master's, and doctoral students in a variety of educational settings, including universities, professional schools, and medical schools. As you consider a career as a professor, recognize that there is more to the professorate than lecturing in front of a classroom each day. Time in the classroom is only the most obvious thing a professor does. A professor's career entails many roles, usually including research and service to the campus and community (advising, committee work, administrative work).

During a typical week, a professor may give lectures, spend time writing an article or book, continue with his or her research by conducting literature reviews and statistical analyses may sit in on faculty meetings, advise students, write letters of recommendation, spend time grading papers, give a talk at a professional meeting, engage in consulting work, serve as an advisor for community agencies, and much more.

Research Careers

A graduate degree in psychology is excellent preparation for a career in research. Research psychologists conduct basic and applied studies of human behavior and may participate in research programs sponsored by universities, government, and private organizations (Kuther & Morgan, 2010). For example, a psychologist working in a university or hospital-based clinic might study smoking cessation; another working in a traumatic brain injury center might study the effects of particular kinds of brain injuries on behavior as well as resilience to brain injury and rehabilitation strategies. Some psychologists work in military research programs, examining the effects of exposure to trauma, for example, while others act as research and development officers at pharmaceutical companies and businesses. Medical schools are emerging as an important employment setting for research psychologists who conduct research and teach medical students. Medical research increasingly relies on contributions from multiple related fields such as anatomy, biochemistry, physiology, pharmacology, and microbiology; as a result, interdisciplinary study is playing an increasingly important role in university life and is leading to more research (and teaching) opportunities for psychologists outside of psychology departments (Balster, 1995). Many research positions are available to master's degree holders, especially in business and private organizations. In academic settings, the doctoral degree offers more flexibility, opportunities for advancement, and opportunities to serve as the primary investigator of federal grants.

Master's degree recipients in research-oriented fields such as quantitative psychology, developmental psychology, general psychology, and experimental psychology, have developed useful methodological and quantitative skills. They are often employed in research positions in university research centers as well as in government, business, and private organizations. Others seek entry into doctoral programs.

Service Delivery (Practice)

Graduate degree holders have a variety of opportunities to engage in service delivery. Mental health professionals with graduate degrees, including clinical and counseling psychologists, engage in a variety of practice activities including, but often not limited to (a) conducting psychotherapy with persons with psychological disorders, crises, or problems of living; (b) administering and interpreting psychological tests of personality, intellect, and vocational aptitude; (c) facilitating psychoeducational and psychotherapy groups; (d) giving talks or workshops on specialty areas; (e) directing and administrating mental health programs; (f) supervising the clinical work of other therapists; and (g) responding to crises or emergency situations (Himelein, 1999; U.S. Bureau of Labor Statistics, 2014).

In order to be licensed as a psychologist the applicant must have completed a doctoral program, obtained 4,000 hours of supervised practice (half prior to obtaining the degree and half post-degree), and pass a national and often state exam. All states permit several forms of licensure for master's trained individuals, usually as counselors, which provides a great deal of autonomy (Actkinson, 2000). If you're considering a master's with the intention of setting up an independent practice, carefully research your options beforehand to ensure that the program you choose provides the experiences needed to be licensed or accredited in your state. Pay attention to specific coursework and especially the number of hours of supervised practice, two factors that licensing and accreditation boards require. The American Counseling Association includes links to licensure boards in all fifty states: http://www.counseling.org/knowledge-center/licensure-requirements/state-professional-counselor-licensure-boards.

Finally, if you are considering a career in school psychology, recognize that the field has very specific requirements for practice. The minimum level of education needed to practice school psychology is a specialist's degree, which falls between a master's and doctoral degree with regard to the amount of time and study. A specialist degree is comprised of sixty credits and 1,500 supervised hours of practice and entails about three years of study. There are many service-delivery options for students interested in earning a graduate degree in psychology. Consider your desired career and look into state certification and licensure requirements as you apply to graduate school to ensure that the degree you earn offers adequate preparation.

EXERCISE 9.1

Practicing with a Master's Degree

1. Opportunities to practice therapy with a master's degree vary by state. Research the requirements of your state. Under what conditions may an individual with a master's in psychology practice? What types of credentialing or licensure are necessary?
2. What other types of master's degrees offer practice opportunities in your state?
3. If you were to pursue a master's degree with the intent of practicing, which degree would you choose and why?
4. Based on your research, with how much independence can an individual with a master's degree practice in your state?

EXERCISE 9.2
Private Practice

Consider some of the realities of working as a therapist or psychologist in private practice. Search the Internet for articles that relay the experiences of therapists. Personal websites and blogs as well as forums might provide useful information. Use your judgment in evaluating the credibility of the information that you find.

1. What sites did you find? Include a brief description of each.
2. What did you learn about private practice? Discuss at least one advantage and one disadvantage.
3. What challenges do practitioners face?
4. How might this apply to you and your career plans?

Other Careers

Research and service-delivery skills come in handy for a variety of careers outside of research and practice settings. Graduate degree holders are found in all of the career settings mentioned in Chapter 7. Below are some additional examples of careers obtained with a graduate degree in psychology.

Administration Graduate degree holders in psychology and related fields work as managers and administrators in hospitals, mental health clinics, government agencies, schools, universities, businesses, and nonprofit organizations, where they may administrate research and applied activities (Bat-Chava, 2000). The ability to effectively administrate in each of these settings is enhanced by the research skills obtained in graduate school. Research skills are essential for evaluating programs and making decisions based on those evaluations. Many administrative positions can be obtained with a master's degree and some experience, especially in smaller institutions and organizations. As in other applied careers, additional opportunities are available to doctoral-level administrators.

Consulting Graduate degree holders in psychology often are hired by organizations to provide consultative services on problems in their area or expertise. Consultative services can include designing a marketing survey, organizing outpatient mental health services, conducting individual assessments, providing expert testimony to a court, and designing webpages, as well as many other activities.

Health psychologists, for example, may be hired as consultants to design and implement programs to help people become healthier, stop smoking, lose weight, or manage stress. Some consultants work in policy: They conduct, interpret, and disseminate research to help national planners and policymakers reach decisions (Flattau, 1998). Trial consultants work in several areas: They may help with jury selection, work with witnesses, or develop effective trial strategy in order to shape juror perceptions (Stapp, 1996). Those trained in forensic or clinical psychology may conduct clinical work in corrections settings, serve as consultants for trial lawyers or as expert witnesses in jury trials, and conduct assessments that are used in trials. As with the other areas that we've discussed, some opportunities are available to master's degree holders, and additional opportunities for advancement are open to doctoral holders.

Business/Human Resources Many graduate degree holders find a career in business, where they select and train employees, engage in human resources development, and develop employee assistance programs. Typical activities include designing and validating assessment instruments, determining the fairness of assessment and vocational tests, particularly for minority applicants, and creating work environments in public and private settings that maximize employee satisfaction (U.S. Bureau of Labor Statistics, 2014).

The research skills honed in graduate school are applicable and valued in a corporate setting, for example, market research (Garfein, 1997). Like other research psychologists, market researchers design studies, construct questionnaires and other research instruments, analyze data, draw conclusions, and write reports. However, instead of conducting and publishing research to advance theory, a market researcher conducts applied research in an effort to help clients become more productive, competitive, and profitable (Kraus, 1996). Business holds a variety of opportunities for master's degree holders because, unlike many other applied careers, doctoral degrees do not necessarily offer much of an advantage over master's degrees. For both master's and doctoral degree holders, advancement becomes possible with additional work experience.

Exercise 9.3
Exploring Psychology Specializations

1. Identify an area of specialization in psychology that interests you. Why does this area interest you? What are typical topics of study within this area?
2. What kinds of jobs do individuals with master's degrees in this area hold? Include information about typical settings, salary, and more.
3. What kinds of jobs do individuals with doctoral degrees in this area hold? Include information about typical settings, salary, and more.
4. How has what you have learned about this specialization influenced your views about graduate study in this area? For example, is a graduate degree a good career option? Which degree offers more opportunities? Conduct a cost-analysis of the pros and cons of seeking a master's degree versus doctoral degree in this specialization.

Media and Publishing Publishing—books, online, and other forms of media—offers opportunities for advanced degree holders in psychology. Some psychologists pursue careers as book acquisitions editors. An acquisitions editor works for a publishing company and engages in a variety of tasks, including reading book proposals, interpreting reviews of proposals, deciding whether to offer book contracts to authors, approaching potential authors with book ideas, discussing works in progress with authors, negotiating journal-publishing agreements with professional societies, and working on practical issues in publishing such as the design of book covers (Amsel, 1996). Others work for media and Internet companies, writing and managing content and content writers. They might solicit, edit, and post articles to websites. Positions in publishing offer opportunities for master's degree holders with interests in writing and the ability to think critically and solve problems effectively. More advanced positions in publishing are held by doctoral degree holders and master's degree recipients with experience in the field.

EXERCISE 9.4

Interesting Careers in Psychological Science

The American Psychological Association has amassed a collection of articles by psychologists who describe their careers in a wide range of settings. Visit the APA page, *Interesting Careers in Psychological Science*, (http://www.apa.org/science/resources/careers/) and choose a specific career.

1. Describe the author's position. What is his or her job and duties?
2. What experience and education led the author to enter this career?
3. What advice do you glean from the article?

In summary, there are many career opportunities for graduate degree holders in psychology. Graduate-level careers span a range of career settings—not simply practice settings. Graduate education translates into more advanced supervisory and leadership roles in business, health care, academic, and other settings, as well as higher salaries. The master's degree provides specific advantages in terms of cost, time to degree, and availability as compared with the doctoral degree. Master's level professionals engage in many of the same activities and in the same places as doctoral level professionals. The doctoral degree, however, offers distinct advantages in academic settings and the ability to use the term *psychologist*. Which degree is right for you depends on your career goals. Consider the careers in this chapter as a starting point for your research and take an active role in pursuing the information you need to make responsible decisions that will meet your specific needs and desires. Remember, however, that the most successful graduates are those who take the reins on their professional development, are open to change, and who are not afraid to explore new and nontraditional avenues.

Suggested Readings

Davis, S. F., Giordano, P. J., & Licht, C. A. (2009). *Your career in psychology: Putting your graduate degree to work.* Hoboken, NJ: Wiley.

Helms, J. L. & Rogers, D. T. (2011). *Majoring in psychology: Achieving your educational and career goals.* New York: Wiley-Blackwell.

Kuther, T. L. & Morgan, R. (2010). *Careers in psychology: Opportunities in a changing world.* Pacific Grove, CA: Wadsworth.

Morgan, R. D., Kuther, T. L., & Habben, C. J. (2004). *Life after graduate school: Opportunities and advice from new psychologists.* New York: Psychology Press.

Sternberg, R. J. (2007). *Career paths in psychology: Where your degree can take you.* Washington, DC: American Psychological Association.

U.S. Bureau of Labor Statistics (2014). *Occupational outlook handbook.* Washington, DC: Department of Labor. http://www.bls.gov/ooh/

Internet Resources (Available at http://www.tarakuther.com)

Interesting Careers in Psychological Science

http://www.apa.org/science/resources/careers/

Psychologists in a wide range of fields share their experiences on the job.

Early Career Psychologists

http://apa.org/careers/early-career/index.aspx

The American Psychological Association provides resources and links for new psychologists. Get a feel for the field by visiting this site.

Psychology Careers for the 21st Century

http://www.apa.org/careers/resources/guides/careers.aspx

This American Psychological Association brochure describes the field of psychology, including employment settings, job outlook, and career preparation.

Master's- and Doctoral-Level Careers in Psychology and Related Areas

http://www.psywww.com/careers/masters.htm

Overview of degrees and careers, by Dr. Markey Lloyd.

Reflection Prompts

What Education You Seek?

Look through your entries written to date. Considering all that you've learned about yourself, what type of career would make you happy? Now consider the information in this chapter. Will a graduate degree help you to achieve your goals? Be honest with yourself.

Comparing Jobs across Degrees

Choose an area of psychology that interests you and brainstorm two or three jobs that fall within that content area. Identify jobs for bachelor's, master's, and doctoral degree recipients. How do the jobs and types of tasks change with the level of education? What do you think about each of these options?

Other Applications

Imagine that you went to graduate school and earned a doctoral degree in psychology, but you will not practice therapy. What would you do? What other activities of psychologists appeal to you, aside from therapy?

Considering Fields

Choose two or three psychology subfields. What is most interesting about the subfield? Drawbacks? Identify two career options for each. How well do these careers fit your interests and skills? Can you see yourself working in each? Why or why not?

Applying to Graduate School in Psychology

Chapter 10

Chapter Outline

Many graduates find that a bachelor's degree in psychology is the foundation for building a successful career. Some students, however, seek to enroll in graduate study in order to pursue the careers discussed in Chapter 9. If you think graduate school may be in your future, plan ahead as graduate admissions is very competitive with about 50% of applicants gaining admission to master's programs and only about 20% to doctoral programs (Kohout & Wicherski, 2010). In this chapter we discuss the nature of graduate school, the application process, and how to compile a successful application.

What Is Graduate School Like?

So what exactly do you do in graduate school? Do you know what to expect? Most new graduate students find that grad school is strikingly different from undergrad because coursework is only one way in which they spend their time. Moreover, classes themselves are different. They are smaller and instruction tends to be student-centered, emphasizing student-generated discussion. Expect fewer tests, many more papers, and a heavy reading load. The reading lists for some classes may seem impossibly long. Classes are a large component of master's programs and the first couple of years of doctoral programs. But grad school entails more than completing a series of classes. The purpose of grad school is to develop a professional understanding of your discipline through independent reading and study—and classes don't fit the bill.

Most of what you learn in grad school will not come from classes, but from other activities, like doing research and, in practice-oriented fields, such as clinical activities. You'll work closely with a faculty member on his or her research. As an apprentice, you'll learn how to define research problems, design and carry out research projects to test your hypotheses, and disseminate your results. The end goal is to become an independent scholar and design your own research program. The extent to which students engage in research varies by field, degree, and program.

Graduate programs in the applied fields, such as clinical, counseling, and school psychology, include training in the clinical skills that will permit graduates to practice psychology. Coursework emphasizes theory and assessment techniques. Students learn how to practice psychology through a series of clinical experiences that begin with observing an experienced therapist. Through supervised experiences graduate students begin to deliver therapy and assessments to individuals and groups. Students are supervised by licensed psychologists, often faculty, and videotaped as well as observed behind a two-way mirror. The amount of clinical training students obtain depend on the program and degree. Students in PsyD programs and others that emphasize practice will receive more supervision and training in clinical skills than will students in research-oriented PhD programs. Graduate students in the applied fields of clinical, counseling, and school psychology acquire hundreds of hours of supervised experience.

Some graduate students, especially those in programs that prepare students for academic careers, obtain teaching experience. Teaching experience usually first comes in the form of teaching assistantships where they assist an instructor by leading discussion sections, conducting tutoring sessions, participating in grading, and presenting some lectures. More experienced graduate students may be instructors responsible for an entire course. Some graduate students are fortunate to take a course or workshop that provides training in teaching skills. Others, unfortunately, learn "on the job." Not all students obtain teaching experience in graduate school.

Advancing through graduate school typically requires completing one or more comprehensive exams that test students' mastery of the field. Master's students may complete comprehensive exams in order to graduate, although exams are not required in every program. Doctoral students will complete at least one set of comprehensive exams. In some programs, students take a set of comprehensive exams at the end of the first year to receive master's degree and then another set after completing all coursework (at the end of the third year) to progress to doctoral candidate status. *Doctoral candidates* have completed all of the academic requirements to earn a doctoral degree, except for the dissertation.

Once a graduate student achieves doctoral candidate status, he or she may formally begin the dissertation. A dissertation represents the culmination of graduate study in which a student constructs a project that will contribute new knowledge to the field, demonstrating significant independent scholarship that advances the field. Students must select a dissertation committee, typically four or five faculty who will advise and judge the dissertation. They select a topic and work closely with a mentor who provides guidance and feedback. The student constructs a proposal, which must be presented to the dissertation committee and defended. Once the proposal is accepted by the dissertation committee students are free to begin their research. Graduate students then spend months or even years collecting, analyzing, interpreting, and writing about their data. The dissertation culminates in a defense in which students present their research to their dissertation committee, answer questions, and support the validity of their work. If all goes well, they walk away from the meeting with a new title and letters behind their name: PhD or PsyD. Master's students usually complete a similar process and write a thesis. The thesis must be a significant project that demonstrates mastery and application of the material, but it typically is not required to make original contributions to the field, entails fewer requirements, and takes less time.

It's easy to see that graduate study entails much more than coursework—and all of these activities take time. The most successful students treat graduate school as a fulltime job, one that doesn't fit the typical 9-to-5 schedule. Many students find that their work spills over into evenings and weekends, especially when they face a deadline. This is because graduate study is not just a matter of taking classes; it's about becoming a professional. In graduate school you will be socialized into your profession. In other words, you will learn the norms and values of your field. Graduate school shapes the mind and leads students to think in new ways. You will learn to think like a professional in your field, whether a scientist, educator, practitioner, or all of these roles.

SHOULD YOU GO TO GRADUATE SCHOOL?

Graduate study isn't the right choice for everyone. Is it right for you? Only you can answer that question. Review Chapter 2 and reflect on your interests, goals, dreams, and abilities. Then consider the following:

Is Graduate Study Needed?

Do you need to attend graduate school to achieve your goals? Some people attend graduate school for the love of learning, others seek career advancement. Can you fulfill your goals with your bachelor's degree? Or is a master's degree needed? Are there alternative ways of achieving your goals? Be honest with yourself. As we've discussed in prior chapters, if you would like to work with people, there are lots of alternatives to a doctoral degree in psychology (and some are preferable for reasons of time and expense). If you decide to attend graduate school, choose the level of education, whether master's or doctoral degree, that offers the training and course work to prepare you for the career to which you aspire.

Do you know why you want to go to grad school? If you're considering pursing a doctorate, why? Some students decide to apply to graduate school to avoid job hunting in a challenging market. Others see attending graduate school as an option to fall back on. Some students focus on the desire to be called, "Doctor"—the prestige. All of these are relevant reasons to consider graduate study, but these reasons alone are not likely to sustain you through the years it takes to earn a degree. Think ahead to a few years after having earned your degree. What are you doing? Will you enjoy your career after graduation?

Are You Prepared for Graduate Study?

Are you prepared for the academic demands of graduate study? Generally it is expected that students will maintain at least a 3.0 average during graduate school. Many programs deny funding to students with less than a 3.33 average. Consider your undergraduate psychology coursework. How comfortable did you feel with these courses? Do you like writing papers? How about library research? Regardless of program, you will spend a lot of your time reading and will write many papers. Students who choose to attend graduate school tend to be more satisfied with their undergraduate courses than students who do not. Do you have good academic habits? Can you juggle multiple tasks, projects, and papers? Can you manage time effectively? Look back over your responses to the assessments in Chapter 4. What did they reveal about your academic habits? Are your habits suited for graduate study?

Are you prepared to take graduate-level methodology and statistics courses? If you are weak in math you may not be able to complete the basic statistical requirements for psychology. If you like math and performed well in your math courses (e.g., with grades of B or higher), then you will be better able to handle graduate-level math. Before you rule out graduate school based on these math requirements, do a little soul-searching. Is your ability in math really weak, or do you just think so? Remember from Chapter 4 that our beliefs about our abilities are powerful influences on our performance. Perhaps if you adjust your studying strategies, or devote more time, you'll find that you're better at math than you think. Are you willing to take on a heavy workload for many years to earn the degree? Are you willing to put much of your personal life on hold? Incur debt? This is a personal decision.

Are you prepared for the personal demands of graduate study? Graduate school entails a greater commitment than undergrad. Gone are the days of skipping classes, waiting until the last minute to write papers, and late-night partying. Excelling in college may have come easily but you likely will find graduate school to be quite different. You'll be surrounded by students who performed just as well and even better than you did in college. The bar is set much higher, and you'll work harder and more consistently than ever before. Successful graduate students are self-reliant, disciplined, committed, and intellectually curious. In addition to the expected academic and professional skills, successful graduate students are social skilled, able to work well with others, and are good at managing their own emotions. Consider the personal demands of graduate study. Are you willing to take on a heavy workload for many years to earn the degree? Are you willing to put much of your personal life on hold? Incur debt?

Speak with professors and graduate students to get a better idea of what's involved in graduate study. Most first-year graduate students are overwhelmed and remark that they had no idea of what they were getting into. Consider this first year student's perspective:

> As an undergraduate, I wish I had spoken with someone about what graduate school is really like. Grad school requires a higher level of dedication, time, professionalism, and maturity. I'm working nonstop. Successful grad students study or work on research, eight hours per day, six to seven days per week. Professors just expect you to read it and get it. Reading lists are long and you're expected to understand and discuss it intelligently. It's a whole other world from the innocence of undergraduate work. It's a ton of work and I feel like I'm in over my head a lot of the time, but I'm glad I'm here.

Does all of this sound overwhelming? Nearly everyone feels that way upon encountering these words. This information is not meant to dissuade you or change your mind, but to provide a more realistic picture of what attending graduate school really entails. Going to graduate school affects the rest of your life. There are both pros and cons to continuing your education. Seek information from multiple sources—this book, the career counseling center, graduate students, professors, and your family. Take your time with the decision. More importantly, trust your judgment and have faith that you'll make the choice that's best for you.

Can You Afford Graduate School?

Without a doubt, higher education is expensive and most people find that graduate study typically is more expensive than their undergraduate degrees. The median annual cost of graduate school in 2013 was about $16,500 ($10,500 for public and $22,000 for private institutions) (National Center for Education Statistics, 2013). Room and board, books, supplies, and fees are additional expenditures.

One of the costs that many students don't consider is the loss of income from full-time employment. Many graduate programs frown on outside employment. Doctoral programs, in particular, often forbid it. Even if holding a job is permitted, most full-time graduate students find that employment is more than they can handle. Part-time students, on the other hand, often can find some time to work, but full-time employment will likely pose great stress to their studies and personal lives. Dealing with the loss of income—or the delay of earning an income—is often easier for students who attend graduate school right out of college, but this is an expense related to graduate study that you should consider. For example, a student who chooses a four-year graduate program over a full-time job with a salary of $40,000 per year forfeits $160,000 of earned income to attend graduate school.

How do students fund graduate school? Funding varies with type of degree and program. Doctoral students are much more likely to obtain department funding for graduate study, typically in the form of research and teaching assistantships, which usually pay for tuition and a small stipend. Research assistants are hired by a professor to work alongside him or her and advance research. Research assistants are usually funded by a professor's grant.

Therefore research assistantships are more common in graduate programs where faculty win grants to conduct research. Doctoral programs that emphasize professional, applied training for practitioners are less likely to offer funding. Teaching assistants are hired to help professors teach their classes. They are more common in universities that have large classes and the funding usually comes from the department or university. Research and teaching assistantships are less common in master's programs.

The majority of students carry some debt after graduation. Given that research assistantships and grant funding is more common in research-oriented graduate programs, it should not be surprising that doctoral recipients in the practice subfields are more likely to report debt after graduation than are those in the research subfields (79% vs. 48%). Among 2009 doctoral recipients in psychology, the median level of debt for those in the practice subfields was $80,000—more than double that for those in the research subfields ($32,000). PsyD recipients incurred even more debt. Graduates with a PsyD in clinical psychology reported a median debt level of $120,000 in 2009. Clinical PhD recipients reported a median level of debt of $68,000 (Michalski et al., 2011). Whether to pursue graduate study is a decision with lifelong financial repercussions.

Selecting Graduate Programs

As you'll soon see, pursuing graduate study in psychology entails many decisions. You'll confront decisions about the type of degree, training models, and then among programs.

Decide among Training Models and Degrees

Graduate programs in psychology follow one of three basic models of training. Choose a program whose model best fits with your interests, because most psychologists engage in the same type of activities that they experienced in their graduate program of study.

Research-Scientist Model (PhD) Programs that follow a research-scientist model focus on molding students into scholars who will make new discoveries and advance the knowledge in their field. From a historical perspective, this was the first training model to emerge as it characterizes the emphases of the PhD, or doctor of philosophy degree. Most of your college professors hold this degree; it is conferred in nearly all academic fields. The PhD in psychology provides training in experimental methods, methodological skill, and a background in a particular specialty area (such as cognitive, social, developmental, and experimental psychology). Individuals trained in the research-scientist model conduct original research, teach, and write about their research findings, typically in the core academic areas of psychology, such as experimental, social and personality, quantitative, physiological, and developmental psychology. PhD recipients tend to be employed as researchers or college and university professors and some work as consultants or conduct research for the government or corporations.

Scientist-Practitioner Model (PhD) Programs adopting the scientist-practitioner model seek to train scholars who integrate their research training with human service. Graduates engage in practice activities and conduct applied and basic research. This model is commonly found in PhD programs in clinical, counseling, school, and industrial psychology. Similar to the research-scientist model, students trained in the scientist-practitioner model receive training in research and methodology; but they take more courses in applied areas and complete more internships and practica than do students trained in the research-scientist model. Graduates trained in the scientist-practitioner model may be employed by hospitals and clinical practices, teach in colleges and universities, medical centers, mental health centers, and in industry and government, and may own private practices. The extent to which a particular psychologist engages in each of these activities depends on his or her job setting and commitment to research; most practicing clinicians do little to no research.

Professional Psychologist-Practitioner Model (PsyD) Graduate programs that adopt the professional psychologist-practitioner model train students to provide psychological services and award the PsyD, a practitioner degree that emphasizes clinical training or the professional model of training. The PsyD and the practitioner model of training place greater emphasis on clinical practice than in the scientist-practitioner model, and much less emphasis on research. PsyD programs train students to be consumers of research rather than producers of it.

PsyD programs tend to be larger than PhD programs, so more students are accepted and your chances of acceptance are much higher. For example, in the 2009–2010 academic year, accredited PhD programs in clinical psychology accepted about 9% of applicants whereas accredited PsyD programs in clinical psychology accepted 31% of applicants (Kohout & Wicherski, 2010). The PsyD degree often is offered at private or professional schools and is generally more expensive than a PhD. Most funding for PhD students comes from faculty research grants. Little research is conducted in PsyD programs, so there are fewer opportunities for funding. Professional programs train students to be educated consumers of research rather than generators of research. Because there is less emphasis on research, PsyD students earn their degrees a little quicker but usually graduate with more debt than do PhD students.

Practice-oriented students often find the curricula of professional programs to be better aligned with their own interests and career aspirations than those of traditional scientist-practitioner programs. Although some have argued that the PhD is more prestigious than the PsyD (Buskist & Sherburne, 1996) and the PhD may be more flexible in terms of career options because of its research basis, you should choose the degree that will prepare you for the career you desire. If you're interested in practicing psychology and do not want to teach in a university setting or conduct research, the PsyD may be for you. However, a master's degree in a helping field can prepare you to engage in many of the same activities—in fewer years and, usually, with less debt. Graduates from professional schools are at a disadvantage only when they apply for positions in research or academic settings. Understand your interests, abilities, and professional goals in order to choose a training model and degree that will prepare you for the career you desire.

Choose a Psychology Subfield

What will you specialize in? This is a crucial question. Unlike college, where you majored in psychology, a general degree, graduate school entails specializing in a particular area of psychology. Carefully consider your area of specialization (e.g., clinical, experimental, developmental, school, and others) because that will determine to which schools and programs you'll apply as well as your likelihood of gaining admission to a program.

How do you choose? Examine your responses to the assessments in this book as well as your reflective writing. Consider your interests. Do you want to work with people? In a laboratory? Teach college? Conduct research? What were your favorite classes in college? On what topics have you written term papers? Seek advice from professors in your department, especially from those in the areas in which you wish to specialize. Chapter 1 notes the major specialty areas of psychology. In order to apply to graduate school you must choose an area in which to specialize. Take your time in making this decision because it will shape your education and career.

Gather Information on Graduate Programs

Once you have a specialty area(s) in mind, it's time to gather program information. How do you get information about programs? Google searches are a good start but you should use a variety of resources. For decades, students relied on a heavy set of educational guidebooks, known as *The Peterson's Guide*, which listed graduate programs in every field, organized alphabetically by university. It was available in the reference section of the library and required strength to lift, good eyesight to read the tiny print, and stamina to leaf through and record the information in one or two library sessions. Fortunately the days of relying on a printed copy of *The Peterson's Guide* are gone as it's available online at http://www.petersons.com/graduate-schools.aspx. You can search by school or subject area.

Each graduate program listing includes a great deal of information including an overview of the program, degrees awarded, number of full- and part-time students, admissions statistics, acceptance rate, tuition and fees, and more.

One of the best sources of information about graduate programs is the APA *Guide to Graduate Study in Psychology.* Updated annually, this book includes information on every psychology graduate program in the United States and Canada. Organized alphabetically by state and by school, this guide provides the following information: criteria for admission; program emphasis; number of faculty; enrollments; and additional admissions information, including the average GPA and GRE scores for each school. An online version is searchable and contains the most up-to-date information about programs. A three-month subscription to the database costs about $20; visit http://www.apa.org/gradstudy/ for more information.

Once you have a list of programs, your next step is to gather more detailed information. Visit the school's website to review the program, degrees, coursework, research and applied opportunities, and faculty. Most graduate programs include admissions statistics such as the acceptance rate and average GRE scores. Before you spend a great deal of time gathering information about graduate programs, consider your priorities and use them as a guide. What field are you interested in? Are you interested more in research or practice? Are there geographic restrictions on where you live?

Exercise 10.1
Learning about Graduate Programs

This exercise will help you begin to consider graduate programs.

1. Identify your priorities with regard to graduate study. Identify a field, degree, and, if relevant, a geographic location.
2. Search for graduate programs in your chosen field. List the program, department and university, specialization, degree, and URL for ten to twelve graduate programs.
3. Brainstorm the factors that you will consider in making selections among graduate programs. How will you make choices?
4. Review the graduate programs that you have selected. Categorize them into programs that are a good fit to your criteria, those that match some criteria, and those that match few criteria.
5. Share your observations about this process.

Evaluate Graduate Programs

All too often students want to go to graduate school "anywhere I'm accepted." It's understandable that students want to get into graduate school, but it's also important to be an educated consumer and look for a program that *you* want, not just one that accepts you. The admissions committee evaluates you as a potential student, but you should evaluate the program to see whether it fits your needs. Is it someplace where you can spend the next few years? Take the time to carefully review and evaluate each graduate program. As you read the information about programs, you'll notice that there are differences among departments in goals, program philosophies, theoretical orientations, facilities, and resources. What are you looking for as you peruse the volumes of information obtained through your research? Basically you're looking to see how well each program matches your goals and aspirations—the "fit" between you and the graduate program. How do you determine fit? As you examine a graduate program, consider the areas listed in the following sections.

Department Emphasis and Program Philosophy What are the program goals? Do they fit with your own? Is the department heavily research oriented, or is it more theoretical or applied? What's the program's theoretical orientation (e.g., cognitive-behavioral, psychoanalytic)? Is the program oriented toward producing researchers? Is it heavily oriented toward theory? Are theory and practice united? Where does the program fall on the scientist-practitioner continuum? Consider:

1. **Faculty research interests and publications.** Do you share interests with any of the faculty? Do the faculty publish often and in refereed journals? Google faculty members to view their webpages. Use Google Scholar or *PsychInfo* to find their publications.
2. **Teaching goals and style.** Can you find any information about how classes are run? Look at the website. Do faculty have their own webpages? Do any of them describe classes or provide resources for students? Try to find out what it's like to be a student in the program. Does it appear to be a student-oriented program?
3. **Information about students and graduates.** Where do graduates go? Do they find jobs in academia, practice, or the "real world"? Do students present at conferences or publish in journals?
4. **Course offerings.** Look over the program course book and requirements to get a feel of what courses you'll take and what you'll learn. This gives you a chance to see some of the program's inner workings, so that you're not surprised once you're admitted.

Program Quality Program quality is difficult to access, because some factors are somewhat subjective. Here are some considerations in evaluating program quality.

1. **Attrition.** What is the attrition rate? Some programs select only a handful of the top students and lose a few of them; other programs take in more students than they can effectively manage and retain few students. Some programs use comprehensive exams to weed out students.
2. **Time to completion.** What is the average time to completion of the degree? In psychology, five to seven years is a normal range. If a program's average time to completion is close to seven years or beyond, you should examine it more closely to determine why.
3. **Logistical resources.** Are there adequate computer facilities, library resources, money for travel to conferences, and other forms of support?
4. **Financial support.** Are research and teaching assistantships used to fund students?

Does it appear to be a quality program? To help you evaluate the overall quality of the program, Table 10.1 presents some characteristics of quality PhD programs.

In addition to program quality, consider the prestige of the department. How much does prestige matter? That depends on what you hope do with your degree. In academia there generally is a correlation between departmental prestige and job quality (Peters, 1992). Doctoral recipients from prestigious departments are more likely to land prestigious jobs (e.g., at research institutions) than are those from less distinguished institutions. Advisors and mentors in prestigious graduate departments often have excellent reputations and important connections that can help you advance in your career. Powerful mentors can write persuasive letters of recommendation, lend authority to student papers, and pull strings because their old classmates, friends, and former students often hold prestigious positions. Though you should also note that powerful mentors often are very busy, so you may have little direct contact with them.

TABLE 10.1 **CHECKLIST: CHARACTERISTICS OF A QUALITY PHD PROGRAM**

- ❑ Program faculty work closely and publish with students
- ❑ Faculty regularly publish in their field and attend conferences at the regional, state, national, and international levels
- ❑ Program is accredited by APA (if clinical, counseling, or school)
- ❑ Program emphasizes research productivity
- ❑ Program faculty are tenured or tenure track
- ❑ Department is large enough to have faculty who represent the major areas in psychology
- ❑ Program is able to support or partially support students through assistantships and other means
- ❑ Program has adequate facilities for research and practica

Adapted from: (Buskist and Sherburne (1996); Keith-Spiegel and Wiederman (2000).

Accreditation Many clinical, counseling, and school psychology programs advertise that they are APA accredited. What does that mean? Recall that the American Psychological Association (APA) is a national association of psychologists. One of APA's many activities is to evaluate practice-oriented psychology programs to ensure that the educational criteria meet the public's needs. APA accredits doctoral programs in the practice areas of clinical, school, counseling, and combined professional-scientific psychology (e.g., some programs in applied developmental psychology seek accreditation).

In order to be accredited, a program must meet the minimum standards for clinical training established by APA. The criteria include faculty credentials, specific coursework, and eligibility for state licensure, adequate research and clinical opportunities, and internships for clinical and counseling students. A site visit confirms that these requirements are met, and they must be maintained over time. If you are applying to clinical, counseling, or school programs, it is in your best interest to be sure that they are accredited because a degree from an APA-approved program carries more weight; students from accredited programs are more successful in competing for clinical internships and jobs. In fact, many states *require* applicants to have earned doctoral degrees from APA programs in order to apply for licensure.

Real Tips for Real Students

Research-Based Programs

Note that programs in scientist-nonpractice areas, such as experimental and social psychology, are *not* part of the APA accreditation program. Accreditation applies *only* to programs that train students to be practicing psychologists. Research programs that do not prepare students to practice psychology are not accredited. If you're applying to a scientist program *do not* look for APA accreditation.

The Application

Once you have narrowed your choice of programs, you're ready to begin the application. Apply to enough programs to have a reasonable chance of being accepted, given your credentials. There is a great deal of competition for entry into doctoral programs in psychology. Plan on applying to six to ten programs and possibly more if you're applying to particularly selective programs (especially in clinical psychology). This can quickly become expensive; application fees are over $50 for most programs. In addition to investing money, plan on investing a significant amount of time on each application.

Most graduate programs use online applications. The process varies but usually you will create a login on the school's website. The online application will include forms for entering your personal information as well as information for all of the components described in the following section. Table 10.2 provides a timetable for applying to graduate school. Now, let's examine the typical components of a graduate application.

TABLE 10.2 **Timeline for Preparing for Graduate School**

First Year

- ❑ Complete your general education mathematics requirements.
- ❑ Begin taking the required methodology and statistics courses in psychology.
- ❑ Take a class in writing.
- ❑ Take several survey psychology classes to learn about the field.
- ❑ Get to know at least one professor outside of class.

Second Year

- ❑ Take a least one more math and science course beyond the general requirements.
- ❑ Learn about the research interests of the faculty and identify potential mentors.
- ❑ Ask a faculty member if you can help in his or her research.
- ❑ Attend a regional psychology conference.
- ❑ If you are interested in the clinical or counseling areas of psychology, seek volunteer experiences.
- ❑ Join Psi Chi and any other campus psychology clubs—and get involved.
- ❑ Get to know at least one other professor outside of class.
- ❑ Ask professors for their opinions on what courses and other experiences you should obtain to prepare for graduate school.

Third Year

- ❑ Participate in an independent research project with a faculty member.
- ❑ If you are interested in the clinical or counseling areas of psychology, seek an internship.
- ❑ Attend a psychology conference.
- ❑ Get to know at least one other professor outside of class.
- ❑ Study for the GRE.
- ❑ Explore graduate programs.
- ❑ Study for the Psychology GRE. Take it either in April of your third year or October of your fourth year.

Summer Prior to Fourth Year

- ❑ Take the GRE.
- ❑ If you have not yet taken it, study for the Psychology GRE.
- ❑ Draft your CV.

TABLE 10.2 **TIMELINE FOR PREPARING FOR GRADUATE SCHOOL**

Summer Prior to Fourth Year

- ❑ Review your transcript for errors.
- ❑ Narrow your list of graduate programs.
- ❑ Begin drafting your admissions essay.

Fourth Year: September

- ❑ Share your list of graduate programs with faculty, ask for input, and ask them if they will write recommendation letters when the time comes (bring your CV).
- ❑ Prepare your admissions essay and get feedback.
- ❑ Finalize your list of graduate programs.
- ❑ Begin online applications.

Fourth Year: October

- ❑ Take the GRE Psychology test, if you have not already.
- ❑ Formally request recommendation letters from faculty.
- ❑ Complete online applications.

Fourth Year: November

- ❑ Finalize your applications (pay attention to deadlines as they may come as early as November and as late as March).
- ❑ Check back with professors and thank them for writing your recommendations.

EXERCISE 10.2

Your Personal Timeline for Applying to Graduate School

Construct your personal timeline for applying to graduate school. Table 10.2 provides a generalized timeline. Consider your own situation.

1. How much time do you have to prepare? Are you a sophomore, junior, or senior?
2. How far along are you in completing required coursework, especially methodology and statistics requirements? What additional coursework do you need to become competitive?
3. Map out your plan for coursework for each semester over the next two years. What will you take in fall? Spring?
4. What out-of-class practical experiences do you need? Will you seek an internship? If so, where does it fall in your two-year plan? Planning ahead is especially important if internships are awarded competitively so that you can be prepared.

(Continued)

EXERCISE 10.2 (Continued)

5. What is your plan for obtaining research experience? Have you gotten to know professors? Have you worked with them on their research? Determine how to obtain these experiences—and how to eventually conduct independent research with a professor.
6. Flesh out your two-year plan. When do you plan to apply to graduate school? Will you carry out your plan in time to apply? If you have extra time, how will you spend it? (I suggest more research!)

Graduate Record Exam: General Test

The Graduate Record Exam (GRE) is a standardized test that all applicants to graduate programs must complete. The GRE General Test is an aptitude test, administered by computer, that measures a variety of skills, acquired over the high school and college years, that are thought to predict success in graduate school. The GRE is only one of several criteria that graduate schools use to evaluate your application, but it is one of the most important. This is particularly true if your college GPA is not as high as you'd like. Exceptional GRE scores can open up new opportunities for grad school. Low GRE scores can remove your application from the admissions pool.

The GRE General Test yields three scores: verbal ability, quantitative ability, and analytical ability. As shown in Table 10.3, the verbal section assesses

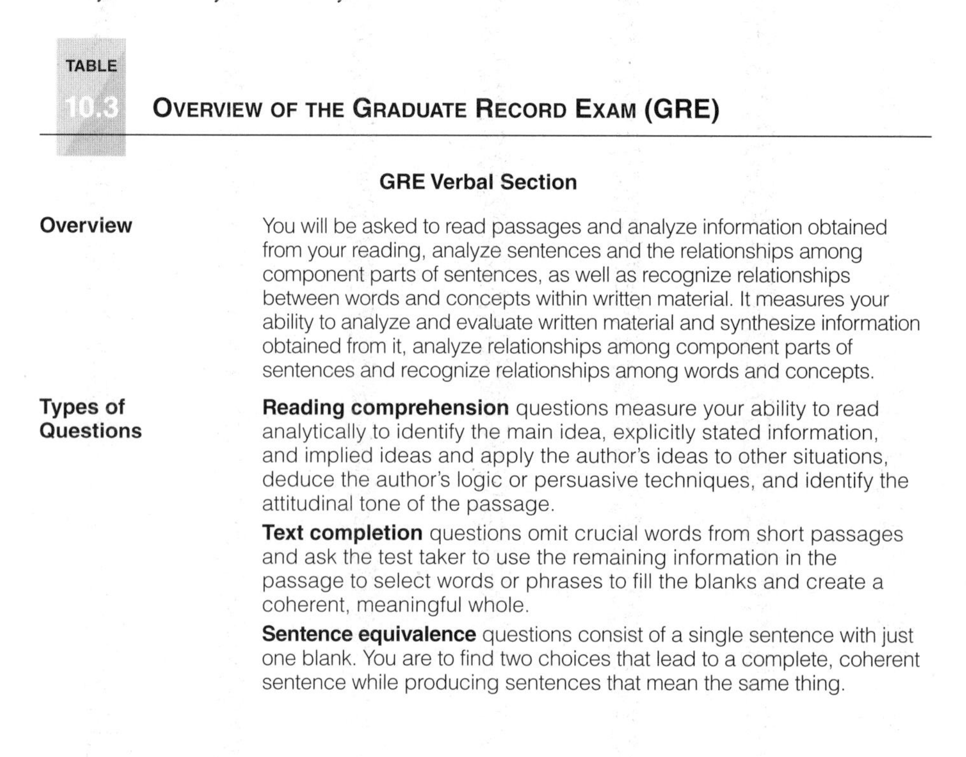

TABLE 10.3 OVERVIEW OF THE GRADUATE RECORD EXAM (GRE)

	GRE Verbal Section
Overview	You will be asked to read passages and analyze information obtained from your reading, analyze sentences and the relationships among component parts of sentences, as well as recognize relationships between words and concepts within written material. It measures your ability to analyze and evaluate written material and synthesize information obtained from it, analyze relationships among component parts of sentences and recognize relationships among words and concepts.
Types of Questions	**Reading comprehension** questions measure your ability to read analytically to identify the main idea, explicitly stated information, and implied ideas and apply the author's ideas to other situations, deduce the author's logic or persuasive techniques, and identify the attitudinal tone of the passage. **Text completion** questions omit crucial words from short passages and ask the test taker to use the remaining information in the passage to select words or phrases to fill the blanks and create a coherent, meaningful whole. **Sentence equivalence** questions consist of a single sentence with just one blank. You are to find two choices that lead to a complete, coherent sentence while producing sentences that mean the same thing.

TABLE 10.3

Overview of the Graduate Record Exam (GRE)

	GRE Quantitative Section
Overview	The quantitative section does not require mathematic skills beyond the high school level. It measures problem-solving ability, focusing on basic concepts of arithmetic, algebra, geometry, data analysis, and data interpretation.
Types of Questions	Problem-solving questions are word problems that assess your understanding of, and ability to apply, arithmetic, algebra, and geometry. **Quantitative comparison** questions ask you to compare two quantities, one in column *a* and one in column *b*. Your task is to determine if they are equal, if one is larger than the other, or if not enough information is presented to make the determination. **Data analysis** questions require use of basic descriptive statistics, the ability to synthesize information, select appropriate data to answer a question, interpret data in graphs and tables, and determine whether the data are sufficient to answer a given question, as well as use elementary probability. **Numeric entry** questions. Rather than multiple choice, questions of this type ask you either to enter the answer as an integer or a decimal in an answer box.
	GRE Analytical Writing Section
Overview	The analytical writing section examines your ability to communicate complex ideas clearly and effectively, support your ideas, examine claims and supporting evidence, sustain a focused and coherent discussion, and effectively use the elements of standard written English.
Subsections	**Analyze an Issue**: This task assesses your ability to think critically about a topic of general interest and to clearly express your thoughts about it in writing. Each issue statement makes a claim that you can discuss from various perspectives and apply to many different situations or conditions. The issue statement is followed by a set of specific instructions. **Analyze an Argument**: This thirty-minute task presents you with an argument. Your task is to critique the argument, assess its claims, and conclude the degree to which it is reasoned.

your ability to understand and analyze written material. The quantitative section tests basic math skills and your ability to understand and apply quantitative skills to solve problems. The analytical writing section examines critical thinking and analytical writing skills. It examines your ability to explain and support complex ideas, and engage in focused and coherent discussion and analysis of arguments. The GRE General Test takes nearly four hours to complete, plus time for breaks and reading instructions.

The GRE General Test is administered by computer year-round. Plan to take the GRE well in advance of application due dates. Generally you should take it in the spring or summer before you apply to grad school.

Remember that it may take a few weeks for scores to be reported to schools. If you take the GRE too late in the fall, the scores may not arrive in time for your application to be considered. Also, you will want to have enough time to retake it if necessary. You can always retake the GRE, but remember that you're allowed to take it only once every 21 days per calendar month. If you retake the GRE you have the option of sending all scores to graduate schools or scores only from a particular test date.

What score should you strive for? The verbal and quantitative subtests yield scores ranging from 130 to 170, in one-point increments. Most graduate schools consider the verbal and quantitative sections to be particularly important in making decisions about applicants. The analytical writing section yields a score ranging from 0 to 6, in half-point increments. Among all test-takers in 2014 the average GRE scores were 152 for Verbal, 149 for Quantitative, and 3.9 for Analytical Writing (Educational Testing Service, 2014). Students who score at the 50th percentile are not likely to gain admission to graduate school. The average GRE scores for incoming students are often listed on program webpages in addition to the APA *Guide to Graduate Study in Psychology.* A quick perusal of graduate websites indicated that graduate programs often vary greatly in their average GRE percentile scores from 79th to 93rd percentile for Verbal scores, 62nd to 84th percentile for Quantitative, and 73rd to 95th percentile for Analytical Writing.

GRE Psychology Test

Many, but not all, doctoral programs require that applicants take the Psychology Test. The GRE Psychology Test consists of 205 questions that tap information from the core psychology courses required in most undergraduate programs. The questions are drawn from commonly offered courses at the undergraduate level and are designed to measure what an undergraduate Psychology major who plans to attend graduate school should know about the field of Psychology. The Psychology Test contains three types of questions that comprise two subscores in addition to an overall total score:

1. **Experimental Psychology subscore**: Experimental or natural science oriented (about 40% of the questions), such as learning, language, memory, thinking, sensation and perception, physiological psychology, ethology, and comparative psychology.
2. **Social Psychology subscore:** Social or social science oriented (about 43% of the questions). These questions are distributed among the fields of clinical and abnormal psychology, lifespan development, personality and social psychology.
3. **General** (about 17% of the questions), including questions on the history of psychology, applied psychology, psychometrics, research design, and statistics. They contribute to the total score only.

The GRE Psychology Test is designed to sample a broad overview of topics in psychology. The best way to prepare is by studying an upper-level introductory psychology textbook. Ask a faculty member for guidance in selecting an appropriate textbook to use.

Unlike the General Test, the GRE Psychology Test is administered only by pencil and paper three times a year, typically in September, October, and April. Ideally, you should take the GRE Psychology Test in April so that you have time to retake it, if needed. Scores are sent several weeks after the test date. If you are taking it as a senior, take it in September to allow enough time for scores to be reported. However, you will not receive your test scores early enough to retake it.

Although the GRE scores are an important part of your application, remember that graduate admissions committees consider many other factors. Many programs will accept students with lower GRE scores if they have strengths in other areas, such as research. How do you communicate your strengths to graduate admissions committees? Admissions essays and personal statements offer you an opportunity to speak directly to the committee.

Admissions Essay

The admissions essay, also known as a letter of intent or personal statement, is often the most difficult part of the application because the task is often ambiguous yet it is very important. Many programs simply ask applicants to describe their interests and career objectives. How do you address such a vague question? Don't get overwhelmed. The essay is your chance to present yourself as you would like to be viewed. The most important determinant of success is the degree to which you match the faculty and program. Faculty look for applicants who are interested in the program, share their research interests, and are prepared to engage in collaborative research or scholarship. Your essay is your chance to show your enthusiasm for the program but especially to highlight how your interests fit with particular faculty members. No matter the question, your job is to show that you're a good fit to the faculty and program. Know as much as you can about the program and faculty—and target your essay to one or two faculty you'd like to work with.

Essay Topics Often programs assign applicants a question or two to answer, or a specific topic on which to write. Keith-Spiegel and Wiederman (2000) have noted that there is a remarkable similarity among essay topics requested by graduate programs. Most questions posed by graduate programs fall into one of several categories (Keith-Spiegel & Wiederman, 2000):

- Career plans. What are your long-term career goals? Where do you see yourself ten years from now?
- General interest areas. What academic or professional areas interest you?

- Research experiences. Discuss areas in which you might like to do research, research experiences you have had, or both. Describe your research interests.
- Academic objectives. Why are you undertaking graduate study? Describe how graduate training is necessary for your goals.
- Clinical or other field experience. Describe your clinical experience. How have your field experiences shaped your career goals?
- Academic background and achievements. Discuss your academic background.
- Personal. Is there anything in your background that you think would be relevant in our evaluation of applicants? Describe your life up to now: family, friends, home, school, work, and particularly those experiences most relevant to your interests in psychology and you. Write an autobiographical sketch.
- Personal and professional development. Describe your values and your approach to life.

Although there are many similarities among essay topics, you should not write a generic essay. Tailor your essay to the specific question and the program. Be sure to save each version of your essay. Many essays ask the applicant to discuss how the program or faculty match his or her individual needs. This means that you must demonstrate that you have researched the program and are familiar with its faculty and curriculum. Explain how the specific program will prepare you for the career you desire, offering clear examples. While writing your essay, remember that your goal is to come across as someone with an interest in the specific program and the potential to succeed.

Content: What to Include in Your Essay The admissions essay is sometimes called a personal statement, but don't take that term literally. Do not get *too personal*. The essay is a professional essay, not a place to discuss your own mental health, experiences with therapy, or heartaches. Instead explain the experiences that have prepared you for graduate school and have led to your decision to apply to graduate school. Use concrete examples whenever possible. Your essay should include at least these four components: your previous research experience, research interests, relevant experience, and career goals (Bottoms & Nysse, 1999).

Discuss the details of your involvement with research. Who supervised the work? Was the research part of a course requirement, for class credit, or as an independent study? Discuss the purpose of the research, including the theory, method, and results. Explain your role. Rather than merely explaining that you entered data for Dr. Smith's research study, for example, show that you have worked to understand the purpose of the research. If the research resulted in class papers, conference presentations, or publications, mention that. If you were an author on a conference presentation or publication, include a copy in your application packet. Discuss how your attitude about research has changed as a result of the experience.

Discuss the areas of psychology that most interest you now. You've already chosen graduate programs to which you'll apply based on the fit between your and the faculty's research interests. For each program, identify faculty whose research interests you and tailor your personal statement so that it will entice faculty with whom you'd like to work. This entails doing your homework first. Read the faculty members' webpages and locate articles they have published. Explain what interests you about the professor's work. State your preferred research interests but also that you are open to studying related areas (if that is true). You are more likely to be accepted at a particular program if you discuss the research interests of several faculty (because not all professors look for new students each year).

Discuss any other relevant experiences. Your statement should also include other relevant experience that pertains to your decision to go to graduate school or makes you qualified for graduate school. Internship experiences and volunteer experiences are included here. Avoid personal emotional self disclosures. That is, it's not a good idea to explain, for example, that your interest in psychology arose from your own experiences in therapy.

Discuss your goals. Explain what you would like to do after graduation. What kind of career do you envision after receiving your degree? Illustrate how the specific program will prepare you for the career that you desire. Personal details that you include about yourself should be relevant to your ability to be a successful graduate student and reflect maturity, adaptability, and motivation.

Writing as Process Writing your admissions essay is a process, not a discrete event. The first step involves preparation—gathering the information needed to compose the essay that sets you apart from the rest. Use the self-assessment and writing techniques that we have discussed throughout this book. Leave yourself plenty of time. Look back over reflective writing, especially your responses to the exercises in Chapter 2. Then sit down and write. Don't censor yourself in any way. Brainstorm and simply write what comes to mind. Begin taking notes on what drives you. Describe your hopes, dreams, and aspirations. What do you hope to gain from graduate study? Given the importance of *carefully* sharing (and often censoring) information that is *too* personal, much of this writing may not make it into the essay, but your goal at this point is to brainstorm.

EXERCISE 10.3

Admissions Essay Prep

Prepare to write your admissions essay by examining your personal history. Identify as much of your personal history as possible so that you can carefully sift through and sort out events and personal items that will strengthen your essay. Consider:

- Hobbies
- Projects you've completed
- Jobs you've held
- Responsibilities
- Personal and academic accomplishments
- Challenges and hurdles that you've overcome
- Life events that motivate your education
- People who have influenced you or motivated you
- Traits, work habits, and attitudes that will ensure your success

Prompt:

1. Choose three topics that you feel are most appropriate to include in an essay. What would you tell an admissions committee regarding these three? How would it bolster your application?
2. Specifically consider a challenge that you have overcome. Do you think the topic is appropriate for your essay? What story would it tell the admissions committee about you?
3. Can you identify a life event that has motivated your education or a person who has influenced you? Choose one and explain whether you think it is appropriate for your essay. What story would it tell the admissions committee about you? Would it be helpful?

Carefully consider your academic record and personal accomplishments. How do the attitudes, values, and personal qualities that you've listed correspond to these experiences? Try to pair them. For example, your curiosity and thirst for knowledge may have led you to conduct independent research with a professor. Consider how your attitudes, personal qualities, and experiences show that you're prepared to excel in graduate school.

Once you have a master list, examine the information. Remember that the information you choose to present can portray you as a positive and upbeat person or as a tired and discouraged student. Think about the image you want to portray, and revise your master list accordingly. Use the revised list as a basis for all of your admissions essays. Remember to be forthcoming about your weaknesses. If your early academic record is weak, explain why. Bright people will be evaluating your application, and they'll spot weaknesses. Don't force them to make assumptions about you. Instead, explain how you've overcome weaknesses. Don't dwell or provide too much backstory. Instead focus on how you've improved.

There's still more information to consider for your admissions essays. Tailor your essay to each program. Show that you're interested and that you've taken the time to learn about each program. If you're truly interested in the graduate programs to which you're applying, take the time to tailor your essay to each program. One size clearly does not fit all.

As you write your essay, occasionally stop to make sure that you're answering the question posed by the admissions committee. Think about the question, the central theme asked, and how it corresponds to your master list of experiences and personal qualities. Some applications offer a string of questions. Pay attention to your responses, and try to avoid being redundant. Remember that this is your chance to present your strengths and really shine. Take advantage of it. Discuss your accomplishments, describe valuable experiences, and emphasize the positive. Show that you're motivated. The committee is composed of professionals who have read hundreds, even thousands of such statements over the years. Make yours stand out.

Curriculum Vitae

Not all graduate programs request a curriculum vitae (CV), but it's always a good idea to provide one. A CV is an academic résumé that summarizes and highlights your scholarly experiences, accomplishments, and interests. Unlike a résumé, which is one page in length, a CV contains more information and grows in length throughout your academic career. The goal is to construct and depict your identity as a scholar.

What goes into a CV? The contents of a CV differ across disciplines and expands as one progresses through graduate school. Your CV probably will not have all of these sections yet, and that is to be expected.

Contact information: Include your name, address, phone, and e-mail for home and office, if applicable. The same rules for professionalism apply (no silly e-mail addresses).

Education: Indicate your college major, type of degree, and the date each degree was (or is expected to be) awarded for each postsecondary school attended. Do not list your high school degree.

Academic achievements: List each award, describe it, and note the granting institution and the date awarded. If you have completed a thesis, list the title and your advisor. If you have only one award (e.g., graduation honors), consider incorporating this information within the education section.

Research experience: List assistantships, practica, and other research experience you have had working under a faculty member. List the institutions at which the research was conducted, the dates during which it was conducted, the topics researched, and any resulting papers or publication.

Teaching experience: If you have teaching experience as a teaching assistant or tutor hired by the university, list it. Most students will not include this section.

Professional experience: List your employment history. List the name of the employer, location, position you held, dates of employment, and a brief description of your duties and responsibilities. The description does not need to be extensive unless it is related to your field of study.

Relevant coursework and technical skills: List statistical and computer programs and data analysis techniques with which you're competent. Consider listing specialized courses. This section is especially relevant for research-oriented doctoral programs. What skills can you "sell" to faculty?

Grants awarded: It's unusual for undergraduate students to have been awarded grants, so don't worry if you don't have anything for this section. If you do, include title of agency, projects for which funds were awarded, and dollar amounts.

Publications: If you have a publication, list it here in APA style. Most students begin writing this section during graduate school. Eventually you'll separate publications into sections for articles, chapters, reports and other documents.

Conference presentations: List any poster presentations that you've given at conferences. It is unusual for a college student to have presented a paper (talk) at a conference, but if you have, list it here. Similar to the section on publications, separate this category into sections for posters and papers.

Research interests: Briefly summarize your research interests with four to six key descriptors. Admissions committees pay attention to your research interests: Are they consistent with what you say in your essay? How well do they fit faculty interests?

Professional affiliations: List any professional societies with which you're affiliated (e.g., Psi Chi, or student affiliate of the American Psychological Association or Association for Psychological Science).

References: Provide names, phone numbers, addresses, and e-mail addresses for your referees. Usually this is left off of CVs but given that you've already requested recommendation letters, include your referees here.

Your CV probably will not include all of these sections. As you organize your CV remember that the education section typically goes first. Order the other items in your CV as you see fit. Keep in mind that the items toward the beginning receive more attention than those later on. Highlight your most important information first. Table 10.4 illustrates a sample CV.

TABLE 10.4 **A Sample CV**

Doug Smith

123 Appletree Lane
Washington, DC
(555) 555-8978
dougsmith@gmail.com

EDUCATION

BA, Psychology — expected 2015
New University, Peartown, IL

GPA: 3.78

HONORS THESIS

Title: College Students' Exposure to Community Violence

Mentor: Martha Jones, PhD

Examined cognitive and psychosocial correlates of college students' self-reports of exposure to violence in their neighborhoods and communities.

RESEARCH EXPERIENCE

Research Assistant — 2012–2013
New University, Peartown, IL
Supervisor: Carla Teach, PhD
Project: Integrating Ethics into the Introductory Psychology Curriculum

Assisted Dr. Teach in conducting her NSF-sponsored research studying ways of teaching ethics in the introductory psychology course. Duties included conducting focus groups with introductory psychology students, administering surveys and entering the data into SPSS.

Research Assistant — Spring, 2012
New University, Peartown, IL
Supervisor: Martha Jones, PhD
Project: Classical Conditioning in College

Assisted Dr. Jones in conducting a study that compared college students and rats with regard to the number of trials to classically condition college students. Responsibilities included maintaining the animal lab, recording observational data, and entering the data into SPSS.

CONFERENCE PRESENTATIONS

Smith, D. & Jones, M. (August, 2015). *College students' exposure to community violence.* Poster session presented at the meeting of the American Psychological Association, Orlando, FL.

Teach, C. & Smith, D. (March, 2014). *Integrating ethics into the introductory psychology curriculum.* Poster session presented at the meeting of the Midwestern Psychological Association, Indianapolis, IN.

(Continued)

TABLE 10.4 **A Sample CV (Continued)**

MANUSCRIPT UNDER REVIEW

Teach, C., Grad, S., & Smith, D. (2014). Teaching psychology students to be ethical. Manuscript submitted to *Teaching of Psychology*.

MANUSCRIPT IN PREPARATION

Smith, D. & Teach, C. (2015). *Psychosocial correlates of exposure to community violence*. Manuscript in preparation.

INTERNSHIPS AND PROFESSIONAL EXPERIENCE

Intern, Center for Violence — 2014–2015
Peartree, IL
Supervisor: Dawn Yoke, PhD

Participated in group sessions with women exposed to domestic violence. Maintained treatment and attendance records.

Peer-Tutor, Statistics for the Behavioral Sciences — 2012–2014
Department of Psychology,
New University, Peartown, IL
Supervisor: Beau Stats, PhD

Tutored students in statistics. Helped students format SPSS files and choose appropriate analyses.

HONORS AND AWARDS

Willerman Award for Excellence in Psychology	2015
College of Arts and Sciences Deans List (Fall and Spring Semester)	2011–2015
Undergraduate Research Travel Award ($200)	2013
Psi Chi	2013
New Psychology Student Award	2012

RESEARCH INTERESTS:

Relationship between community violence and adolescent risk taking
Development of interventions to help people exposed to violence
Decision making in college students

RELEVANT COURSEWORK AND SKILLS

Research Methods
Statistics
Advanced Statistics
Ethics in Animal Research
Ethics in Research with Human Participants
Honors in Developmental Psychology
Advanced Issues in Moral Development
Experience with SPSS

WORK EXPERIENCE

Assistant Child Care Provider, ChildrenRUs — 2012–2014
Hometown, IN

TABLE 10.4 A Sample CV

Supervisor: Kitty Richards

Provided care for children ages 2 to 5. Responsibilities included curriculum planning and communication with parents.

Cashier, Tasty Deli
Hometown, IL
Supervisor: Anna Testi

Maintained the cash register, checked out customers, maintained stock

PROFESSIONAL AFFILIATIONS

American Psychological Association, Student Affiliate
Association for Psychological Science, Student Member

REFERENCES

Martha Jones, PhD
Department of Psychology
Peartown, IL
(555) 555-1234
Jones@NewU.edu

Carla Teach, PhD
Department of Psychology
Peartown, IL
(555) 555-5678
Teach@newu.edu

Dawn Yoke, PhD
Center for Violence
Peartown, IL
(555) 555-9101
YokeD@viocenter.org

Exercise 10.4

Create Your CV

Convert your résumé into a curriculum vitae. Choose the areas that apply to your experiences and convert your résumé into a CV that is at least two pages long.

Letters of Recommendation

Every graduate program requires applicants to submit three letters of recommendation. What is a letter of recommendation? It's a letter, written by a faculty member, that discusses the personal qualities, accomplishments, and experiences that make you unique and perfect for the programs to which you've applied. Don't underestimate the importance of these letters. While your transcript, standardized test scores, and admissions essay are vital components of your application, an excellent letter of recommendation can bolster a weak application. The letter of recommendation gives admissions committees information that isn't found elsewhere in the application.

Nearly all graduate programs accept electronic recommendation letters. Typically after an applicant completes an online application and lists faculty contacts, they get an e-mail with a link to a form to submit.

Who Should You Ask? Deciding who will write your recommendation letters often is difficult. Consider faculty members, administrators, internship or cooperative education supervisors, and employers. But remember that it's faculty who will be reading the recommendation letters (and they've been through graduate school), so faculty tend to write the most credible recommendation letters.

Appleby, Keenan, and Mauer (1999) examined recommendation forms from the application packages of 143 graduate programs in clinical, experimental, and industrial-organizational psychology. The applicant characteristics that faculty were requested to discuss and rank were identified and categorized. About 40% of the 802 characteristics referred to personal characteristics; about one-third referred to acquired skills; and about one-quarter referred to intellectual abilities or knowledge. The top characteristics that recommendation forms asked faculty to discuss are listed in Table 10.5. As you can see, grad programs are interested in more than your academic abilities.

The persons you ask to write your letters should:

- Know you well
- Have known you long enough to write with authority
- Know your work
- Describe your work positively
- Have a high opinion of you
- Know where you are applying
- Know your educational and career goals
- Be able to favorably compare you with your peers
- Be well known
- Be able to write a good letter

Keep in mind that no one faculty member will satisfy all of these criteria. Aim for a set of letters covering the range of your skills. Letters should include your academic and scholastic skills, research abilities and experiences, and applied experiences (e.g., cooperative education, internships, and related work experience). When you approach potential recommenders, ask if they know you well enough to write a meaningful letter. Pay attention to their demeanor. If you sense reluctance, thank them and ask someone else. Remember that it is best to ask early in the semester. As the end of the semester approaches, faculty may hesitate because of time constraints.

TABLE 10.5 **TOP CHARACTERISTICS ASSESSED BY RECOMMENDATION FORMS**

Motivation
Intellectual/scholarly ability
Research skills
Emotional stability and maturity
Writing skills
Speaking skills
Teaching skills or potential
Ability to work with others
Creativity
Knowledge of area of study

Source: Appleby, Keenan, and Mauer (1999).

Help Your Referees The best thing you can do to ensure that your letters cover all the bases is to provide your referees (those who will write your letters of recommendation) with all the necessary information. Start from scratch, pretending that you have just met and that they know nothing about you. Give them the info you'd like included. Frame the material, highlighting what you think is most important. Make an appointment to speak with each of your referees. Give them plenty of time, preferably a month at minimum. Ask each professor about his or her preference for receiving material in hard or electronic copy. If he or she chooses a hard copy, provide one folder with all of your background information neatly arranged. If your professors request an electronic copy, offer it by e-mail or cloud service such as Dropbox. Organize the material into one folder and clearly label each file. Don't make your referee open multiple files to find what he or she needs. What do you include?

- Transcript
- CV
- GRE scores
- Courses you've taken with them and grades that you've earned
- An excellent paper from their class
- Thesis or other capstone paper
- List of research experiences and explanation of each
- Internship and other applied experiences
- Honor societies to which you belong
- Awards you've won
- Relevant work experience
- Professional goals

- Due date for the application
- Copy of the application recommendation forms

Confidentiality The recommendation forms supplied by graduate programs require you to decide whether to waive or retain your rights to see the recommendations. As you decide whether to retain your rights, remember that confidential letters tend to carry more weight with admissions committees. In addition, many faculty members will not write a recommendation letter unless it is confidential. Other faculty may provide you with a copy of each letter, even if it is confidential. If you are unsure of your decision, discuss it with your referees.

What Do Graduate Admissions Committees Look For?

As you think about what's important to you in a graduate program and how to compile your application, consider the flip side: What do graduate admissions committees look for in applicants? Let's consider the four major components of a grad school application: GPA, GRE scores, admissions essay, and letters of recommendation. All of these are required but their relative importance varies, as shown in Table 10.6, and often in ways that surprise students.

Important Criteria for Evaluating Applicants (as Rated by Faculty Members)

1. The fit or match between the applicant's interests and skills and the program's goals
2. Research experience (especially research resulting in the publication in a scholarly journal of a paper presented at a professional conference)
3. Interest expressed by one or more members of the selection committee in working with a particular applicant
4. The clarity, focus, and content of the applicant's admission essays
5. Experience as research assistant
6. Writing skills
7. Knowledge about, and interest in, the program
8. Number of statistics, research methodology, and hard science courses taken
9. Prestige and status of faculty in undergraduate department, especially of those who are writing letters of recommendation
10. Potential for success as judged by interview
11. Honors and merit scholarships

Adapted from: Bonifazi, Crespi, and Rieker (1997); Keith-Spiegel, Tabachnick, and Spiegel (1994).

Grade point average and standardized test scores are important to your application but less so and in different ways than students typically believe. Typically the question with regard to grades and test scores is if they are good enough: Do they make the cut? Frequently grades and test scores are used as cutoff criteria to weed applicants out. This is particularly true in graduate programs that receive a large numbers of applicants, such as clinical programs that typically receive hundreds of applications for a handful of slots. The files of applicants who do not make the cut don't make it to the admissions committee and are never viewed. Your GRE scores provide information about how you rank among your peers (that's why it's important to do your best!).

Admissions essays or personal statements are critical to your application, and the most important part. This is where you introduce yourself in a statement in which you describe yourself and your intentions for graduate study. Committees look at the quality of writing but the content is more important. The key is how well your interests match those faculty and program. They accept students who desire the training the program provides. Also students who have interest that match the faculty's can work with them. Applicants with excellent qualifications can be weeded out if they don't match the program or faculty. In this case an applicant who is less qualified but matches very well can get in. Once you make the cutoff interests matter more than grades. Faculty read personal statements very closely because they reveal lots of information about applicants. Your essay is an indicator of your writing ability, motivation, ability to express yourself, maturity, passion for the field, and judgment. Admissions committees read essays with the intent to learn more about applicants, to determine if they have the qualities and attitudes needed for success, and to weed out applicants who don't fit the program.

The other critical part of your application, in addition to your essay, are letters of recommendation. They provide an outside perspective on your ability and interests. Letters from faculty provide a context in which you consider your application. Who you choose matters. They should have something significant to say about you. Generally speaking, letters written by professors known to committee members tend to carry more weight than those written by "unknowns." Letters written by well-known people in the field, if they signify that they know you well and think highly of you, can be very helpful in moving your application toward the top of the list. But one that is written by someone who knows you and provides clear examples is more important.

The Interview

Some programs conduct phone or Skype interviews, some conduct on-site interviews, and some don't interview at all. What happens if you're invited to interview? How do you prepare? What are admission committees looking for?

The interview gives admission committees an opportunity to meet candidates and see the people behind the GPAs and GRE scores. It's a chance for them to meet you, to see how you react under pressure, and to assess your verbal and nonverbal communication skills. The interview might range from half an hour with one or two faculty to a full day or more filled with meetings with students and faculty. Activities might range from small group discussions to larger group interviews and even social hours or parties.

Interview Prep

How do you prepare for the interview? Learn as much about the program as possible. Review the program description, department webpage, and faculty webpages. Understand the program's emphasis, and be aware of the faculty's research interests. Consider how you will answer common interview questions, such as the following:

- Why are you interested in our program?
- What do you know about our program?
- What are your career goals?
- Why did you choose a career in psychology?
- What are your research interests? Describe your research experience. Regarding research, what are your strengths and weaknesses?
- What are your academic strengths? What was your favorite course, and why?
- What do you like best about yourself?
- Who would you like to work with? Why?
- Describe the accomplishment you're most proud of.
- If you were to begin a research project now, what would be the topic?
- Describe your theoretical orientation.
- Discuss your experiences in clinical settings. Evaluate your clinical abilities.
- What are your strengths and weaknesses?
- Tell us about yourself.

Consider how you might answer each of these questions, but don't memorize answers. Instead, be prepared to speak extemporaneously so that you're ready for interview curveballs. To gain confidence, practice with family, friends, or in front of the mirror.

Don't forget that this is your opportunity to ask questions too. In fact, admission committees expect you to ask questions, so prepare some thoughtful questions about the program, faculty, and students. Use this opportunity to learn about the program and whether it meets your needs. During your visit, try to get a sense of the department's emotional climate. What do graduate students call professors? Doctor? Or do they use first names? Are students competitive with one another? Try to get a sense of whether the atmosphere matches your personality. Is it excessively formal? Would you be happy there?

Real Tips for Real Students

Quick Primer on What to Wear

Neatness is the rule. A suit in a dark color is the easiest and safest way to approach the what-to-wear dilemma. Err on the side of overdressing than underdressing, but don't worry if you don't have a suit. Men can wear slacks, a button-down shirt, and one or more of the following: tie, pullover sweater, or blazer. Women can wear slacks or a skirt with a modest top or a conservative dress. Practical comfortable shoes are the rule for both men and women. Don't look like you're trying. Minimize accessories. Fair or not, sometimes applicants who look too pulled together or "too good" are not taken seriously. You want to be remembered for your ideas, not your fashion sense. Also, be sure that your clothes fit and that you don't show unnecessary skin. Finally, pass the smell test. Don't wear perfume, cologne, or stinky products that might distract your interviewers. Some people are sensitive to smells and heavy perfume might unconsciously sway them against you.

Skype Interviews

Many graduate programs are moving toward conducting interviews by video conferencing via platforms like Skype. Skype interviews permit graduate programs to interview students cheaply and efficiently—and perhaps even squeeze even more applicant interviews in than they would in real life. An interview for admission to graduate study, regardless of whether it's on campus or by Skype, means that the admissions committee is interested in you and is your opportunity to demonstrate your fit to the faculty and graduate program. Treat a Skype interview like a campus interview: Dress up. Also do a practice run with a friend so that he or she can give you feedback on what you look and sound like (and what's in the background). Skype interviews pose special challenges. Overcome them:

Be prepared. Plug in your laptop. Do not rely on its battery. Also, have the phone number for the admissions chair at hand in case tech problems arise. Log out of messaging programs, Facebook, and other apps with sound notifications. Mute notifications in Skype. Make sure that you will not be interrupted by any sounds on your computer. Whatever you hear, your interviewers hear.

Attend to visuals. What will the committee see behind you? Pay attention to your background. Posters, signs, photos, and art can detract from your professional demeanor. Don't give professors an opportunity to judge you on anything other than your words and persona. Choose a well-lit space.

Make eye contact. Sit at a desk. The camera should be level with your face. Sit far enough away that your interviewer can see your shoulders. Look into the camera, not at the image on the screen—and certainly not at yourself. If you look at the image of your interviewers, you'll appear to be looking away. Challenging as it may seem, try to look at the camera to simulate eye contact.

Be heard. Be sure that the interviewers can hear you. Know where the microphone is located and direct your speech toward it. Speak slowly and pause after the interviewer finishes speaking. Sometimes video lag can interfere with communication, making it harder for interviewers to understand you or making it appear as if you are interrupting them. Eliminate any potential sources of background noise, such as barking dogs, crying children, or insensitive roommates.

Skype interviews share the same purpose as old-fashioned in-person interviews: An opportunity for the graduate admissions committee to get to know you. Preparing for the technological aspects of video interviews can sometimes overshadow the basic interview preparation that will help you learn about the program and put your best foot forward. As you prep, don't forget to focus on the content of the interview.

Application Outcomes

When can you expect to hear from programs? Every program has a different method and style of handling admissions. Some programs review applications and make decisions early, and others wait. How quickly applications are reviewed depends on a variety of factors including the number of applications received, how many people are on the committee, academic demands, conferences, holidays, how well the members of the committee work together, and so on. Most programs inform applicants of their status by mid-April, but you might hear from programs earlier or later.

Being Accepted

You've received good news. Congratulations! Most programs inform applicants of their acceptance from March through early April. In most cases, your decision on whether to accept an offer is due by April 15. Once you decline an offer, it can be passed along to someone else who is waiting, so do not hold onto offers that you don't plan on accepting. As soon as you have two offers, decide which to decline. Each time you receive a new offer, decline your least preferred offer so that you're not holding on to offers that you don't intend to accept. How do you decide which to decline? Consider your priorities. Know what you are accepting. Don't be surprised because you made assumptions about financial support, housing, or assistantships. Ask about financial aid, housing, and assistantships. Compare acceptance packages to decide among programs. Don't be afraid to do some negotiating, because they've decided that they want you. Help them make it possible for you to accept by explaining any financial limitations that might impede accepting their offer. How do you decline a graduate program? E-mail a letter explaining that you appreciate their interest, but will not be accepting their offer. Mail a hard copy of the letter as well.

Dealing with Rejection

What if you're not accepted? It is difficult to be told that you are not among a program's top choices. From a statistical standpoint, you have lots of company as rejection rates are as high as 91% in clinical psychology programs. Most graduate programs must split hairs in making decisions as there are many highly qualified applicants. As we discussed it usually comes down to fit—how well does an applicant fit a particular faculty member's needs. Regardless, a rejection letter is difficult, especially if you were invited for an interview. Yet often programs interview two to three times as many students as they can enroll.

Why are students rejected? Most simply, because there aren't enough slots; graduate programs in psychology receive far more applications from qualified candidates than they can accept. Why were you eliminated by a particular program? There is no way to tell, but in many cases applicants are rejected because they didn't fit the program. For example, an applicant to a research-scientist program who didn't read the program materials carefully might be rejected for indicating an interest in practicing therapy.

You might find it difficult to inform family, friends, and professors of the bad news, but it is essential that you seek social support. Allow yourself to feel upset and acknowledge your feelings, and then move forward. If you are rejected by every program you've applied to, reassess your goals, but don't necessarily give up.

- Did you select schools carefully, paying attention to fit?
- Did you apply to enough programs?
- Did you complete all parts of each application?
- Did you spend enough time on your essays?
- Did you have research experience?
- Did you have field experience?
- Did you know your referees well, and did they have something to write about?
- Were most of your applications to highly competitive programs?

Your answers to these questions may help you determine whether to reapply to a greater range of programs next year, or to apply to a master's program instead, as either a first step toward the doctoral degree or as an end in itself. Or you may want to choose another career path. If you are firmly committed to attending graduate school in psychology, consider reapplying next year; but don't send out the same application. Use the next few months to improve your academic record, seek research experience, and get to know professors. Apply to a wider range of schools (including "safety" schools), select programs more carefully, and thoroughly research each program.

Suggested Readings

American Psychological Association (2007). *Getting in: A step-by-step plan for gaining admission to graduate school in psychology.* Washington, DC: Author.

American Psychological Association (2015). *Graduate study in psychology: 2015 edition.* Washington, DC: Author.

Appleby, D. C., Keenan, J., & Mauer, E. (1999, Spring). Applicant characteristics valued by graduate programs in psychology. *Eye on Psi Chi, 3*(3), 39.

Kracen, A. C. & Wallace, I. J. (2008). *Applying to graduate school in psychology.* Washington, DC: APA.

Kuther, T. L. (2004). *Getting into graduate school in psychology and related fields: Your guide to success.* Springfield, IN: C. Charles Thomas.

Norcross, J. G. & Sayette, M. A. (2014). *Insider's guide to graduate programs in clinical and counseling psychology.* New York: Guilford.

Privitera, G. J. (2015). *Getting into grad school: A comprehensive guide for psychology and the behavioral sciences.* Thousand Oaks: Sage.

Silvia, P. J., Delaney, P. F., & Marcovitch, S. (2009). *What psychology majors could (and should) be doing: An informal guide to research experience and professional skills.* Washington, DC: APA.

Internet Resources (Available at http://www.tarakuther.com)

Applying to Graduate School

http://www.apa.org/education/grad/applying.aspx

A collection of advice from the American Psychological Association.

gradPSYCH

http://www.apa.org/gradpsych/index.aspx

Magazine for graduate students, by the American Psychological Association. Frequently includes advice for undergraduates.

How I Got into Stanford

http://howigotintostanford.com/

Now PhD, Eran Magden shares his advice, as a graduate student, on how to get into graduate school, as well as his experience as a successful applicant.

GRE Homepage

http://www.gre.org

Get information about the GRE from the source.

How to Get In: Your Guide to Applying to Graduate Programs

http://www.columbia.edu/cu/psychology/dept/resources/getin3.html

Collection of links curated by the psychology department at Columbia University.

Mitch's Uncensored Advice for Applying to Graduate School in Clinical Psychology

http://www.unc.edu/~mjp1970/Mitch%27s%20Grad%20School%20Advice.pdf

Dr. Mitch Prinstein shares valuable advice from his experience as a faculty member who teaches in a clinical psychology PhD program.

Psi Chi

http://www.psichi.org/

The International Honor Society in Psychology offers resources on graduate school. Specifically, peruse the Psi Chi magazine, *Eye on Psi Chi,* for a variety of resources.

About Graduate School

http://gradschool.about.com

I maintain this site, which is part of the About.com network. Here, you'll find information for graduate school applicants, current students, postdoctoral fellows, and faculty in all disciplines, including psychology.

Reflection Prompts

Why Graduate School?

Where does graduate education fit into your life? What goals will it help to accomplish? What are the costs of graduate school? It is sometimes said that as one door of opportunity opens, another closes. What door will close when you enter graduate school? What will you miss out on in your years of graduate study?

Where Do I Stand and What Must I Do?

Imagine that you are to apply to graduate school. What steps are entailed? What preparation is needed? Do you have the necessary academic, research, and/or applied experiences? What are your strengths as an applicant? Weaknesses? Everyone can improve in some area. Consider ways of addressing the weaknesses in your application.

Recommendation Letters

If I were to ask for letters of recommendation right now, who would I choose? How would I make this choice? Who would be able to speak about my competencies? What can I do to strengthen these relationships? What if I can't identify three faculty? What specific things can I do to establish working relationships with faculty?

References

Actkinson, T. R. (2000). Master's and myth: Little-known information about a popular degree. *Eye on Psi Chi, 4*(2), 19–21, 23, 25.

Adler, A. (2010, April). Talking the talk: Tips on giving a successful conference presentation. *Psychological Science Agenda*. Retrieved from http://www.apa.org/science/about/psa/2010/04/presentation.aspx

American Psychological Association. (2010). *Ethical principles of psychologists and code of conduct*. Washington, DC: Author. Retrieved from http://www.apa.org/ethics/code/principles.pdf

American Psychological Association. (2010). *Publication manual of the American Psychological Association*. Washington, DC: Author.

American Psychological Association. (2013). *APA guidelines for the undergraduate psychology major: Version 2.0*. Retrieved from http://www.apa.org/ed/precollege/undergrad/index.aspx

Amsel, J. (1996). An interesting career in psychology: Acquisitions editor. *Psychological Science Agenda*. Retrieved January 19, 2015, from http://www.apa.org/careers/resources/profiles/amsel.aspx

Appleby, D. (1997). *The handbook of psychology*. New York: Longman.

Appleby, D. (1999). Choosing a mentor. *Eye on Psi Chi, 3*(3), 38–39.

Appleby, D. (2001). The covert curriculum: The lifelong learning skills you can learn in college. *Eye on Psi Chi, 5*(3), 28.

Appleby, D. C., Millspaugh, B. S., & Hammersley, M. J. (2011). An online resource to enable undergraduate psychology majors to identify and investigate 172 psychology and psychology-related careers. *Office of Teaching Resources in Psychology*. Retrieved from http://teachpsych.org/Resources/Documents/otrp/resources/appleby14.pdf

Appleby, D. C., Keenan, J., & Mauer, E. (1999, Spring). Applicant characteristics valued by graduate programs in psychology. *Eye on Psi Chi, 3*(3), 39.

Atkins, D. C., & Christensen, A. (2001). Is professional training worth the bother? A review of the impact of psychotherapy training on client outcome. *Australian Psychologist, 36*(2), 122–130. doi:10.1080/00050060108259644

Balster, R. L. (1995). An interesting career in psychology: Behavioral pharmacologist. *Psychological Science Agenda*. Retrieved January 19, 2015, from http://www.apa.org/careers/resources/profiles/balster.aspx

Bare, J. K. (1988). A liberal education. In P. J. Woods (Ed.), *Is psychology for them? A guide to undergraduate advising* (pp. 39–41). Washington, DC: APA.

Bat-Chava, Y. (2000). An interesting career in psychology: Research director for a non-profit organization. *Psychological Science Agenda*. Retrieved January 19, 2015, from http://www.apa.org/careers/resources/profiles/bat-chava.aspx

Bonifazi, D. Z., Crespi, S. D., & Rieker, P. (1997). Value of a master's degree for gaining admission to doctoral programs in psychology. *Teaching of Psychology, 24*, 176–182.

Bornstein, M. H., & Arterberry, M. E. (1999). Perceptual development. In M. H. Bornstein & M. E. Lamb (Eds.), *Developmental psychology: An advanced textbook* (231–274). Mahwah, NJ: Erlbaum.

Bottoms, B. L., & Nysse, K. L. (1999). Applying to graduate school: Writing a compelling personal statement. *Eye on Psi Chi, 4*(1), 20–22.

Bureau of Labor Statistics. (2013). The job market for recent college graduates in the United States. *Economics Daily*. Retrieved from http://www.bls.gov/opub/ted/2013/ted_20130405.htm

Buskist, W., & Sherburne, T. R. (1996). *Preparing for graduate study in psychology: 101 questions and answers*. Needham Heights, MA: Allyn & Bacon.

CareerBuilder. (2014). *Number of employers passing on applicants due to social media posts continues to rise, according to New CareerBuilder Survey*. Retrieved from http://www.careerbuilder.com/share/aboutus/pressreleasesdetail.aspx?sd=6/26/2014&id=pr829&ed=12/31/2014

Carnevale, P. A., & Cheah, B. (2013). *Hard times: College majors, unemployment, and earnings, 2013*. Washington, DC: Center on Education and the Workforce, Georgetown University. Retrieved from https://georgetown.app.box.com/s/9t0p5tm0qhejyy8t8hub

Cooley, E. L., Garcia, A. L., & Hughes, J. L. (2008). Undergraduate research in psychology at liberal arts colleges: Reflections on mutual benefits for faculty and students. *North American Journal of Psychology, 10*(3), 463.

Davis, S. F. (1995). The value of collaborative scholarship with undergraduates. *Psi Chi Newsletter, 21*(1), 12–13.

DeGalan, J., & Lambert, S. (1995). *Great jobs for psychology majors*. Chicago, IL: VGM Career Horizons.

Dweck, C. S., Walton, G. M., & Cohen, G. (2011). *Academic tenacity*. White paper prepared for the Gates Foundation. Seattle, WA. Retrieved from http://web.stanford.edu/~gwalton/home/Publications_files/DweckWaltonCohen_2014.pdf

Educational Testing Service. (2014). *General test percentage distribution of scores within intended broad graduate major field based on seniors and nonenrolled college graduate*. Retrieved from http://www.ets.org/s/gre/pdf/gre_guide_table4.pdf

Flattau, P. E. (1998). *An interesting career in psychology: Policy scientist as an independent consultant*. Retrieved January 19, 2015, from http://www.apa.org/careers/resources/profiles/flattau.aspx

Garfein, R. (1997). *An interesting career in psychology: International market research consultant*. Retrieved January 19, 2015, from http://www.apa.org/careers/resources/profiles/garfein.aspx

Goldstein, R. (2010). Major developments in undergraduate psychology. *Observer, 23*(3). Retrieved from http://www.psychologicalscience.org/index.php/publications/observer/2010/march-10/major-developments-in-undergraduate-psychology.html

Grover, S. F. (2006). Undergraduate research: Getting involved and getting into graduate school (A student's perspective). *Eye on Psi Chi, 11*(1), 18–20.

Himelein, M. J. (1999). A student's guide to careers in the helping professions. *Office of Teaching Resources in Psychology*. Retrieved January 19, 2015, from http://teachpsych.org/resources/Documents/otrp/resources/himelein99.pdf

Holland, J. L. (1959). A theory of vocational choice. *Journal of Counseling Psychology, 6,* 35–45.

Jessen, B. C. (1988). Field experience for undergraduate psychology students. In P. J. Woods (Ed.), *Is psychology for them? A guide to undergraduate advising* (pp. 79–84). Washington, DC: APA.

Kahn, N. B. (1992). *More learning in less time: A guide for students, professionals, career changers, and lifelong learners*. Berkeley, CA: Ten Speed Press.

Karlin, N. J. (2000). Creating an effective conference presentation. *Eye on Psi Chi, 4*(2), 26–27.

Keith-Spiegel, P., Tabachnick, B. G., & Spiegel, G. B. (1994). When demand exceeds supply: Second order criteria used by graduate school selection committees. *Teaching of Psychology, 21,* 79–81.

Keith-Spiegel, P., & Wiederman, M. W. (2000). *The complete guide to graduate school admission: Psychology, counseling, and related professions*. Mahwah, NH: Erlbaum.

Kohout, J., & Wicherski, M. (2010). *2011 graduate study in psychology*. Washington, DC: American Psychological Association. Retrieved from http://apa.org/workforce/publications/11-grad-study/applications.aspx?tab=2

Krannich, R. I. (2005). *Nail that resume: Great tips for creating dynamite resumes*. Woodbridge, VA: Impact Publishers.

Kraus, S. K. (1996). *An interesting career in psychology: Market research consultant*. Retrieved February 1, 2001, from http://www.apa.org/science/ic-kraus.html

Kuther, T. L., & Morgan, R. D. (2010). *Careers in psychology: Opportunities in a changing world*. Belmont, CA: Wadsworth.

Landrum, E. (2008). Evaluating the undergraduate research assistantship experience. *Eye on Psi Chi, 12*(3), 32–33.

Landrum, R. E. (2009). *Finding jobs with a psychology bachelor's degree: Expert advice for launching your career*. Washington, DC: APA.

Landrum, R. E., & Nelsen, L. R. (2002). The undergraduate research assistantship: An analysis of the benefits. *Teaching of Psychology, 29*(1), 15–19.

Lewis, P., & Rivkin, D. (1999). *O*NET interest profiler: Reliability, validity, and self-scoring*. Raleigh, NC. Retrieved from http://www.onetcenter.org/dl_files/IP_RVS.pdf

Lloyd, M. A. (1997). *Entry level positions obtained by psychology majors*. Retrieved January 19, 2015, from http://www.psywww.com/careers/entry.htm

Lloyd, M. A. (2000). *Master's- and doctoral-level careers in psychology and related areas*. Retrieved January 19, 2015, from http://www.psychwww.com/careers/masters.htm

LoCicero, A., & Hancock, J. (2000). Preparing students for success in fieldwork. *Teaching of Psychology, 27,* 117–120.

Lock, R. D. (1988). *Taking charge of your career direction*. Pacific Grove, CA: Brooks/Cole.

Mathie, V. A. (2006). Preparing for research presentations: Now is the time! *Eye on Psi Chi, 11*(1). Retrieved from http://www.psichi.org/?111EyeFall06hMathie

Mayne, T. J., Norcross, J. C., & Sayette, M. A. (1994). Admission requirements, acceptance rates, and financial assistance in clinical psychology programs. *American Psychologist, 12,* 806–811.

Meyer, M. (1985). *The little, brown guide to writing research papers*. Glenville, IL: Scott, Foresman and Company.

McGovern, T. V., & Carr, K. F. (1989). Carving out the niche: A review of alumni surveys on undergraduate psychology majors. *Teaching of Psychology, 16*, 52–57.

McGovern, T. V., Furumoto, L., Halpern, D. F., Kimble, G. A., & McKeachie, W. J. (1991). Liberal education, study in depth, and the arts and sciences major: Psychology. *American Psychologist, 46*(6), 598–605.

Michalski, D., Kohout, J., Wicherski, M., & Hart, B. (2011). *2009 Doctorate Employment Survey*. Washington, DC: APA Center for Workforce Studies. Retrieved from http://www.apa.org/workforce/publications/09-doc-empl/report.pdf

Mueller, P. A., & Oppenheimer, D. M. (2014). The pen is mightier than the keyboard: Advantages of longhand over laptop note taking. *Psychological Science, 25*(6), 1159–1168. doi:10.1177/0956797614524581

Myers, I. B., McCaulley, M. H., Quenk, N. L., & Hammer, A. L. (1998). *MBTI manual: A guide to the development and use of the Myers-Briggs Type Indicator* (3rd ed.). Palo Alto, CA: Consulting Psychologists Press.

National Association of Colleges and Employers. (2000). *Ideal candidate has top-notch interpersonal skills, say employers*. Retrieved August 19, 2000, from http://www.naceweb.org/press/display.cfm/2000/pr011800.htm

National Association of Colleges and Employers. (2014a). *Job outlook 2014*. Washington, DC: Author.

National Association of Colleges and Employers. (2014b). *NACE salary survey*. Washington, DC: Author.

National Center for Education Statistics. (2013). *Digest of education statistics, 2012*. Washington, DC: Author.

National Center for Education Statistics. (2014). *The condition of education, 2014*. Washington, DC: Author. Retrieved from http://nces.ed.gov/pubsearch/pubsinfo.asp?pubid=2014083

National Science Foundation. (2012). *National survey of recent college graduates; survey year 2010*. Washington, DC: Author. Retrieved from http://ncsesdata.nsf.gov/recentgrads/2010/

National Science Foundation. (2014). *Survey of doctorate recipients: Survey year 2013*. Washington, DC: Author. Retrieved from http://ncsesdata.nsf.gov/doctoratework/2013/

Pauk, W., & Fiore, J. (2000). *Succeed in college!* New York: Harper & Row.

Peters, R. L. (1992). *Getting what you came for: The smart student's guide to earning a Master's or a PhD*. New York: Noonday Press.

Pittenger, D. J. (2005). Cautionary comments regarding the Myers-Briggs Type Indicator. *Consulting Psychology Journal: Practice and Research, 57*(3), 210–221. doi:10.1037/1065-9293.57.3.210

Powell, J. L. (2000). Creative outlets for student research or what do I do now that my study is completed? *Eye on Psi Chi, 4*(2), 28–29.

Rajecki, D. W. (2012). Psychology baccalaureates at work: Major area subspecializations, earnings, and occupations. *Teaching of Psychology, 39*(3), 185–189.

Richardson, M., Abraham, C., & Bond, R. (2012). Psychological correlates of university students' academic performance: A systematic review and meta-analysis. *Psychological Bulletin, 138*(2), 353.

Robinson, F. P. (1970). *Effective study*. New York: Harper & Row.

Roche, M. W. (2010). *Why choose the liberal arts?* Notre Dame, IN: University of Notre Dame Press.

Rosnow, R. L., & Rosnow, M. (2008). *Writing papers in psychology*. Belmont, CA: Wadsworth.

Rotter, J. B. (1990). Internal versus external control of reinforcement: A case history of a variable. *American Psychologist, 45*(4), 489.

Ruff, E. A., Reardon, R. C., & Bertoch, S. C. (2007). *Technical report 47: Creating a research database on Holland's theory and practical tools.* Tallahassee, FL: Center for the Study of Technology in Counseling and Career Development, Florida State University. Retrieved from http://www.career.fsu.edu/content/download/185506/1608303/TR47.pdf

Ryan, R. M., & Deci, E. L. (2000). Self-determination theory and the facilitation of intrinsic motivation, social development, and well-being. *American Psychologist, 55*(1), 68.

Scott, J. M., Koch, R. E., Scott, G. M., & Garrison, S. M. (1999). *The psychology student writer's manual*. Upper Saddle River, NJ: Prentice Hall.

Seligman, M. E. (1995). The effectiveness of psychotherapy. The consumer reports study. *American Psychologist, 50*(12), 965–974. Retrieved from http://www.ncbi.nlm.nih.gov/pubmed/8561380

Singleton, D., Tate, A. C., & Kohout, J. L. (2003). *2002 Master's, Specialist's, and Related Degrees Employment Survey*. Retrieved January 19, 2015, from http://www.apa.org/workforce/publications/02-mas-spec/index.aspx

Sleigh, M. J., & Ritzer, D. R. (2007, Spring). Undergraduate research experience: Preparation for the job market. *Eye on Psi Chi, 11*(3), 27–30.

Society for Research in Child Development. (2007). *Ethical standards in research*. Washington, DC: Author. Retrieved from http://www.srcd.org/about-us/ethical-standards-research

Stapp, J. (1996). *An interesting career in psychology: Trial consultant*. Retrieved January 15, 2015, from http://www.apa.org/careers/resources/profiles/stapp.aspx

Sternberg, R. J. (1993). *The psychologist's companion*. New York: Cambridge University Press.

Strong, E. K., Jr., Donnay, D. A. C., Morris, M. L., Schaubhut, N. A., & Thompson, R. (2004). *Strong interest inventory, revised edition*. Mountain View, CA: Consulting Psychologists Press.

Taylor, M. S. (1988). Effects of college internships on individual participants. *Journal of Applied Psychology, 73*, 393–401.

US Bureau of Labor Statistics. (2009). *Current population survey*. Washington, DC: US Department of Labor.

US Bureau of Labor Statistics. (2014). *Occupational outlook handbook*. Washington, DC: Department of Labor. Retrieved from http://www.bls.gov/ooh/

Walfish, S., & Turner, K. (2006). Relative weighting of admissions variables in developmental psychology doctoral programs. *Eye on Psi Chi, 10*(4). Retrieved January 19, 2015, from https://www.psichi.org/?104EyeSum06bWalfish

Walter, T. J. (2007). The undergraduate psychology internship: Benefits, selection, and making the most of your experience. *Eye on Psi Chi, 11*(3). Retrieved from https://www.psichi.org/?113EyeSpr07cWalter

Wong, L. (2015). *Essential study skills*. Stamford, CT: Cengage.

Index

Page numbers followed by "*t*" indicate a table.